DISTINCTIVE CUISINE OF CHINA

Chef Chu's

DISTINCTIVE CUISINE OF CHINA

Lawrence C. C. Chu

Van Lachlan & Lange

Harper & Row, Publishers, Inc.
New York, Hagerstown, San Francisco, London

Library of Congress Catalog
Card Number 83-47845
ISBN 0-06-181158-0

Managing Editor
Linda Brandt

Art Director
James Stockton

Photographers
Nikolay Zurek, color
Leo Holub, black/white

Research Editor
Cynthia Wordell

Text Contributors
Susan Wels
Karin Shakery
Winslow Briggs

Illustrator
Cyndie Clarke-Huegel

Production
Meredith Bauman
Carolyn Cline
Sue Mathison

Typesetter
Frank's Type, Mountain View
and Jack Burns

Printer
Interprint for
Dai Nippon, Tokyo

Props for Photography
Belinda Chung
B. K. Collections, Los Altos

Special thanks to those whose
hospitality and personal effort
contributed to this book: Kay Daley,
Rick Smolan, Carolyn Caddes, Robert
& Ruth Halperin, Mark Day of Good
Cooks & Company, Deborah Fife,
Peter Mansfield, Patsy Ishiyama,
Rob Kinsey, Glenn & Nancy Mueller,
Alice Wong, Bill & Mary Cox,
Alexandra Morrall, Olivia Dawson,
Janice Kim, Eric Fry, Scooter
Mitchell, Eric Wong, and Emperor
Bennett Ho.

Acknowledgements

謹以此書 獻給愛妻
璐德，感謝她為我辛勞持家；
以及事業上的最佳伴侶，做為
我們結婚十二年的禮物。

America is such a bountiful country—rich in land, products, and opportunities. It is a country where a person can dream and where, with a lot of hard work and a little bit of luck, dreams can come true.

This book—a vehicle through which I can share my professional knowledge developed over twenty years and more—has been one of my great dreams. I am grateful to the people who have made it possible.

Most of the recipes in this book have been handed down through the centuries by chefs who have kept culinary secrets alive through their sheer love of cooking. I have learned from them by inheriting traditions they established. I have learned greatly from all the chefs I have worked with, especially my colleagues and mentors: H.T. Chu, my father and source of inspirations, Alec Cline, teacher and advisor; and Chef Chen Shiang Shen, master chef and close associate.

All this knowledge, still, would not make a book but for the team that has come together, working so closely and with such kind attention that they are now family: Ciddy Wordell, my developmental editor and patient scribe; Linda Brandt, my food editor and masterful coordinator; two superior photographers, Nikolay Zurek and Leo Holub; polished book designer, James Stockton; talented primary writer and editor Susan Wels who was assisted by Kay Daley, Karin Shakery, and Debby Fife; researcher, Carolyn Cline and Belinda Chung; and my publishers, who not only made it come to be, but also insisted on absolute authenticity in recipes and graphic presentations. Their energy and resourcefulness have guaranteed the quality of this work.

Running a restaurant seven days a week, as chef, manager, and host, requires a zealous devotion on my part made possible only because of a generously tolerant family whose presence by my side I cherish.

Though mentioned last, they generally come first in my mind: the patrons of Chef Chu's Restaurant.

Hsieh hsieh.

Lawrence C. C. Chu

New Year's feast pictured on the following pages include (clockwise, from top): antique basket laden with fresh oranges and kumquats; deep-fried pastry buns; an assortment of treats—fresh kumquats, candied lotus seeds, dried lichee nuts, candied lotus root, preserved kumquats, and dried winter melon seeds; eight treasure rice pudding (page 191), rich in color and flavor; deep-fried sesame buns, filled with sweet bean paste and symbolizing wealth; Hunan honey-glazed ham (page 121), a prized and dramatic presentation; whole roast duck, purchased in a Chinatown specialty shop; fragrant duck (page 41), a cold plate that may be prepared in advance; steamed kirin fish (page 101), symbolizing prosperity; mixed Chinese vegetables (page 150); and a section of roast suckling pig, which can usually be purchased freshly roasted from a specialty shop in Chinatown. Red paper envelopes, tucked inside decorative jar, hold small presents of money for children and younger friends to ward off the unwanted effects of aging that each New Year brings!

■

Table of Contents

Introducing Chef Chu

He is in his thirties, very personable, attractive, has boundless energy, is attentive, creative, and successful. Born in Szechuan, China, he lived in several countries before moving to San Francisco. In 1970, he opened a restaurant in Los Altos, 40 miles south of the city. Small to begin with, it expanded over the years to serve a growing and sophisticated clientele that now numbers 800 a day. He is a masterful chef, an adroit teacher of his cuisine, and a very likeable individual. This is his book, a work in progress for two years, a sharing of culinary "secrets" resulting from more than twenty years of experience. The publishers are pleased to introduce Lawrence C. C. Chu, Chef.

"Of course you can cook as well as I can," Chef Chu will tell an inquiring patron at his restaurant. "Many people are afraid to cook Chinese food because they think they need special equipment and unusual ingredients. That's not so. Chinese cooking is as much a philosophy, a technique, as it is a particular piece of equipment or combination of flavors. Anyone can prepare a good Chinese meal at home with a good sauté pan and simple ingredients usually on hand. If you like to eat Chinese food, you shouldn't hesitate to discover the pleasure of preparing it."

Pleasure, philosophy, and technique are three words that fit Chef Chu. *"Haw tze* is a Chinese saying that means loving to eat and experiment with different foods. That's how I am. Food is one of the great pleasures of my life, and my restaurant is my child—my other five children and my wife understand that," he grins. And Chef Chu's patrons understand, too, as the quality of cooking and the presentation of food at his restaurant reflect his care and zest for perfection. The sheer pleasure of eating is paramount in the mind of this restaurateur and his staff.

"To enjoy good food," insists Larry Chu, "you must be relaxed, in a good mood, and in the proper atmosphere." In his bustling but comfortable, two-storied California restaurant, he has set himself the task of seeing to it that each of his guests is in the proper spirit. As diners stream through the door into the warm, russet-walled lobby, he is usually there to greet them, shaking hands with old friends and introducing himself to new ones. Rarely found relaxing, he couples the roles of host and chef often.

After remembering to scrawl a special birthday message in Chinese on a sign board by the door to welcome an 82-year-old grandmother and her banquet party, he enters the active kitchen to prepare several dishes, emerging periodically to present his breathtaking banquet entrées, explaining each delicacy with appropriate flourish. "Is everything all right? Are you enjoying yourselves?" he will ask, stopping at tables. The mood, like the food, is carefully tended.

The bustling kitchen, open to full view, adds its own excited energy as dinner hour peaks. Waiting customers crowd the glass wall, watching the furious motions of white-capped

Chef Lawrence C. C. Chu, 1982.

10

heads and flashing hands. Waiters dart in and out, blue flames shoot up under woks, steam furls beneath the faucets, and dishes hiss and sizzle to completion in 20 seconds of intense heat. In the noisy confusion, there are pockets of calm: a cook cleaves a duck and plunges it into snapping hot oil, a pastry cook folds won-ton envelopes filled with crabmeat, a chef delicately carves the crisp amber skin of a Peking duck.

Through all of this, Larry Chu circles ceaselessly, watching, checking, testing, encouraging. From time to time, he pauses in the kitchen to eat a bowl of green noodles with concentrated pleasure or to watch his banquet chef prepare a complicated speciality. "I teach my chefs," he says, "and they teach me." He cooks beside them, too, rolling up his sleeves to carve a white rose from a radish or to put the final touches on a steaming dragon fish, moments before it is carried to the table.

It is only well toward midnight that Larry Chu allows himself to stop, sitting quietly over supper with his staff. He has been at the restaurant since 10 o'clock in the morning, scheduling, ordering, planning, and filling in where needed. Now he collapses in a chair, scribbling absently on a piece of paper while his cooks and assistants help themselves to plates of braised chicken and winter melon.

He is proud of his work, proud of the restaurant he built with almost single-minded effort over the past twelve years. He thinks of one day opening another *Chef Chu's* farther south, to serve customers who now drive distances to his restaurant. But that is in the future. For now, he is content to run one restaurant and focus his extra energy on teaching

others how to enjoy the pleasures of Chinese cooking.

Since 1976, Chef Chu has held Chinese cooking classes in the restaurant's cooking studio, and nearly every Saturday he is there, in his white hat and apron, demonstrating to capacity audiences how to prepare his favorite recipes. During class, he cooks and chatters, irreverently sharing every secret and shortcut in preparation.

He concentrates on teaching methods that are unique to Chinese cooking, and techniques that he has developed himself—techniques distinctively his, that distinguish his style of cooking from that of his peers. "Once you understand the purpose of various techniques and cooking methods, forget about theory," he tells his students. "Use your nose, eyes, ears, hands, and taste buds to cook. Be sensitive to the wok aroma,

Saturday and evening classes are always filled to capacity with students eager to learn the Chef's techniques for preparing their favorite recipes.

and the color, flavor, and texture of what you are creating." Most of all, he advises students to practice so that they develop confidence and a good sense of timing. "The important thing," he advises them, "is to get everything out of your hands, so that you can enjoy yourself!"

Larry Chu is open to new ideas that will make Chinese cooking easier, faster, more convenient for American cooks. He enrolled in a food technology program at a local college to study Western culinary techniques, and has no reluctance about putting American technology to work. "It is good to try new methods," he asserts. "The important thing is that the food taste good."

In his own simple white and oak-grained kitchen at home, he relies on such American utensils as an electric frying pan, a sauté pan, an electric rice cooker, and an electric deep-fat fryer. A microwave oven is set into the kitchen wall, and he is currently testing its usefulness in Chinese cooking. "Right now," he says, "it is mainly good for heating things up, but I'm still experimenting."

Most of his own cooking and entertaining is done at the restaurant, where he and his staff prepare banquets and catered dinners for customers and friends. At home, a housekeeper does the cooking, although Larry Chu normally creates one elaborate meal a month for his extended family. The family's fare normally consists of simple favorites such as noodles or dumplings. Breakfast is often rice porridge with toppings of peanuts, dried fish, and bean curd. Although the children, ranging

13

The key to making delicious soup is a rich, flavorful broth—in this case, it's chicken.

in age from 3 to 9½, are rarely allowed to come to the restaurant, his wife, Ruth, frequently stops by school to bring them hot lunches of won-ton soup from *Chef Chu's* kitchen.

He came to the restaurant business naturally, from a family that loved good food and enjoyed experimenting with different styles of cooking. Born in 1944 in the wartime Chinese capital of Chungking in the province of Szechuan, he moved with his family to Taiwan in 1949. His father, a

well-traveled palace architect and designer, prized good cooking and brought to it an adventurous and open mind.

Food images fill Larry Chu's memories of the crowded city of Taipei, where the family resided. Peddlers jammed the streets, pushing carts of steaming won-ton soup and *char siu bao* from door to door. Street vendors sold flavored ices on nearly every corner, and eating places were always packed with people dining on the spicy regional cooking of Taiwan.

At age 14, he left Taipei for Hong Kong to study photography. Living there alone for three years, he dined out frequently, exploring the immense variety of Chinese cuisine in the cosmopolitan British colony.

While he was there, his parents emigrated to the United States, and Larry Chu joined them in San Francisco in 1963. After a year, he enrolled in a university architectural program and began earning money by working nights at San Francisco's famed *Trader Vic's* restaurant.

At the time, he recalls, restaurant work was "just a job" but cooking fascinated him, and so he decided to learn the basics of the restaurant business from the bottom up. But his real education and culinary expertise began in 1965 when his father decided to open a Chinese restaurant in Menlo Park.

From the beginning, his father's *Mandarin House* was a success. It was the first Chinese restaurant on the San Francisco Peninsula to feature Mandarin cuisine, and Larry Chu left *Trader Vic's* to help his father operate the business. He was tutored in cooking there by an elderly Chinese cook, "the most talented chef" he says, he has ever encountered. "That was my first training ground," he recalls.

In 1969 Larry Chu decided to go out on his own. With his savings, his newly-gained experience, and a small loan from his parents, he opened a "bare-boned" food-to-go stand in a small, well-located storefront in Los Altos. He ran it with the help of one cook and his optimistic fiancée, Ruth.

Though the restaurant offered only a dozen items, they quickly found that customers were asking for dishes not on the menu. "People seemed to enjoy the food we cooked," Larry remembers. "They were always curious when Ruth or I fixed something different for ourselves, and seemed anxious to try new things." On a minimal budget, the Chus decided to lease the storefront next door, put in some tables, and began expanding their menu slowly.

The first year and a half were difficult, but when favorable newspaper reviewers discovered them, the restaurant began to thrive. Larry and Ruth Chu took over additional space next door, thus doubling their seating capacity; the popularity of the restaurant kept pace. In 1974, they built a large, well-ventilated, stainless steel kitchen, and then in 1976, they added banquet facilities on the second floor.

Chef Chu's is still in part a family-run operation—Ruth keeps the books, and his brother, Norman, man-

As chef de cuisine, Larry Chu must oversee the general operation of the restaurant, including purchasing and scheduling.

15

ages the banquet room. "Because we were inexperienced in the beginning," he explains, "our families taught us to always treat the customer as our guest. We always served more rather than less, and we found that our business grew by word of mouth." He still takes personal pride in his customers' comfort and insists that "it is better to put extra food on their plates, than pay for advertising."

If asked what makes *Chef Chu's* different from most other Chinese restaurants, Larry has a ready answer, but one based on experience and proven by his establishment's long-standing reputation. "Consistency," he says firmly. "If you enjoy what you eat here once, you expect to enjoy it the next time you come. You will not be disappointed. Many restaurants rely on the reputation of their chefs, and unfortunately, chefs are notorious for coming and going. Since I am the *chef de cuisine,* and not just an employee whose interest is monetary, *Chef Chu's* reputation is my reputation—I am Chef Chu."

If his customers' respect for his reputation is essential to his restaurant's success, so are the respect, loyalty, and happiness of his staff. According to Larry Chu, it is impossible to cook good food if you are feeling sad or angry, and he sees keeping the cooks' spirits high as one of his main responsibilities. In the morning, when he breezes through the back door of the sunny kitchen, he greets the crew with a barrage of jokes and he constantly passes through the kitchen during the day, diffusing quarrels and making sure the mood is bouyant. Too much laxity, however, is discouraged. If a cook is slouching at the stove, he is likely to be reprimanded: "Stand straight while you are cooking! Stand like a chef!"

Just as Larry Chu blends Western techniques and equipment with Chinese cooking styles, so has he found a useful model in European kitchen organization. His kitchen staff, behind the steam and seeming confusion of activity, is a tightly-organized group in which everyone knows his duties specifically and thoroughly. While the kitchen staff's basic organization resembles that of many Chinese restaurants, its discipline and titles have been adopted by Larry from the French.

As *chef de cuisine,* Larry Chu oversees the general operation of the restaurant and does all purchasing and scheduling. His *sous chef,* or kitchen manager receives all supplies and oversees the staff and the cooking. Next come eight stir-fry or *sauté cooks;* two hors d'oeuvre cooks specializing in potstickers, soups, and similar items; a pastry cook; and a portion assembler who gathers together all the ingredients required for each dish and passes them to the appropriate cook for braising, steaming, or stir-frying. Beneath the cooks are three kitchen helpers who clean vegetables and prepare basic ingredients.

On a par with the *sous chef* is Chef Chang, a renowned banquet chef specializing in Hunan cuisine, whom Larry Chu brought to the United States from Taiwan. Together, Larry Chu and Chef Chang plan banquet menus, and Chang executes them, proudly bringing forth glistening

Friendly greeting by host Lawrence Chu awaits diners at Chef Chu's restaurant. Tempting seafood dinner includes: seaweed soup (page 59), Foochow clams (page 105), and Hangchow poached cod (page 100).

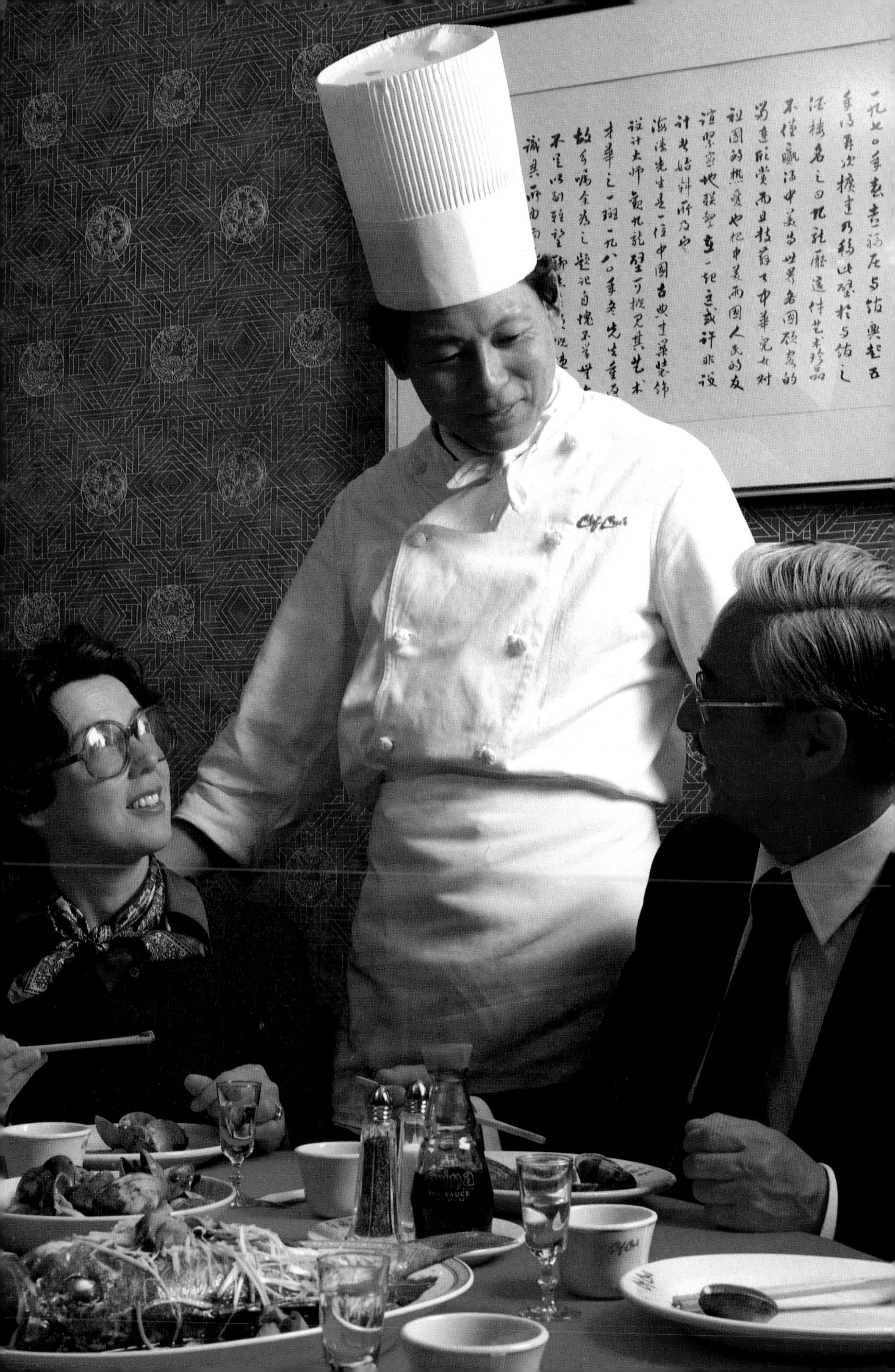

dishes such as eel sautéed with Chinese cucumber, ham with lotus seeds, savory green noodles, shrimp with salty egg yolk, and tender bok choy and scallops simmering in a delicious chicken broth.

As chef, restaurateur, caterer, and teacher, Larry Chu has little time for his quiet pleasures, such as the San Francisco Light Opera, reading, and rare, unhurried vacations at the beach. Sundays are devoted to Ruth and the children, but the restaurant claims more than equal attention. "It's hard, sometimes," he says, "but Ruth and I both know that how well we do depends on how much we care about, know about, and give to the restaurant."

Part of his effort to stay knowledgeable and involved includes exposing himself to new ideas and challenges. "Education," he says, "is just like rowing a boat upstream. If you don't keep rowing, the boat goes backwards." He keeps abreast of Western and Eastern cooking by dining out and traveling, as far as Europe and China, to meet the world's best chefs and learn their techniques.

His greatest pleasure, however, is in teaching others to cook with confidence. He plans to build a bigger cooking studio to accommodate larger classes, but even so, he will only be able to share his recipes and expertise with a few; so to spread the word and the ease of Chinese cooking, Larry has written this book, hoping others will learn how creative and enjoyable gourmet Chinese cooking can be.

A wide, full-length mirror, suspended overhead, enables students to get a better glimpse of the Chef in action (at left). Consulting with Chef Chu is Chef Chang, the restaurant's banquet chef who specializes in regional dishes from Hunan. Here he offers suggestions for an upcoming banquet serving a dozen guests with as many different courses.

Chinese Ingredients *Pictured on pages 20 and 21*

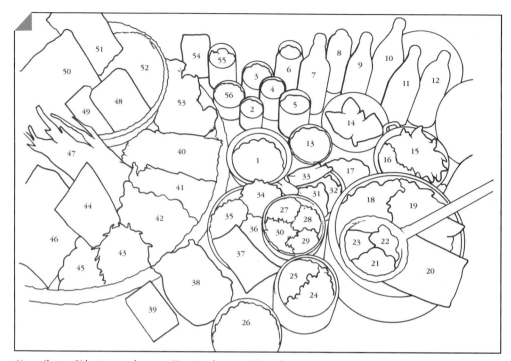

1) quail eggs, 2) button mushrooms, 3) water chestnuts, 4) mushrooms, 5) hoisin sauce, 6) preserved ginger, 7) soy sauce, 8) sesame oil, 9) light soy sauce, 10) and 11) red rice vinegar, 12) rice wine, 13) five-spice powder, 14) bamboo shoots, 15) licorice chips, 16) peanuts, 17) preserved plums, 18) and 19) dried mushrooms, 20) dried seaweed, 21) cardamom seed, 22) dried scallops, 23) sea cucumbers, 24) lotus seeds, 25) black beans, 26) dried shrimp, 27) fennel seeds, 28) crushed chili peppers, 29) and 30) star anise, 31) cardamom seeds, 32) dried abalone, 33) Chinese cinnamon, 34) hair seaweed, 35) black sesame seeds, 36) sesame seeds, 37) pressed bean curd, 38) and 39) tea, 40) rice sticks, 41) dried Chinese greens, 42) red dates, 43) tiger lily (golden needles), 44) red dates, 45) dried lichee nuts, 46) dried shark's fin, 47) dried bean curd skins, 48) wheat flour, 49) spicy rice, 50) rice sticks, 51) dried sugar cane, 52) rice, 53) dry noodles, 54) dried bean curd skins, 55) button mushrooms, 56) shredded bamboo shoots.

Before you begin....

A new cookbook will tempt the confident cook to plunge in immediately with the testing of an interesting recipe. **Please may I ask you to read the following before you begin?**

There are two principles in successful Chinese cooking: **visualizing** the dish before preparation begins and good **timing** during the actual cooking.

To make sure that you are able to **visualize** the dish and the process, we have devised a recipe format which is easy to read, step-by-step. The ingredients appear in the order in which you will need them. If an ingredient is to be marinated, the marinade spices will follow immediately after the ingredient. Preparation instructions are easy to spot and follow the same sequence as the listing of ingredients so that you need not look back and forth. The method of cooking appears in bold—such as steaming, oil blanching, deep-frying, stir-frying—so you can see at a glance how many major steps are involved and the eventual appearance and textures your dish will have. The various methods of preconditioning and cooking are described in detail beginning on page 196. The most valuable information appears on these pages. If I have any "chef's secrets" or tips to pass on, these are the most important.

Please read each recipe carefully, including the notes in which I try to alert you to common pitfalls and there's no need to stumble in them! Also, before you begin, have your serving plate or bowl ready. Having read the recipe, you'll be able to visualize the outcome so select the most appropriate receptacle: If large long pieces of food are involved, select a long plate; if the pieces are round, a round plate; if there are juices, a plate with a lip. Using the appropriate plate in which to serve your dish will add to the success of your presentation. And, with food which requires quick cooking, having the receptacle ready when you remove the pan from the stove is a good idea. The color of ingredients may determine the color of your plate. If there are many colors, and a "busy" feeling is generated, use a white plate. (If Chinese cooking is not infrequent in your home, you might consider adding Chinese tableware to your cupboard. The photographs which appear in this book feature authentic Chinese porcelain in natural, unstylized settings.)

Timing is not just how long the cooking time should be. By timing I mean the ability to cook with your senses.

Use your nose to smell the aroma because the aroma tells you when to proceed. The Chinese will often say, "Bring out the wok aroma, which, literally means cook the green onion and garlic until fragrant." The nose is very important.

Use your eyes to see the color changing or the smoke appearing or the steam rising or the sauce thickening—your eyes will help you create the dish you have envisioned.

Use your ears to hear the rice sizzling or the broth bubbling—to know when to move on to the next step.

And use your mouth to make the ultimate sensory evaluation—to tell you if the spices, seasonings and juices of the ingredients have been properly married and that the best flavor has been achieved.

Learning this kind of timing takes much trial and error, but your common sense and good judgment will always be the ingredients needed to succeed as an accomplished Chinese cook.

L.C.

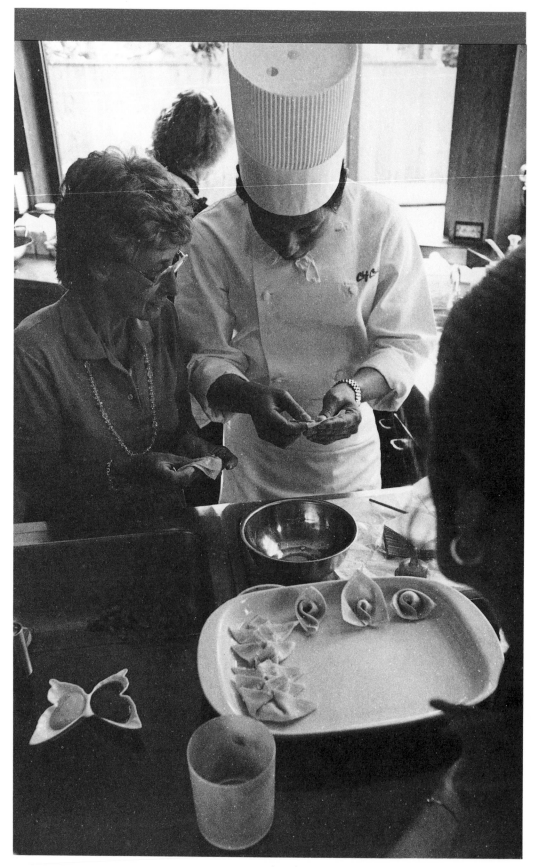

APPETIZERS
& COLD PLATE

The etiquette of a Chinese dinner party, or of a family meal in a Chinese home, differs greatly from the American tradition. Unlike the Western practice of serving hors d'oeuvres during the social exchanges which precede a meal, Chinese hospitality in a dinner party commences rather promptly at the table.

Since it would not do to bring one's guests to an empty table, several dishes of appetizers are already displayed on the table when guests are seated.

In a banquet setting, the array of appetizers is likely to include at least half a dozen small, delicate dishes with nuts, dried fruits, and little sweet cakes. At a family meal, the appetizers are more likely to include smoked fish, a spicy cold chicken, and colorful arrangements of cold vegetables.

These hot and cold appetizers must be artfully arranged as they offer guests their first view of dinner and promises of the splendid meal which is in store. Their appearance and flavors should stimulate the appetite while pleasing the eye. And, on a more practical note, their presence on the table allows guests to begin savoring the meal while the cook attends to the last-minute dishes.

The host may introduce wine at the beginning of the meal and raise the first toast to guests. Chinese wines are distilled from grains and are quite potent. They somewhat resemble whisky or liquer, and one must acquire a taste for them. I find my guests prefer a nice Gewurtstraminner or Zinfandel!

The appetizers that appear in this section are very versatile—they may be served in the traditional Western style, prior to sitting at the table, and make excellent items for picnics, boat parties, or tailgates. They will give your children great cheer when they find them in lunch boxes, too. Look for other serving suggestions in the notes.

Cold plates are also versatile. Many can be served alone as one-dish meals, such as Lobster with Four Flavors, and make a nice addition to the repertoire of light luncheon fare.

Cold vegetable dishes are also excellent as salads and as condiments to accompany Western meals. Served slightly chilled in the Chinese style, these vegetables are light and crunchy, and enhanced by delicately piquant dressings.

Three or four appetizers or cold plates are a must at a Chinese banquet. They may be skipped in an informal meal, although I would encourage you to tantalize your guests with at least one.

Making won-tons may seem difficult at first—one's thumbs seem to get in the way! Nevertheless, a few instructions from the Chef in person and you can wrap two won-tons per minute—a great group activity.

25

Crab & Cheese Puffs   *Pictured on page 33*

Crispy, crunchy on the outside, these uniquely-shaped appetizers are so pretty they need no decoration when served. The inside is a delicious, subtle combination of flaked crab meat and softened cream cheese.

Makes: 24 appetizers
Cooking time: 15 minutes

FILLING

  2 ounces cooked crab meat, lightly flaked (or cooked baby shrimp)
  1 small package (3 oz.) cream cheese, at room temperature
     Pinch salt
     Pinch white pepper

 24 won-ton wrappers
     Beaten egg

     Vegetable oil, for deep-frying

     Chinese Hot Mustard Sauce (page 212) and Chef Chu's Dipping Sauce (page 212)

Combine FILLING ingredients well.

To assemble, put 1 teaspoon filling in center of wrapper, seal edges with egg, and fold as illustrated below.

To deep-fry, heat 4 cups oil in wok (or electric deep-fat fryer) to 350°. Fry, a few at a time, for 1½ minutes or until puffy and golden brown. Offer mustard and dipping sauces at the table.

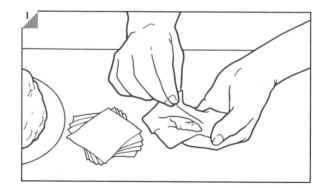

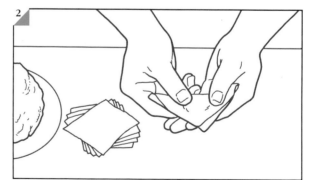

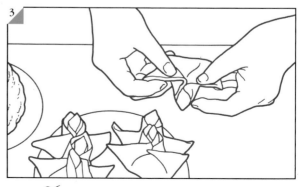

Place 1 teaspoon filling in center of wrapper and 1) fold to form triangle. 2) Push filling into center and seal edges together. Lightly brush center of triangle with beaten egg and 3) bring corners together, forming a butterfly.

26

Golden Coin Shrimp

Many items on a Chinese menu suggest "happiness" or "long life." That is because we are rather superstitious and believe in symbols of good luck. In placing a meal before friends, we take advantage of the opportunity to wish our guests well. The "gold coin" symbolizes wealth, a good wish, and this appetizer of shrimp, ham, and onion is rich with good tastes, too.

Makes 20 appetizers
Cooking time: 10 minutes

½ pound shrimp, shelled and deveined

MIXTURE
1 egg
1 tablespoon cornstarch
¼ teaspoon minced fresh ginger
½ teaspoon sugar
¼ teaspoon salt
Pinch white pepper

6 slices white bread
2 green onions (tops), minced
2 tablespoons finely chopped ham (or black sesame seeds)

Vegetable oil, for deep-frying

Tomato rose (or other vegetable carving)

Using a food processor or by hand, finely chop shrimp and MIXTURE ingredients and mix until a paste consistency is reached. Using a cookie cutter, cut each slice of bread into 4 circles (each about 1½-inches in diameter).

To assemble, spread about 2 teaspoons paste on each bread circle. Sprinkle half the circle with onion and the other half with ham.

To deep-fry, heat 3 cups oil in a heavy 12-inch skillet or straight-sided frying pan to 350°. Gently lower circles into oil, paste side up. Deep-fry for 2 to 3 minutes until bottoms brown; carefully turn over for 30 seconds, then turn back and remove. Drain on paper towels and arrange on serving platter. Garnish with tomato rose.

• Notes •

1. Twenty appetizers fit perfectly in a 12-inch skillet.

2. If you don't want to be deep-frying when your guests arrive, make this in advance and reheat in a preheated 250° oven for 5 minutes.

Curry Beef Puffs

My children don't always approve of my new concoctions, but this variation for fried Won-Ton got their high marks. The light aroma of curry whets the appetite.

Makes: 48 appetizers
Cooking time: 15 minutes

- 3 tablespoons vegetable oil
- ½ small white onion, coarsely chopped
- ⅓ pound lean ground beef

SEASONINGS

- 1 tablespoon dry sherry
- 2 teaspoons curry powder
- 1 teaspoon sugar
  Pinch salt
  Pinch white pepper

  Cornstarch paste

- 4 dozen won-ton wrappers
  Beaten egg

  Vegetable oil, for deep-frying

  Chinese Hot Mustard Sauce (page 212) and Chef Chu's Dipping Sauce (page 212)

To stir-fry, set wok (or wide frying pan) over high heat for 1 minute until hot. Add oil and swirl sides to coat. When oil is hot, add onion and stir-fry for 30 seconds. Add beef, stirring to separate, and cook for 1 minute. Add SEASONINGS and stir well. Bring to a boil and thicken with 1 tablespoon cornstarch paste. Remove and pour into a fine strainer to cool.

To assemble, cut won-ton wrappers into 3½-inch circles using a canape cutter or empty soup can. Cover to prevent drying. Moisten edge of 1 wrapper with egg and spoon 1 teaspoon filling in center. Fold in half to make half-circle. Lightly pinch to seal edges. Repeat with remaining wrappers, covering to prevent drying out.

To deep-fry, heat 4 cups oil in a wok (or electric deep-fat fryer) to 350°. Carefully, fry puffs, about a dozen at a time, until golden brown. Serve with mustard and dipping sauces.

• *Notes* •

1. Try making won-ton rings from the leftover won-ton wrapper trimming. Deep-fry them and serve with Sweet & Sour Sauce for dipping.

2. To make ahead, place uncooked appetizers on a cookie sheet dusted with cornstarch and cover with a damp towel.

Fried Won-ton *Pictured on page 33*

Did you know that when you eat won-ton you are "swallowing clouds"? That's the literal translation of the Chinese words, and, if you see the delicate won-ton in soup, the description is quite perfect. This recipe calls for the simple meat dumplings to be crisply fried until deep golden brown then offered with Sweet and Sour Sauce for dipping.

Makes: 48 appetizers
Cooking time: 15 minutes

FILLING

- ¼ pound ground pork
- 1 green onion, finely chopped
- 1 tablespoon dry sherry
- ½ teaspoon sugar
- ¼ teaspoon salt
  Pinch white pepper
  Dash sesame oil

- 4 dozen won-ton wrappers
  Beaten egg

  Vegetable oil, for deep-frying

  Sweet & Sour Sauce (page 213) for dipping

Mix FILLING ingredients thoroughly in a bowl.

To assemble, place ¼ teaspoon filling in the center of each won-ton wrapper. Fold as illustrated below.

To deep-fry, heat 4 cups oil in wok (or electric deep-fat fryer) to 350°. Deep-fry won-ton, a dozen at a time, for about 1½ minutes or until golden brown. Serve with sauce for dipping.

• Notes •

1. In the restaurant, I use egg roll wrappers cut in fourths instead of buying won-ton wrappers since I need them for egg rolls anyway. Unused wrappers may be frozen or wrapped in foil and refrigerated up to 1 week.

2. Use very little filling—¼ teaspoon is best—because the meat has to cook through quickly without overcooking the wrapper.

3. Uncooked won-ton may be frozen individually on cookie sheets first, then stored in plastic bags in freezer until ready to use.

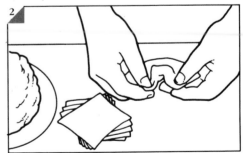

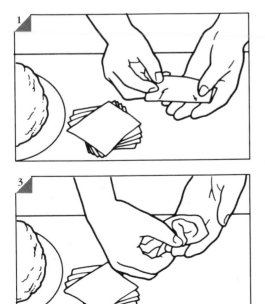

Place ¼ teaspoon filling in center of wrapper and 1) fold in half lengthwise. Lightly brush left side with beaten egg and 2) bring right side over on top. 3) Press firmly, making sure right and left corners are sealed.

Crispy Shrimp Balls   *Pictured on page 33*

Prawns, fresh ginger, green onion, and bacon are finely chopped together and then shaped into small balls. Each one is rolled in soft, homemade croutons and then deep-fried until lightly golden.

Makes: 20 appetizers
Cooking time: 10 minutes

MIXTURE

- ½ pound medium-size prawns, shelled and deveined
- 1 strip bacon, coarsely chopped
- 1 green onion (white part)
- ¼ teaspoon minced fresh ginger
- 1 water chestnut, coarsely chopped (optional)

SEASONINGS

- 1 egg, slightly beaten
- 3 tablespoons flour
- ½ teaspoon baking powder
- ¼ teaspoon salt
  Pinch white pepper

- 2 cups coarsely-cubed bread croutons

  Vegetable oil, for deep-frying

  Chinese Hot Mustard Sauce (page 212) and Chef Chu's Dipping Sauce (page 212)

With a food processor or knife, finely chop MIXTURE ingredients until a paste consistency is reached. Add water chestnut and SEASONINGS and mix thoroughly; let stand for 10 minutes.

To shape, dip hand in water (as necessary) to prevent sticking. Grab a handful of mixture (about ¼ cup) and squeeze out 1-inch balls from the top of your fist as illustrated below. Roll each ball in a tray filled with bread croutons, covering completely. Lightly squeeze outside of ball so that croutons stick; set aside.

To deep-fry, heat 3 or 4 cups oil in wok to 275°. Add balls, all at once, and then raise oil temperature to 350°. Continue frying for 2 to 4 minutes or until golden brown. Remove and drain on paper towels.

To serve, arrange on serving platter with small bowls of mustard and dipping sauces at the table.

• Notes •

1. To make fresh croutons, trim crusts from 4 slices bread and then cut into cubes about ¼-inch thick. Allow them to dry for about 5 minutes in a 300° oven.

2. If using a food processor to prepare paste, use steel knife blade and only process for about 1 minute.

3. This is almost a double-frying process. The balls cook at a lower temperature to retain their shape as well as heat the inside; the higher temperature is required to brown the outside.

Dip hand in water to prevent sticking. Then 1) grab handful of mixture and squeeze out 1-inch balls from top of fist. With spoon, lower balls into tray and 2) roll them in croutons to cover evenly.

Phoenix Tail Fried Prawns   *Pictured on page 33*

These butterflyed prawns, quickly deep-fried to be crunchy on the outside but succulent and flavorful inside, are worthy of their majestic name. Serve with my special dipping sauce.

Makes: 26 to 30 appetizers
Cooking time: 20 to 30 minutes

- 1 pound medium-size (26–30 count) prawns

BATTER
- 1 cup flour
- ⅓ cup cornstarch
- 1 cup water
- 1 egg
- 2 tablespoons oil
- ½ teaspoon baking powder
- Pinch salt

MARINADE
- ¼ teaspoon salt
- Pinch garlic powder
- Pinch white pepper

Vegetable oil, for deep-frying

Lemon slices
Chinese Hot Mustard Sauce (page 212) and
Chef Chu's Dipping Sauce (page 212)

Mix together BATTER ingredients until the consistency of heavy cream. Let stand ½ hour.

Shell prawns, leaving tails attached. Split down the back, removing black vein, to butterfly. Rinse in cold water to clean thoroughly, drain and pat dry.

Combine MARINADE ingredients with prawns and let stand for 10 minutes.

To deep-fry, heat 4 cups oil in wok (or electric deep-fat fryer) to 300°. Grab prawns by the tail, dip into batter to coat, and drop into oil. Deep-fry, a few at a time, for 2 minutes. When all prawns have been fried, increase oil to 350°. Return prawns, all at once, to oil and deep-fry 1½ to 2 minutes longer until golden brown. Remove with strainer and drain on paper towels.

To serve, arrange prawns decoratively on platter and garnish with lemon slices at both ends of platter. Serve with mustard and dipping sauces at table.

• *Notes* •

1. If you want to make prawns ahead of time, deep-fry just once until lightly browned; then do the second frying at serving time.

2. When choosing fresh prawns, look for ones with a light grey-blue tinge to the shell and translucent flesh.

Spring Rolls *Pictured on facing page.*

Chinese New Year usually occurs at the end of winter and signals the beginning of spring when vegetables are young, tender, and succulent. Many are gathered for this delicious appetizer. (The following recipe includes pork and shrimp but vegetarian spring rolls are excellent, too. To make, simply replace missing ingredients with more black mushrooms.)

Makes: 36 appetizers
Cooking time: 30 minutes

- 2 dried black mushrooms

- 3 tablespoons vegetable oil
- 1 green onion (white part), finely chopped
- ¼ cup cooked and peeled shrimp
- ¼ cup shredded Chinese Barbecued Pork (page 39)

VEGETABLES
- 2 stalks celery, diagonally sliced and shredded
- 1 small head regular cabbage, shredded
- 1½ cups bean sprouts
- ½ cup shredded bamboo shoots

SEASONINGS
- 2 tablespoons dry sherry
- 1 teaspoon salt
   Pinch white pepper
   Pinch Chinese five-spice

   Dash sesame oil

- 12 spring roll wrappers (see page 206)
   Beaten egg

   Vegetable oil, for deep-frying

   Chinese Hot Mustard Sauce (page 212) and Chef Chu's Dipping Sauce (page 212)

Soak mushrooms in warm water for 20 minutes; drain, remove stems, and shred.

To stir-fry, set wok (or wide frying pan) over high heat for 1 minute until hot. Add oil and swirl to coat sides. When oil is hot, add green onion and cook until fragrant. Add shrimp and pork; cook 2 minutes. Stir in VEGETABLES, sprinkle with SEASONINGS, mix well, and continue stir-frying for 3 minutes longer. Remove from heat to test for doneness. (Bean sprouts should be slightly wilted yet still crunchy.) Return to heat, add sesame oil, and toss gently. Pour into colander to drain; let cool.

To assemble, place wrapper with one point toward you. Moisten upper edges with egg. Spoon about 3 tablespoons filling in center of wrapper and fold bottom up and over filling to cover. Fold over left and right corners so they meet in the center. Then, roll up, jellyroll-style, sealing final corner. Repeat with remaining wrappers; cover with plastic wrap as you go to prevent drying.

To deep-fry, heat 4 cups oil in wok (or electric deep-fat fryer) to 350°. Carefully, put 4 or 5 rolls in oil and deep-fry for 3 to 4 minutes or until golden brown on all sides. Remove and drain on paper towels. Check to see that oil temperature is 350° before doing next batch.

To serve, cut rolls into thirds. Serve with mustard and dipping sauces at the table.

Sailors and landlovers alike enjoy portable sampling of Chinese appetizers. Tempting array includes (clockwise, from top): tea-smoked duck (page 84) with steamed bread (page 176); barbecued spareribs; Phoenix tail fried prawns with dipping sauce (page 31); sliced and whole spring rolls (above); crispy shrimp balls (page 30); and plate of fried won-ton (page 29) and crab & cheese puffs (page 26). Photographed at St. Francis Yacht Club, San Francisco.

Swordstick Beef

If your party is outdoors, here's a perfect way to involve your guests. These marinated appetizers allow your friends to gather around one or more hibachis or grills and cook at their pleasure.

Makes: 24 appetizers
Cooking time: 10 minutes

1 pound flank steak, sliced against grain ¼- by 1- by 2-inches thick

MARINADE

 3 tablespoons soy sauce
 2 teaspoons dry sherry
 2 tablespoons Hoisin sauce
 1 green onion (white part), minced
 1 tablespoon vegetable oil
 1 teaspoon sesame oil
   Pinch white pepper

24 six-inch bamboo skewers
 3 tablespoons vegetable oil (for pan-frying only)

Combine MARINADE ingredients in a bowl; add beef strips and mix well. Let stand for about 20 minutes. Lift out strips and thread 3 or 4 pieces on each skewer (reserve marinade for grilling).

To grill, arrange skewers on grill over hot coals and cook, rotating frequently and basting with marinade, for 1 to 2 minutes or until desired doneness is reached.

Or, to **pan-fry,** set wok over high heat for 1 minute until hot. Add oil and swirl pan to coat sides. When oil is hot, lay beef skewers around sides of wok; cook, turning often and basting with oil, until desired doneness is reached.

• *Notes* •

1. You'll be able to slice the beef easily if you partially freeze it first.

2. Use reserved marinade rather than vegetable oil for basting when cooking on a grill over hot coals.

Parchment-wrapped Chicken

This is one of my favorites because my mother used to offer these quick snacks to us when we lived in China. She often substituted chicken with beef or fish—it really doesn't matter what you use. The result is a very tender, juicy, and tasty morsel tucked inside a parchment envelope.

Makes: 12 appetizers
Cooking time: 5 minutes

- 1 whole chicken breast, split, boned, and cut into 12 pieces

MARINADE

- 1 tablespoon soy sauce
- 1 tablespoon dry sherry
- ½ teaspoon minced green onion (white part)
- 1 tablespoon Hoisin sauce
- 1 thumb-size slice fresh ginger, minced
  Pinch Chinese five-spice

- 12 sprigs Chinese parsley (cilantro), cut in pieces
- 12 pieces parchment paper (or aluminum foil), cut into 6-inch squares

  Sesame oil

  Vegetable oil, for deep-frying

Combine chicken with MARINADE ingredients and let stand for 20 minutes.

To assemble, brush each square of parchment with sesame oil. Wrap 1 piece of chicken and 1 piece of parsley inside. Fold in half to form a triangle; then fold over edges a few times to seal completely and twist corners. Or fold in another decorative way illustrated below.

To deep-fry, heat 4 cups oil in a wok (or electric deep-fat fryer) to 350°. Drop in wrapped chicken, push down to submerge in oil using a strainer, and cook for about 2 minutes. Remove and drain well on paper towels. Allow to cool a few seconds before opening carefully. Eat out of hand.

• Notes •

1. Make sure wrappers are folded securely. If you don't have a tight seal, the envelopes will pop open once they're submerged in hot oil.

2. Just like my mother, you can substitute beef or pieces of fish for the chicken.

3. Wrapping bundles in different shapes such as triangles or crescents is practical and fun—especially if you serve more than one kind at a time.

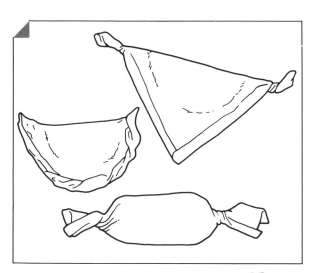

Three ways to fold parchment include (clockwise, from top): triangle with folded sides and twisted corners; candywrapper-style with twisted ends; and crescent-shaped with curved crimped edge.

Tantalize the eye and appease the appetite of hungry guests by offering colorful assortment of cold meat and vegetables. Pictured are (clockwise, from top): blanched asparagus, tossed with sesame oil and garlic; five-spice beef, a staple of northern China (page 42); tender baby corn; sherry-flavored Shanghai braised mushrooms (page 45); Buddhist vegetarian chicken, a delicate deception of bean curd skins, soy, and onion (page 49); hot & spicy prawns (page 94); and in center, Hunan delicacy candied pecans (page 43).

Phoenix Wings

Simple drumsticks easily become the dramatic wings of the mythical bird. Very popular, you'd be well-advised to double the quantity.

Makes: 12 appetizers
Cooking time: 15 minutes

6 chicken wings

MARINADE

1 green onion (white part), minced
¼ teaspoon minced fresh ginger
1 tablespoon dry sherry
½ teaspoon salt
Pinch curry powder
1 egg
¼ cup cornstarch

Vegetable oil, for deep-frying

Sweet & Sour Sauce (page 213) or Lemon Sauce (page 69)

Break chicken wing at joint; twist joint, inside out, to expose bone. Separate to make 2 pieces. Cut off wing tip, remove smaller bone; push meat to end of remaining bone creating a "drumstick" as illustrated below.

Combine MARINADE ingredients with chicken in the order listed and let stand for 10 minutes.

To deep-fry, heat 4 cups oil in a wok (or electric deep-fat fryer) to 350°. Add chicken and fry for 8 to 10 minutes or until golden brown. Remove and drain.

To serve, arrange drumsticks in a circle on serving plate. Place sauce in a small bowl in center.

• *Notes* •

1. For easier handling, hold chicken wings with a towel while breaking the joint.

2. Chinese gourmets consider the chicken wing the tastiest part of the chicken—the meat is sweet, has substance, yet is tender.

3. Phoenix wings are great for picnics, and a nice treat in school lunch boxes.

1) Using a towel to prevent slipping, break chicken wing at joint. 2) Twist joint, inside out to expose bone, and push meat down to end, creating a "drumstick."

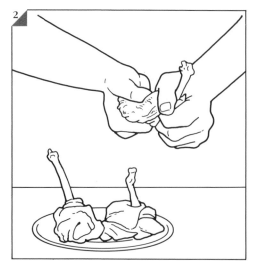

Chinese Barbecued Pork

This colorful, red-glazed pork makes many appearances in the Chinese diet—as a delectable snack, as a bright garnish in soups, on dumplings, or in fried rice. If you are in Chinatown, don't resist the temptation to try the freshly cooked barbecued pork on display. This recipe calls for the pork to be oven-roasted just like the original Cantonese specialty.

Makes: 40 to 50 appetizers
Cooking time: 1 hour

1½ to 2 pounds pork shoulder butt, trimmed and cut into 2- by 2- by 5-inch-size strips

MARINADE
¼ cup light soy sauce or ½ teaspoon salt
1 tablespoon dry sherry
½ teaspoon Chinese five-spice
½ teaspoon garlic powder
¼ teaspoon curing salt (optional)

COATING
½ cup catsup
½ cup sugar
½ teaspoon salt
½ teaspoon red food coloring (optional)
¼ teaspoon egg yellow food coloring (optional)

Toasted sesame seeds

Chinese Hot Mustard Sauce (page 212) and Chef Chu's Dipping Sauce (page 212)

Combine MARINADE ingredients and rub into meat. Cover and allow to stand for at least 2 hours or preferably overnight.

Combine COATING ingredients and mix with meat. Set aside for 2 hours.

To roast, preheat oven to 350°. Pour 1 cup water in a roasting pan. Remove pork from sauce (reserve for basting) and lay strips on a rack. Set rack in pan close to but not touching the water. Roast for 30 minutes, brushing occasionally with reserved sauce. Turn strips over, baste again, and continue roasting for 30 minutes longer.

To serve, sprinkle sesame seeds lightly on top of sliced pork and offer mustard and dipping sauces at the table.

• Notes •

1. I recommend using pork shoulder butt rather than the more common pork butt because it has a greater proportion of lean meat.

2. Slightly frozen meat is easier to cut into strips.

3. Chinese barbecued pork is an ingredient in many other recipes. Try doubling the recipe and freezing the extra pork for later use. It will keep for several months in the freezer.

4. Good in sandwiches, too.

5. For barbecued spareribs, substitute 2 to 3 pounds meaty ribs for pork butt. Score surface of ribs and cut into sections; marinate and roast as directed.

Sweet & Sour Cold Radishes   *Pictured below*

Eat the garnish? Why not when it is as good as these radishes. Simple to prepare, this colorful vegetable can stand on its own, complement Szechuan Cold Cucumbers, or serve as a garnish with Smoked Fish, Barbecued Squab, and other fancy dishes.

Makes: 6 servings
Pickling time: 40 minutes

1 pound large radishes
1 tablespoon salt

SEASONINGS

2 tablespoons white vinegar
2½ tablespoons sugar
¼ teaspoon salt

Trim off root and stalk ends and cut radishes in half lengthwise. With red side exposed, thinly slice each half lengthwise, taking care not to cut all the way through at one edge (see fan-cut, page 149). Cover radishes with salt, mix gently, and let stand for 20 minutes.

To cold mix, drain radishes well by gently forcing out excess water by hand and return to bowl. Add SEASONINGS and refrigerate for 5 minutes.

To serve, remove radishes and drain slightly. Carefully spread open slices into a fan shape and arrange on serving platter.

•   *Note*   •

Use these fan-shaped radishes as a colorful garnish when serving any entrée.

Fancy-cut, fan-shaped sweet & sour radishes (above) and Szechuan cucumbers, (page 41), presented on antique Chinese embroidery, make bright accompaniment to any meal.

Szechuan Cold Cucumbers   *Pictured on facing page*

The piquant, clear taste of these crunchy cucumbers heightens the appetite. It is served as a first course, or "cold plate," but may be offered as a salad or condiment.

Makes: 6 servings
Pickling time: 1 hour

8 slender (or pickling) cucumbers
½ teaspoon salt

SEASONINGS

1 clove garlic, sliced
2 teaspoons hot Chili Paste, page 203
1 tablespoon red rice vinegar
1 tablespoon sesame oil
2 teaspoons sugar
   Pinch freshly ground roasted Szechuan peppercorns (page 212)

Cut off and discard ends of cucumbers. Cut into slices using fan-cut (see illustration page 149). Place in bowl, sprinkle with salt, and refrigerate for 1 hour.

To cold mix, drain cucumbers well and return to bowl. Add SEASONINGS, mix well, and let stand for 10 minutes before serving.

• *Notes* •

1. You may substitute English cucumbers if you wish, although they tend to have less crunch.

2. Excellent condiment for curries, or Congee (see page 172).

Fragrant Duck   *Pictured on page 6*

Rubbed with Chinese spices then steamed to become trim and tender, this first-course dish is worthy of your most impressive dinner party.

Makes: 8 to 10 servings
Cooking time: 1 hour

1 fresh duck (4 to 5 lbs.), cleaned

MARINADE

2 green onions (including tops), cut in pieces
2 thumb-size chunks fresh ginger, crushed
2 star anise, broken
3 tablespoons dry sherry
2 tablespoons roasted Szechuan peppercorns
4 tablespoons salt
¼ teaspoon curing salt (optional)

   Chinese parsley (cilantro)

Combine MARINADE ingredients and rub into duck, both inside and out. Cover and refrigerate at least 8 hours or overnight.

To steam, place duck on rack inside steamer; cover and steam over boiling water for 1 hour or until juices run clear when pierced in the thigh. Remove, discarding spices clinging to duck; then cool and refrigerate.

To serve, cut cold duck into major sections; then cut into ½-inch-thick slices, including the bone. Reassemble on serving platter to recreate the original shape as illustrated on page 85. Garnish with Chinese parsley leaves.

• *Notes* •

1. Curing salt, available at Oriental markets, firms up the meat as well as gives it some color.

2. Serve all or part of the duck at one time; refrigerate remainder for 2 weeks.

Five-spice Beef *Pictured on page 37*

Originating in Northern China, this dish was practically considered a staple food because the spices used preserved the meat and therefore made refrigeration unnecessary. A different version found in the Southern part of China uses this beef as a filling for dumplings similar to ravioli.

In a restaurant, the Master Sauce is very important. It's similar to a sourdough starter in that if properly treated, it can be used and added to for many years. Traditionally, it's offered as a gift to someone just beginning as a homemaker.

Makes: 8 to 10 servings
Cooking time: 2 hours

- 2 beef shanks (1–1½ lbs. each) or 2 or 3 pounds bottom round
- 1 teaspoon salt
- 1 teaspoon Szechuan peppercorns
- 1 tablespoon dry sherry
- ¼ teaspoon curing salt (optional)

MASTER SAUCE
- 4 quarts water
- 2 knobs fresh ginger, crushed
- 4 green onions, tied in knots

In a cheesecloth bag put:
- 6 star anise
- 1 teaspoon Szechuan peppercorns
- 1 teaspoon fennel seed
- 2 pieces preserved tangerine peel
- 5 cardamom seeds
- ½ teaspoon whole cloves

- 1½ cups dark soy sauce
- ½ cup sugar
  Dash sesame oil
  Chinese parsley (cilantro)

Prick meat all over with a fork. Rub in salt, Szechuan peppercorns, sherry, and curing salt. Let stand for 1 hour.

In a deep pot, bring water to a boil. Add MASTER SAUCE ingredients including cheesecloth bag. Reduce heat and simmer, uncovered, for about 30 minutes. Stir in soy sauce and sugar; keep warm.

To water-blanch, put beef in boiling water and blanch for 3 minutes. Remove and drain, discarding any peppercorns sticking to sides; then add to master sauce. Bring mixture to a boil, reduce heat, cover, and simmer for 1 to 1½ hours. Remove meat from sauce (reserve sauce for other uses) and refrigerate until cold.

To serve, cut meat across the grain in ⅛-inch-thick slices. Arrange decoratively on platter, sprinkle with sesame oil, and garnish with parsley leaves.

• *Notes* •

1. You can adjust the flavor of the MASTER SAUCE to suit your own taste by increasing or decreasing the amounts of spices and seasonings.

2. Serve this cold by itself, or as part of any combination cold plate.

3. It's important to remove the cheesecloth bag before storing the MASTER SAUCE. If properly cared for, the sauce can be reused over and over (for more information, see page 198 and 205).

4. Try it in sandwiches or as a buffet cold cut.

Hunan Candied Pecans   *Pictured on page 36*

This dish calls for your keen eye—first to judge color when deep-frying, then to appreciate the rich glaze when finished. Here is a Hunan delicacy and an elegant snack.

Makes: 4 cups
Cooking time: 20 minutes

1 pound fresh pecans, shelled
2 quarts boiling water

COATING
½ cup water
1 cup sugar
Pinch salt

Vegetable oil, for deep-frying

To water-blanch, drop pecans into boiling water for 2 minutes and then drain.

To coat, heat COATING ingredients in a wok until boiling. Mix in pecans, reduce heat to medium, and cook for about 5 minutes. Stir vigorously and watch carefully so that sugar doesn't burn. When sugar is completely dissolved and becomes carmelized, remove pecans and pour into strainer to drain off excess sugar.

To deep-fry, immediately heat 1½ quarts oil in clean wok to 300°. Add pecans, and cook for 5 minutes, stirring often. Raise temperature gradually to 350°; pecans will reach a deep chocolate-brown color and will start to float to the surface.

Remove, drain well, and place in a shallow pan to cool. Shake pan often to prevent pecans from sticking. When coating turns glossy, blot pecans with paper towels to remove excess oil. When completely cooled, store nuts in a tightly-sealed container or plastic bag in refrigerator or cool place.

• *Notes* •

1. The purpose of blanching is to remove the pecans' bitterness as well as bleach their color.

2. Deep-frying first at 300° gets rid of any moisture remaining in the pecans; raising the temperature to 350° enables the sugar to form a glaze on the outside.

3. Deep-frying at the right oil temperature is the key to success—if the temperature is too high in the beginning, the pecans will burn right away.

4. I don't recommend using an electric deep-fat fryer since the temperature is difficult to control.

Shanghai Smoked Fish

Not smoked at all, this recipe typifies the unique style found in Chinese cooking. First deep-fried then braised in a spicy anise sauce, the snapper takes on a smoky look during cooking. This fish is so unique, guests never seem to have enough of it.

Makes: 6 to 8 servings
Cooking time: 30 minutes

- 2 pounds fish steaks (rock cod, halibut, or red snapper)

MARINADE
- 2 tablespoons soy sauce
- 1 tablespoon dry sherry
- 5 thumb-size slices fresh ginger, crushed
- 2 green onions, cut in pieces

  Vegetable oil, for deep-frying

SPICES
- 2 tablespoons vegetable oil
- 1 teaspoon Szechuan peppercorns
- 2 star anise
- 4 thumb-size slices fresh ginger
- 1 green onion, cut in pieces
- 1½ cups water or Rich Chicken Broth (page 52)

SEASONINGS
- 3 tablespoons soy sauce
- 1 tablespoon dry sherry
- 3 tablespoons sugar
- ¼ teaspoon salt

- 2 teaspoons white vinegar
- ¼ teaspoon Chinese five-spice
- ½ teaspoon sesame oil

  Chinese parsley (cilantro)

Combine MARINADE ingredients and rub onto fish. Let stand 10 minutes.

To deep fry, heat 2 cups oil in a wok (or electric deep-fat fryer) to 375°. Cook fish in batches, maintaining oil temperature, for 5 to 7 minutes or until dark brown on outside yet firm inside. Remove fish and drain, discarding oil.

To braise, heat wok over high heat for about 1 minute until hot. Add 2 tablespoons oil and swirl to coat sides. When oil is hot, add remaining SPICES and cook until fragrance emerges. Add water, bring to a boil, and cook over medium heat for 5 minutes. Add SEASONINGS, bring to boil, and continue cooking for about 5 minutes more.

Add fish to sauce, mixing gently to coat. Stir in vinegar and Chinese five-spice. Continue cooking 5 more minutes, stirring gently and constantly, until sauce thickens. Stir in sesame oil, remove from heat, and cool to room temperature. Cover and refrigerate until serving.

To serve, remove fish from sauce, discarding any spices clinging to sides, and transfer to serving platter. Garnish with leaves of Chinese parsley.

• Notes •

1. Serve as a cold plate, or on top of Fresh Noodles (page 162), or in a soup.

2. Normally you can reuse oil after deep-frying; however, in this recipe the oil becomes dark and odorous, so discard it.

Shanghai Braised Black Mushrooms   *Pictured on page 36*

There is no flavor that rivals the woodsy, subtly aromatic black mushroom. Although most frequently used in combination with other vegetables and meats, here it stands alone braised in sherry, soy, and a dash of sesame oil. Delicious cold and hot.

Makes: 6 to 8 servings
Cooking time: 30 minutes

- 2 dozen large dried black mushrooms
- 3 tablespoons vegetable oil
- 6 thumb-size slices fresh ginger
- 2 green onions (including tops), cut in pieces

SAUCE

- 5 tablespoons soy sauce
- 2 tablespoons dry sherry
- 1½ cups Rich Chicken Broth (page 52), or chicken bouillon
- 1 tablespoon sugar
- 1 tablespoon sesame oil

Presoak mushrooms in warm water for 20 to 30 minutes. Drain and remove stems.

To braise, heat wok over high heat for about 1 minute until hot. Add oil and swirl to coat sides. When hot, add ginger and onions and cook for 30 seconds until fragrant. Stir in SAUCE ingredients and then add mushrooms. Bring to a boil, reduce heat, and simmer, stirring occasionally to prevent burning, for 20 minutes or until liquid is absorbed. Mix in sesame oil, remove from heat, and cool.

To serve, discard ginger and green onion. Arrange mushrooms, cap-side up, on platter or as part of any combination cold plate.

Variation: Black Mushrooms & Bamboo Shoots (Winter Delicacy). Just before braising mushrooms, add 1 cup bamboo shoots, cut into bite-size pieces using rolling cut (page 194).

• *Notes* •

1. Mushrooms should be just as soft and dark on the outside as inside when completely cooked.

2. This dish is wonderful when served hot, too. A good accompaniment to roast meats.

3. Don't stir in the mushrooms before the sauce because they will toughen.

Spicy Hot Garlic Chicken

Delightful in summertime, my highly-spiced, Szechuan-style chicken is served cold as an appetizer at the restaurant. However, some of my students tell me they enjoy serving it as an entrée as well.

Makes: 8 to 10 servings
Cooking time: 30 minutes

- 1 broiler-fryer chicken (about 3 lbs.)

SAUCE
- 2 teaspoons minced fresh ginger
- 2 small cloves garlic, minced or pressed
- 2 green onions (including tops), minced
- ⅓ cup soy sauce
- 2 teaspoons hot Chili Oil, page 212 or purchased
- 3 tablespoons red rice vinegar
- 1½ tablespoons sugar
- 1 teaspoon sesame oil
  Pinch freshly ground roasted Szechuan peppercorns (page 212)

  Chinese parsley (cilantro)

To cook, place chicken in enough boiling water to cover and cook for 10 minutes. Turn off heat and let stand for 10 minutes more. Remove chicken, rinse under cold water, and refrigerate until cold.

Bone chicken completely, except for wings, keeping meat in large pieces and leaving skin on. Slice meat ½-inch thick and reassemble on serving platter to recreate original shape (see illustration, page 85).

To serve, combine SAUCE ingredients well in a bowl and spoon over chicken. Garnish with parsley leaves.

Variation: Mild Onion Chicken. For a milder sauce, combine 2 teaspoons minced fresh ginger, 1 minced green onion (including top), 1 tablespoon salt, and ½ cup vegetable oil. Spoon over chicken as directed above.

• *Notes* •

1. Yes, chicken will cook through by using this rapid boiling and steeping method. Make sure the water is boiling before immersing the chicken completely. Do not overcook.

2. This dish keeps well. Try any leftover chicken as topping for soup noodles.

Lobster With Four Flavors

Thin slices of perfectly cooked lobster are surrounded by four tantalizing sauces for dipping. A dish for a banquet, a meal in itself, or a new way to serve your catch at a beach party.

Makes: 6 to 8 servings
Cooking time: 30 minutes

- 2 lobster tails (10 oz. each), or 2 whole California lobsters
- 2 cucumbers diagonally sliced ⅛-inch thick
- ½ teaspoon salt
  Bamboo skewers

Insert skewers lengthwise through lobster tails to prevent curling. Cover lobster with water, bring to a boil, and cook for 8 to 10 minutes. Drain, remove skewers, and refrigerate.

Meanwhile, mix cucumber slices with salt and let stand 15 minutes. Drain well and refrigerate.

In four separate bowls, combine ingredients for GINGER SAUCE, HOT & SPICY SAUCE, PONG-PONG SAUCE, and CHEF CHU'S DIPPING SAUCE.

(continued)

GINGER SAUCE

- 1 teaspoon minced fresh ginger
- ¼ cup red rice vinegar

HOT & SPICY SAUCE

- ½ teaspoon minced fresh ginger
- 1 small clove garlic, minced or pressed
- 1 -inch section of green onion (white part), minced
- 3 tablespoons soy sauce
- 2 teaspoons hot Chili Oil, page 212 or purchased
- 1 teaspoon red rice vinegar
- 2 teaspoons sugar
  Pinch freshly ground roasted Szechuan peppercorn
  Dash sesame oil

PONG-PONG SAUCE

- 1 tablespoon creamy peanut butter or sesame paste
- ½ teaspoon minced fresh ginger
- 1 -inch section of green onion (white part), minced
- ½ clove garlic, minced or pressed
- 1 tablespoon soy sauce
- 1 teaspoon red rice vinegar
- 1 teaspoon hot Chili Oil, page 212 or purchased
- ½ teaspoon sesame oil
- ½ teaspoon sugar

CHEF CHU'S DIPPING SAUCE

- 3 tablespoons catsup
- 1 tablespoon soy sauce
- ½ teaspoon minced fresh ginger
- ½ clove garlic, minced or pressed
- 1 teaspoon sugar

To serve, remove and discard lobster shells; slice meat ¼-inch thick. Overlap cucumber slices to form a circular bed in center of serving platter. Arrange lobster slices on bed, leaving the decorative tips of the cucumber showing. Place two bowls of sauce at each side of platter to serve.

Variation: Prawns With Four Flavors.
Cook 1 pound of prawns (21–25 count) in boiling water; drain, shell, and split in half lengthwise. Arrange on platter, tails out, on bed of cucumbers and serve with the four sauces.

• *Notes* •

1. English cucumbers (water-blanched) or bean sprouts may be substituted for cucumbers.

2. This would make a delightful meal in itself, for luncheon parties or a summertime supper.

Pong-pong Chicken

"Pong-pong" means stick and the name of this dish suggests that the tender chicken became so because it had had a beating. The julienned strips of chicken also resemble match sticks—so take your choice. Most Chinese dishes bear names that describe their appearance or method of cooking. Eating is a straightforward, serious business! And this recipe for Pong-pong chicken is seriously hot and delicious.

Makes: 6 to 8 servings
Cooking time: 30 minutes

2 cups cooked chicken meat
2 cups bean sprouts

SAUCE
3 tablespoons peanut butter or sesame paste
3 tablespoons soy sauce
1½ teaspoons sugar
3 tablespoons chicken broth
1 teaspoon minced fresh ginger
1 green onion (white part), minced
1 clove garlic, minced or pressed
1 tablespoon red rice vinegar
1 tablespoon hot Chili Oil, page 212 or purchased
1½ teaspoons sesame oil

Chinese parsley (cilantro)

Shred cold chicken into match-stick-size pieces; set aside.

To water blanch, cook bean sprouts in boiling water for 1 minute; run under cold water and drain.

Combine SAUCE ingredients thoroughly. Arrange bean sprouts on serving platter and cover with shredded chicken; refrigerate until cold.

To serve, spoon sauce over chicken and garnish with Chinese parsley leaves.

• *Note* •

You can substitute either regular or English cucumbers for bean sprouts. Shred as directed but do not water-blanch.

Buddhist Vegetarian Chicken   *Pictured on page 36*

The Buddhist philosophy, which reveres all creatures, is the source of a widely popular school of cuisine featuring vegetarian dishes. Nutritious, they are deceptive, too, as many are designed to imitate meats, such as this delicate concoction of soy bean curd skins flavored with onion and soy sauce, then steamed, cooled, and cut into pieces that resemble thin slices of chicken.

Makes: 6 to 8 servings
Cooking time: 2 hours

---

4 large frozen bean curd
   skins (page 202), thawed

MIXTURE
1 green onion (including
   top), minced
⅓ cup soy sauce
1 small piece fermented
   bean curd
1 teaspoon sugar
1 tablespoon sesame oil

String
Sesame oil
Vegetable flower
   (optional)

Combine MIXTURE ingredients in a small bowl to form a paste.

To assemble, lay 2 flat sheets of bean curd on top of each other. Brush surface with half of the mixture. Fold 3 sides of the sheet into the center, then roll up jelly-roll fashion toward the non-folded edge. Continue rolling almost to edge but then fold that edge back onto roll so that sauce is not forced out. Wrap string, diagonally, around roll 4 or 5 times; secure at end and then reverse process and wrap back, 4 or 5 times, to original starting point. Secure tightly. Repeat for second roll.

To steam, place both rolls on rack in steamer; cover and steam over boiling water for 2 hours. Allow to cool.

To serve, cut off string and cut each roll diagonally into 1-inch pieces. Sprinkle with sesame oil and garnish with vegetable flower, if desired.

• *Notes* •

1. You'll find bean curd skins in frozen section of Oriental markets.

2. In addition to the soy mixture, try spreading sheets with chopped dried shrimp or preserved mustard green *(jah choy)* before rolling.

·SOUPS·

A formal Chinese meal may involve ten or more courses, and the order in which they are served is surprisingly different from the sequence of a Western-style meal. Soup, for example, is not served first but last, and sometimes between courses to clear the palate or indicate the end of courses. At a family meal, soup appears along with the main dishes.

Chinese soups are varied—from the light and clear Egg Flower Soup to the meaty Chengdu Beef Soup, from the pungent flavor of Hot & Sour Soup to the delicately prepared Fish Blossom Soup. They can offer drama to your dinner, too. To draw exclamations from your guests, try Sizzling Rice Soup. Five-willow Shark's Fin Soup, usually prepared and served only for special or festive occasions as part of a banquet, combines pieces of chicken, ham, and shredded abalone with bits of fresh vegetables in a rich, flavorful broth. Shredded shark's fin that has been reconstituted from a dried state, is the final ingredient of this masterful soup.

While many other ethnic cuisines offer a variety of their soups cold, Chinese generally prefer to serve soup hot. However, there is a kind of soup that is served lukewarm. It is a milky, almond-flavored soup that is quite a delicacy and so usually saved for banquets or special guests and served as a midday snack.

The recipes that follow offer some of the very best among the many different kinds of Chinese soups. When preparing them, I strongly suggest you take the first (and most important) step by cooking a rich broth. My recipe for a flavorful broth appears on the following page (am I emphatic enough?): Rich Chicken Broth.

After making the broth (remember, this can be done well in advance and in large batches), you'll notice that many of the remaining instructions—slicing or dicing fresh vegetables or shredding meat—are completed rather quickly.

You will be able to tell from a quick glance at the recipe which soups are simple to prepare and which require your patience. When in doubt, check through the notes for they will suggest how much can be done in advance. Several soups are such "show stoppers" that you might plan a fairly simple meal around one such soup, saving energy and time without sacrificing the appealing quality of your menu.

Soup, served in a bowl smaller than a rice bowl, follows American custom and is offered at the onset of a meal.

51

Rich Chicken Broth

A good, rich-tasting chicken broth is essential in Chinese cooking so in my restaurant I make no exceptions. I always use 4- to-5-pound chickens because I'm preparing food in such volume, but you can use a regular broiler-fryer if you prefer. I firmly believe a good broth needs no additives. So why not take a little time (and not much effort) and prepare this chicken broth?

Makes: 8 servings
Cooking time: 1½ hours

- 1 roasting chicken (4 to 5 lbs.), or about 4 to 5 pounds chicken bones (wings, neck, back, carcass)
- 4 quarts water
- ½ white onion, cut up
- 4 knobs fresh ginger, crushed

To par-boil, place chicken (or bones) in an 8-quart stockpot. Cover with boiling water and cook for 5 minutes to get rid of the scum. Pour chicken into a colander, rinse under cold water, and return chicken to pot.

To cook, add water and vegetables. Bring to a boil, reduce heat, and simmer uncovered for about 1 hour. Occasionally skim surface as needed. Remove from heat and cool; then strain well before using.

• Notes •

1. As I mentioned, this recipe produces a rich broth that is the basic stock for many of my other soups. If you prefer not to make it or you don't have the time, always use chicken bouillon (cubes) in water rather than the less flavorful, canned chicken broth.

2. Save your chicken bones! You can use them to make broth instead of a whole chicken.

3. Since the vegetables are added only for flavor, use tips and ends of onions and knobs of ginger root. I mention this since I was once told by a student that she couldn't find "knobs" of ginger at her market.

4. If you make broth several hours ahead of serving time, let it cool with the bones still inside. If made several days in advance, try freezing it in ice cube trays; when frozen, store cubes in a sealed freezer bag (1 ice cube equals ¼ to ⅓ cup broth).

Hot & Sour Soup

Chef Ku Lang, my teacher, best friend, and in my opinion, the greatest chef in the world, loved and prepared this soup often. The ingredients I use are slightly different than the ones he used in China, but the flavor remains the same. This rich soup has an extra kick offered by the white pepper and vinegar added just before serving—maybe the secret for its popularity in America as well as China.

Makes: 8 servings
Cooking time: 20 minutes

12 pieces tiger lily buds
1 dried tree mushroom (black fungus)

MARINADE

1 teaspoon soy sauce
¼ teaspoon cornstarch
½ teaspoon vegetable oil

¼ pound pork butt, cut in strips ⅛-inch by 1½-inches

2 quarts Rich Chicken Broth (facing page), or chicken bouillon
2 tablespoons shredded bamboo shoots
½ carton (16 oz.) bean curd (firm tofu), cut in strips
1 tablespoon dry sherry
Salt to taste
Cornstarch paste
2 eggs, beaten
2 tablespoons soy sauce
2 tablespoons vegetable oil

6 tablespoons red rice vinegar
1½ teaspoons white pepper
Chopped green onion
Dash sesame oil

Soak tiger lily and tree mushroom in warm water for 20 minutes. Cut tiger lily in half; shred tree mushroom.

Combine MARINADE ingredients with pork in the order listed; mix well and set aside.

To cook, bring chicken broth to a boil. Add pork, tiger lily, mushroom, and bamboo shoots. Return to boil, skimming occasionally. Add bean cake, sherry, and salt. Stir in 3 to 4 tablespoons cornstarch paste and continue cooking until reaching the consistency of creamed soup. Slowly drizzle eggs into broth in a thin stream; gently fold in soy sauce and oil. (If you wish, you may set aside at this point.)

To serve, mix rice vinegar and pepper in a large soup bowl or tureen. Pour in soup and stir. Sprinkle with chopped onion and sesame oil; serve immediately.

• Notes •

1. Red rice vinegar produces the sour aroma. NEVER cook vinegar, just mix it in. The white pepper provides the hot "kick" in our soup. You can adjust the flavor to suit your taste by increasing or decreasing the amount of vinegar and pepper used.

2. For a vegetarian version, leave out the pork and substitute vegetable bouillon for broth.

3. I sometimes get carried away and add fresh shrimp and slices of canned abalone. This makes the soup expensive, but delicious and worth it.

Pork & Preserved Mustard Green Soup

The Chinese love this soup! Crunchy preserved mustard greens add a unique, slightly salty flavor to the clear broth. Shredded bamboo shoots, thin strips of marinated pork, and shredded black mushrooms are added just before serving.

Makes: 8 servings
Cooking time: 15 minutes

2 dried black mushrooms

MARINADE
1 teaspoon soy sauce
¼ teaspoon cornstarch
½ teaspoon oil

¼ pound pork shoulder butt, boned and cut in strips ⅛-inch by 1½-inches

2 quarts Rich Chicken Broth (page 52), or chicken bouillon
1 large chunk (4 oz.) preserved mustard green, shredded
⅓ cup shredded bamboo shoots
Salt and white pepper to taste

1 -inch section green onion (white part), thinly shredded on the diagonal
Dash sesame oil

Soak mushrooms in warm water for 20 minutes; remove stems and shred.

Combine MARINADE ingredients with pork in the order listed; mix well after each addition and let stand for 10 minutes.

To cook, bring broth to a boil and add pork, mushrooms, mustard green, and bamboo shoots. Return to boil and skim thoroughly until broth is clear. Continue cooking for about 3 minutes.

To serve, pour soup into serving bowl or tureen and sprinkle with green onion and sesame oil.

• *Notes* •

1. Szechuan preserved mustard green is quite different from fresh mustard green; it has a definite crunchy flavor as well as saltier taste. You can purchase preserved mustard green in cans or airtight packages.

2. Skimming thoroughly is essential because this soup should appear clear when served.

Winter Melon Blossom Soup

Typically, winter melon is available only at Oriental markets; you can buy it whole or in sections. For an extra special occasion, Chinese cooks often use the whole melon as a serving container, carving a design that symbolizes luck or good fortune on the outer rind. The soup itself is full of cooked ham, chicken, crab, mushrooms, and pieces of melon.

Makes: 8 to 10 servings
Cooking time: 30 minutes

- 2 dried black mushrooms
- 1 pound section of winter melon
- 2 quarts Rich Chicken Broth (page 52), or chicken bouillon

MEATS

- 2 tablespoons diced cooked ham
- ¼ cup diced cooked chicken
- ¼ cup crabmeat, flaked

SEASONINGS

- 1 teaspoon dry sherry
  Salt and white pepper to taste

  Cornstarch paste
- 2 egg whites

  Minced Virginia ham (optional)

Soak mushrooms in warm water for 20 minutes; remove stems and dice. Remove melon rind and seeds; cut melon into crouton-size pieces or scoop out with melon ball spoon.

To par-boil, drop melon in enough boiling water to cover and cook for 10 minutes or until completely soft and almost transparent. Remove and drain.

To cook, bring broth to a boil and add melon, mushrooms, MEATS and SEASONINGS. Return to a boil, skimming occasionally. Stir in 2 tablespoons cornstarch paste and continue cooking until consistency of creamed soup is reached. Beat egg whites until foamy and gently fold into soup. Remove from heat, stirring gently.

To serve, pour soup into large soup bowl or tureen and garnish with minced ham, if desired.

• *Note* •

You can keep cooked melon balls in cold water until ready to use in the soup.

For festive occasion, scoop meat from entire winter melon and use shell as serving tureen. Carve fancy design on outer rind, if desired.

Fish Blossom Soup *Pictured on facing page*

Popular in Taiwan, this festive soup becomes the star attraction when brought to the table. Hot chicken broth is poured (carefully) over thin slices of raw fish fillets, fried won-ton wrappers, and pieces of lettuce. It's an unusually beautiful soup to prepare because once the broth is poured, the fish turns white and flaky as it cooks before your eyes.

(A word of caution: don't dump the broth in all at once and don't pour it from very high up. I did *both* the first time we tried to take the picture. I splattered liquid all over, ruining the satin tablecloth and was not asked to try again when this photo was shot.)

Makes: 8 servings
Cooking time: 10 minutes

- 5 won-ton wrappers
- 1 rock cod or red snapper fillet (about ½ lb.), skinned
- 2 quarts Rich Chicken Broth (page 52), or chicken bouillon

SEASONINGS

- 1 tablespoon dry sherry
  Salt and white pepper to taste

- ¼ head Iceberg lettuce, torn into bite-size pieces
- 2 thumb-size slices fresh ginger, finely shredded
- 1 green onion (white part), finely shredded
- 1 tablespoon sesame seeds, crushed
- 1 tablespoon roasted peanuts, crushed

Cut each won-ton wrapper into four triangles. Deep-fry until golden brown as directed on page 29; set aside to drain on paper towels.

Cut fish fillet into ¼-inch-thick slices and carefully butterfly. Bring chicken broth to a boil, skimming fat if necessary. Add SEASONINGS and keep hot.

To assemble, place lettuce in a large serving bowl or tureen. Sprinkle with ginger and onion. Layer fried won-ton wrappers on top. Arrange fish decoratively in a circular pattern on top and sprinkle with sesame seeds and peanuts.

To serve, bring serving bowl to the table. Carefully, oh so carefully, pour piping hot broth over all.

• *Notes* •

1. Remember, the broth must be piping hot when poured in order to cook the raw fish.

2. If you want to simplify the fancy cutting technique for the fish, just slice the fillet into ⅛-inch-thick slices.

Delicate ingredients of fish blossom soup—lettuce, ginger, onion, fried won-ton wrappers, peanuts, and paper-thin slices of fish—await final touch of steaming chicken broth to be poured over all. Displayed in an antique bowl with lotus famille rose design.

Sizzling Rice Soup

Can soup sing? When golden rice crust is dropped into a hot broth, the results are dramatic. Timing is critical, so read through this recipe carefully.

Makes: 6 servings
Cooking time: 20 minutes

12 medium-size prawns, shelled, deveined, and split in half lengthwise

MARINADE
Pinch salt
Pinch white pepper
1 small egg white
¼ teaspoon cornstarch
1 tablespoon vegetable oil

1½ quarts Rich Chicken Broth (page 52), or chicken bouillon

VEGETABLES
24 canned sliced button mushrooms
12 snow peas, diagonally sliced in half
12 slices water chestnuts
12 slices bamboo shoots
6 slices carrot

SEASONINGS
1½ teaspoons dry sherry
Salt to taste
Pinch white pepper

Vegetable oil, for deep-frying

6 small chunks rice crust (page 171)

Combine prawns with MARINADE ingredients in the order given; mix gently, and set aside.

To cook, bring chicken broth to a boil. Add prawns and VEGETABLES and cook, skimming occasionally, for 1 minute. Adjust flavor by adding SEASONINGS.

Meanwhile, have wok ready for deep-frying.

To deep-fry, heat 2 cups oil in wok (or electric deep-fat fryer) to 375°. Carefully drop in rice and deep-fry for about 30 seconds or until golden brown. Quickly remove and transfer to a plate.

To serve, bring golden rice crust and hot broth to the table. Drop chunks of rice into soup and serve while soup is still "singing."

• *Notes* •

1. A rich chicken broth is essential to this soup. If using canned chicken broth, enrich the flavor by adding 1 teaspoon (1 cube) chicken bouillon.

2. Rice crust (taken from the bottom of the rice pan) must be deep-fried at 375° to achieve the best results.

3. Abalone, cooked ham, or thin slices of chicken can be added to the broth, if desired.

4. Timing is very important. While waiting for oil to reach 375°, pour hot soup in a large soup bowl or tureen.

5. Since this requires your last minute attention, serve Lion's Head, and Szechuan String Beans to follow as they can be prepared and await service.

Bean Sprout & Sparerib Soup

This Shanghai-style family soup is a meal in itself. While drinking the broth, the bean sprouts and spareribs may be removed with chopsticks, dipped in a sauce of chili paste and soy, and eaten along with the soup.

Makes: 8 servings
Cooking time: 2 hours

1 pound meaty spareribs
3 quarts water

SEASONINGS

2 green onions, tied in knots
1 thumb-size chunk fresh ginger, crushed
2 cups soybean sprouts
2 tablespoons dry sherry
Salt and pepper to taste

With a cleaver or sharp knife, cut spareribs into 1½-inch cubes.

To par-boil, place ribs in enough boiling water to cover and cook for 3 minutes. Remove, pour out water, and return ribs to pot.

To cook, add 3 quarts water, onions, and ginger. Bring to a boil, reduce heat, cover, and simmer for 1 hour. Skim off fat occasionally.

Meanwhile, pick off and discard end of root on each sprout. Rinse under cold water and drain. Add to soup, cover, and continue simmering for about 1 hour more. Add sherry and adjust seasonings before serving.

• *Note* •

Soybean sprouts, available at Oriental markets, are topped by a large yellow bean and are different than the mung bean sprouts found at most supermarkets.

Egg Flower Soup

Fluffy yellow egg blossoms and firm red tomato wedges in a rich chicken broth—delicious.

Makes: 8 servings
Cooking time: 10 minutes

2 quarts Rich Chicken Broth (page 52), or chicken bouillon
2 medium-size tomatoes, peeled and cut into wedges
2 tablespoons cooked peas

SEASONINGS

1 teaspoon dry sherry
Salt and white pepper to taste

Cornstarch paste
2 eggs, slightly beaten

Chopped green onion
Dash sesame oil

Bring chicken broth to a boil. Add tomatoes, peas, and SEASONINGS. Thicken slightly with 1 tablespoon cornstarch paste. Slowly pour in eggs, turn off heat, and stir gently until egg starts to float on top.

To serve, transfer to a large serving bowl or tureen and top with green onion and sesame oil.

Variation: Seaweed Soup (*pictured on page 17*). Tear 8 to 10 sheets of dried seaweed into bite-size pieces and add to soup right after eggs.

Chengdu Beef Soup   *Pictured on facing page*

Though rarely served in restaurants, this nutritious soup is very popular in Chinese homes.

Makes: 8 servings
Cooking time: 2 hours

1 pound beef stew, cut in 2-inch cubes

3 quarts water
1 large white turnip, cut into chunks with a rolling cut
1 thumb-size chunk fresh ginger, crushed
2 green onions, tied in knots

2 tablespoons dry sherry or rice wine
Salt and white pepper to taste

Soy sauce
Chili Paste

To par-boil, place meat in enough boiling water to cover and cook for 3 minutes. Pour through colander to drain and return meat to pot.

To cook, add 3 quarts water, turnip, ginger, and onion. Bring to a boil, reduce heat, cover, and simmer for 2 hours, skimming occasionally. Remove ginger and onion; add sherry, salt and pepper, adjusting seasonings if necessary.

To serve, pour into large soup bowl or tureen and offer different sauces for dipping.

• *Notes* •

1. Chinese often prefer beef with some gristle such as beef shanks.

2. A heavy pot, such as cast iron, is helpful for better heat distribution during the cooking.

3. Fresh spinach or other vegetables may be added to the soup at the last minute.

Spicy Ma Po's bean curd, a protein-rich Szechuan dish (page 157), combines with simple boiled rice (page 171) and nutritious Chengdu beef soup to make hearty homestyle Chinese meal. Served on traditional blue blossom china.

Five-willow Shark's Fin Soup

The most auspicious of old traditional banquets in China would include a rare catch from the mountains and a prize from the sea—the bear's palm and the shark's fin. To offer these gifts to one's guests would honor them, indeed. Today, the gift from the sea is still available and may be given, but it is a delicacy as expensive as sturgeon caviar. This recipe makes your investment worthwhile.

Makes: 8 to 10 servings
Cooking time: 3 hours

- ½ box (4 oz.) dried shark's fin
- 4 dried black mushrooms

- 2 quarts water
- 6 thumb-size slices fresh ginger
- 2 green onions, tied in knots
- 2 tablespoons dry sherry

- 2 quarts Rich Chicken Broth (page 52), or chicken bouillon

MEATS
- ½ cup shredded cooked chicken
- 2 thin slices cooked ham, shredded
- 1 piece canned abalone, shredded (optional)

VEGETABLES
- ½ cup shredded bamboo shoots
- 1 green onion (white part), minced
- ½ teaspoon minced fresh ginger

- 1 tablespoon dry sherry
- ½ teaspoon salt
  Pinch white pepper
- 5 snow peas, cut lengthwise in thin strips
  Cornstarch paste
- 1 tablespoon soy sauce
- 1 teaspoon vegetable oil

- 3 sprigs Chinese parsley (cilantro), chopped

Soak shark's fin in warm water for 1 hour; remove and set aside. Soak dried mushrooms in warm water for 30 minutes; drain, remove stem, and shred.

Place 2 quarts water in a pot and add ginger, green onion, sherry, and presoaked shark's fin. Bring to a boil, reduce heat, cover and simmer for 1½ hours. Remove shark's fin (remove any hard gristle) and drain; discard green onion and ginger.

To cook, bring chicken broth to a boil and add prepared shark's fin, mushrooms, MEATS, and VEGETABLES. Return to a boil and stir in sherry, salt, pepper, and snow peas. Gradually, stir in 3 tablespoons cornstarch paste and continue cooking until thickened. Stir in soy sauce and vegetable oil.

To serve, pour soup into a large soup bowl or tureen and garnish with Chinese parsley. Serve immediately.

Shrimp Ball Soup

Rich clear broth with crunchy snow peas and tasty morsels of shrimp balls.

Makes: 6 to 8 servings
Cooking time: 15 minutes

MIXTURE

- ½ pound medium-size prawns, shelled and deveined
- 1 strip bacon, chopped
- 1 green onion (white part), minced
- ¼ teaspoon minced fresh ginger

- 1 egg, slightly beaten
  Pinch baking soda
- ¼ teaspoon salt
  Pinch white pepper

- 2 quarts Rich Chicken Broth (page 52), or chicken bouillon
- 4 to 5 canned mushrooms, sliced
- 10 snow peas, ends trimmed
- 1 tablespoon dry sherry
  Salt and white pepper to taste

- 1 green onion (white part), diagonally sliced ¼-inch thick

With a food processor or knife, finely chop MIXTURE ingredients as needed until paste consistency is reached. Add egg, baking soda, salt, and pepper; mix thoroughly and let stand for about 10 minutes. Meanwhile, bring a large pot of water to a boil, reduce heat to simmering and keep ready for blanching shrimp balls.

To shape, grab a handful of mixture and squeeze out 1-inch balls from top of fist as illustrated below. As balls are shaped, quickly drop them into simmering water. Remove balls after about 1 minute and drop in cold water.

To cook, bring chicken broth to a boil. Add mushrooms and peas and cook for 1 to 1½ minutes. Stir in sherry, shrimp balls, and season with salt and pepper. Garnish with onion to serve.

Dip hand in water to prevent sticking. Then 1) grab handful of mixture and squeeze out 1-inch balls from top of fist. 2) As they are shaped, lower balls into simmering broth for 1 minute.

Won-ton Soup   *Pictured below*

Without question, this is the most requested Chinese soup in America. In China it is served as an afternoon snack or for a late night supper, but seldom as a soup for dinner.

Makes: 6 servings
Cooking time: 30 minutes

FILLING

- ½ pound lean ground pork
- 1 green onion (including top), minced
- 1 tablespoon dry sherry
- 1 teaspoon sesame oil
- ½ teaspoon sugar
- ¼ teaspoon salt
  Pinch white pepper

- 1½ quarts Rich Chicken Broth (page 52), or chicken bouillon

- 2 dozen won-ton wrappers
  Beaten egg
- 1½ quarts water

  Dash sesame oil
  Chopped green onion

Optional toppings:
  sliced barbecued pork, boiled prawns, snow peas, black mushrooms, sliced water chestnuts, or bite-size pieces of Chinese cabbage or fresh spinach

Combine FILLING ingredients; mix well and set aside.

Pour chicken broth in pan to reheat; skim off any fat and season with salt and pepper, if necessary. Cover and simmer over very low heat until ready to serve.

To assemble, spoon about 1 teaspoon filling in center of won-ton wrapper, brush edge with beaten egg, and fold as illustrated on page 29.

To cook, bring water to a boil and drop in won-tons. When water begins to boil, add another 1 cup water to reduce the temperature. When water reaches second boil (about 3 minutes) and won-tons start to float, remove them with a strainer and transfer to a large soup bowl or tureen.

To serve, pour hot chicken broth over won-ton; sprinkle with sesame oil and chopped onion. Garnish with your favorite topping.

• *Notes* •

1. Don't overcook won-tons or the noodle quality and texture will be lost. Don't allow water to come to a rolling boil because this might cause wrappers to break.

2. Won-ton may be cooked ahead of time. Drain well and mix with 1 tablespoon oil until serving, or cover with cold water and refrigerate.

Shark's Fin Chicken Soup

This recipe is a variation of Five-willow Shark's Fin Soup on page 62. The only difference is that the shredded ham and abalone have been removed as well as some of the vegetables.

Makes: 8 to 10 servings
Cooking time: 3 hours

½ box (4 oz.) dried shark's
    fin

1 broiler-fryer chicken
3 quarts water
1 thumb-size chunk fresh
    ginger, crushed
1 green onion, tied in knot
5 dried black mushrooms
¼ cup shredded bamboo
    shoots
1 tablespoon dry sherry

SEASONINGS
½ teaspoon salt
    Pinch white pepper
1 tablespoon soy sauce

    Cornstarch paste
2 sprigs Chinese parsley
    (cilantro), chopped

Prepare shark's fin as directed in Five-willow Shark's Fin Soup, page 62.

To par-boil, place chicken in enough boiling water to cover and cook for 5 minutes. Pour into colander, rinse under cold water, and return chicken to pot.

Add 3 quarts water, ginger, and onion. Bring to a boil, reduce heat, cover, and simmer for 1½ hours, skimming occasionally.

Meanwhile, soak dried mushrooms in warm water for 30 minutes. Drain, remove stems, and shred.

When chicken is cooked, remove (reserving broth for other use) and cool; then bone, discarding skin, and shred.

To cook, remove and discard ginger and onion from broth. Add prepared shark's fin, black mushrooms, bamboo shoots, and sherry. Cook for 2 to 3 minutes and then add chicken and SEASONINGS. Gradually, stir in 4 tablespoons cornstarch paste and continue cooking until the consistency of creamed soup is reached.

To serve, transfer to a large soup bowl or tureen and garnish with Chinese parsley.

·POULTRY·

In China, poultry is purchased alive and killed by the vendor or by the cook later at home. This tradition guarantees freshness—the first shrewd step toward serving a good meal.

When examining fresh poultry in China, one would touch the breast to determine whether the fowl is plump or bony, to estimate the overall weight, and to judge its age—whether premature or overgrown.

In the United States, most markets sell refrigerated chicken. Choosing the freshest is difficult; however, try to select a chicken with a yellower color to its skin, as this kind tends to be tastier. Since there are different types of chicken to choose from, do not let size affect your buying, as that does not guarantee tenderness.

Here are a few guidelines: *Fryers* or *broilers,* usually weighing 2 to 3 pounds, are good for braising, barbecuing, or deep-frying; *Roasters,* 3 pounds and up, are chickens generally used in restaurants. They are tender and tasty and excellent for making broth. And, because they have more meat, they are the ideal choice when boned chicken is called for.

Since most recipes in this cookbook specify boned chicken, your best buy is a roaster even though it is more expensive. Roasters weighing 5 pounds will yield about 3 pounds of bones and 2 pounds of meat while a fryer (about 3 pounds) will produce only 1 pound of meat.

Ducks found in American markets are frozen, and while they are quite adequate, a fresh duck is far superior. If you live near a metropolitan city in which there is a Chinatown, a trip to a Chinese butcher is well worth the trouble. There is no easy way to tell how fat a frozen duck is, but when selecting among fresh ducks, look for the plumpest candidate with the least amount of fat.

Poultry seems to make an appearance in virtually every Chinese meal. There are many ways it may be cooked and it can assume a great variety of textures and tastes, from light and velvety to bold and spicy. Cooking time can run the gamut, too, and on days when time is of the essence, quick, stir-fry dishes will allow you to serve a tempting meal in less than 30 minutes. Working people who attend my cooking classes tell me that they have found chicken breasts "on standby" in their refrigerator or freezer to be an essential ingredient for quickly-prepared meals—slice or dice, stir-fry, and dinner is virtually ready.

Presentation of a dish is most important. Here the Chef carefully arranges freshly-steamed buns on a plate with Tea-smoked Duck.

Shredded Chicken Salad

There are a number of steps to this popular dish, but the results are worth them. Shredded chicken, actually hand-torn, combined with lettuce, crunchy rice sticks, peanuts and sesame seeds, green onions, fragrant cilantro, and a snappy sauce.

Makes: 8 servings
Cooking time: 25 minutes

½ broiler-fryer chicken,
   (about 1½ lbs.)
   Cornstarch

   Vegetable oil, for deep-
   frying

2 ounces rice sticks, broken
   into sections

SAUCE

1 tablespoon hot powdered
   mustard
1 tablespoon water
1 tablespoon sesame oil

½ head iceberg lettuce,
   shredded
10 to 12 sprigs Chinese
   parsley (cilantro)
1 green onion (white part),
   slivered
½ teaspoon Chinese Five-
   spice Salt (page 212)

2 tablespoons crushed
   roasted peanuts
1 teaspoon toasted sesame
   seed

Rinse chicken under cold water; drain well and dust with cornstarch.

To steam, place chicken on rack in steamer; cover and steam for 10 minutes. Remove and cool.

To deep-fry, heat 4 cups oil in a wok (or electric deep-fat fryer) to 350°. Add rice sticks in two batches. Deep-fry for just a few seconds until rice puffs. Remove and set aside.

Return oil temperature to 350°. Add chicken and deep-fry for about 7 minutes until golden brown. Remove and set aside.

Prepare SAUCE by combining mustard with water; then stir in sesame oil.

To assemble, remove bone (but not skin) from warm chicken and shred meat by hand or with a cleaver. Place shredded lettuce on one side of a large salad bowl and hot mustard sauce on the other. Break parsley into small pieces, twisting stems over lettuce to bring out the juice. Drop parsley and green onion on lettuce; then mix chicken thoroughly with mustard sauce. Sprinkle five-spice salt over entire mixture before tossing chicken and lettuce together. Combine peanuts and sesame seed with half of the rice sticks; crush slightly. Sprinkle over top and serve with remaining rice sticks on the side.

• Notes •

1. When you leave chicken bones intact during deep-frying, it prevents the meat from shrinking.

2. Dusting the chicken with cornstarch creates a tasty, crispy skin during deep-frying. I prefer using it for this salad but you may want to remove it.

3. It's important to add all the ingredients to the salad bowl in the order listed.

4. Many of my students ask what kind of powdered mustard I prefer; my favorite is Colman's Hot Mustard.

Lemon Chicken

I offer you another one of my four-star dishes. Breast of chicken, lightly coated with batter and deep-fried, is topped with a tangy lemon sauce that's so refreshing.

Makes: 6 servings
Cooking time: 45 minutes

3 whole chicken breasts, split, boned, and skinned

MARINADE
¼ cup water
1 tablespoon dry sherry
¼ teaspoon garlic powder
¼ teaspoon salt
Pinch Chinese five-spice

BATTER
½ cup flour
1 cup cornstarch
¼ teaspoon baking powder
1 cup water
1 teaspoon vegetable oil

LEMON SAUCE
1 lemon
1 cup water
½ cup Rose's Lime Juice
¾ cup sugar
¼ teaspoons salt
2 drops yellow food coloring (optional)

Cornstarch
Vegetable oil, for deep-frying

Cornstarch paste
1 tablespoon vegetable oil

1 cup shredded lettuce
Lemon slices
Maraschino cherries, halved

Lightly score both sides of chicken breasts making a crisscross pattern. Combine MARINADE ingredients with chicken; let stand for 10 minutes.

In a bowl, place BATTER ingredients except oil. Using a whisk, beat continuously until the consistency of heavy cream is reached. Stir in oil, mix well, and let stand for 20 minutes.

Cut lemon in fourths; squeeze juice (discarding seeds) into a saucepan, dropping lemon into pan as well. Stir in remaining SAUCE ingredients, bring to a boil, remove and set aside.

To deep-fry, remove chicken from marinade and lightly coat with cornstarch. Heat 4 cups of oil in a wok (or electric deep-fat fryer) to 275° to 300°. Coat chicken in batter, draining off excess. Lower into wok by sliding pieces down the sides; deep-fry for 3 to 4 minutes (about 80% done) until a crust is formed. Remove and drain. (The above procedure may be done in advance.)

Reheat lemon sauce; stir in 2 to 3 tablespoons cornstarch paste and cook until thickened. Stir in 1 tablespoon oil; keep warm.

To deep-fry again, raise oil temperature in wok to 350°, discarding any pieces of batter from the first frying. Add chicken, all at once, and cook for 3 to 4 minutes until golden brown. Remove and drain.

To serve, place lettuce on a large serving platter. Cut chicken into 4 pieces crosswise and place on lettuce bed. Spoon sauce over chicken and garnish with lemon slices and cherries. Offer any extra sauce at the table.

• Notes •

1. Because the chicken should be crunchy on the outside yet juicy and tender on the inside, we've developed a "double-frying" process. The first frying, when the oil temperature is lower, actually cooks the chicken and causes a crust to form on the outside. The second frying at a higher temperature is what produces that special crunchy crust.

2. The lemon sauce should have a sharp, tangy taste and be the consistency of syrup.

3. I always tell my students to double the recipe for lemon sauce; it stores beautifully in the refrigerator for several months.

69

General's Spicy Hot Chicken

General Chua, a famous Chinese general from the Hunan Province, is reported to have concocted this dish over 100 years ago. It's hot, spicy, and quite tempting. You'll probably enjoy it as much as he did!

Makes: 6 servings
Cooking time: 10 minutes

1 whole chicken breast, split, boned, and skinned

MARINADE

1 tablespoon soy sauce
1 teaspoon cornstarch

SAUCE

1 tablespoon white vinegar
1 tablespoon soy sauce
1 tablespoon dry sherry
½ teaspoon sugar
½ teaspoon salt
1 teaspoon cornstarch paste

Vegetable oil, for blanching

3 dried red chili pods, broken and seeds from pods

SEASONINGS

1 green onion (white part), chopped
½ teaspoon minced fresh ginger
1 clove garlic, minced or pressed

2 teaspoons sesame oil

Pound chicken slightly with a mallet to tenderize; then cut into ¾- by ¾-inch pieces. Combine MARINADE ingredients with chicken in the order listed; set aside.

Combine SAUCE ingredients thoroughly; set aside.

To oil-blanch, set wok over high heat for about 1 minute. Add 2 cups oil and heat to 350°. Add chicken and blanch for 3 or 4 minutes until golden brown. Remove and drain, reserving oil.

To stir-fry, remove all but 2 tablespoons oil from wok. Reheat, swirling pan to coat sides. Add chili pods and seeds; stir-fry for about 30 seconds until browned. Return chicken and add SEASONINGS, stir-frying for another 30 seconds. Pour in sauce and cook until thickened. To serve, stir in sesame oil.

• *Note* •

Chili pods are browned to produce the aroma while the seeds are used to make the dish spicy and hot. Take care not to burn the seeds or let them get too dark.

Minced Chicken In Lettuce Cups

Classic but simple to prepare, this beautiful dish is also elegant to serve. The chicken and black mushrooms are scooped into lettuce to be eaten out of hand.

Makes: 6 to 8 servings
Cooking time: 15 minutes

- 4 or 5 dried black mushrooms
- 1 whole chicken breast, split, boned, and skinned

MARINADE
- Pinch salt
- Pinch white pepper
- 1 egg white
- ½ teaspoon cornstarch
- 1 tablespoon vegetable oil

- 1 head iceberg lettuce

- Vegetable oil, for deep-frying
- 1 ounce rice sticks, broken into small pieces

SAUCE
- 1 tablespoon dry sherry
- 1 tablespoon oyster sauce
- 3 tablespoons Hoisin sauce
- ¼ teaspoon salt
- Pinch white pepper

- 2 ounces ground pork
- 1 green onion (white part), minced
- ½ cup coarsely chopped bamboo shoots
- 2 water chestnuts, coarsely chopped
- 2 tablespoons roasted peanuts, crushed

Soak mushrooms in warm water for 20 minutes; remove, drain, and coarsely chop.

Mince chicken and combine with MARINADE ingredients in the order listed; let stand for 10 minutes.

Cut 1-inch off the end of lettuce head. Peel off large leaves and trim with scissors to make circles about 4 or 5 inches in diameter.

Combine SAUCE ingredients thoroughly; set aside.

To deep-fry, heat 2 cups oil in a wok (or electric deep-fat fryer) to 350°. Add rice sticks, little by little, and fry for about 15 seconds until puffed. Remove immediately, drain, and transfer to a large serving platter.

To oil-blanch, turn off heat until oil in wok is reduced to 300°. Add chicken, stirring to separate. Remove and drain.

To stir-fry, remove all but 3 tablespoons oil from wok. Reheat, swirling pan to coat sides. Add pork, stirring to separate. Add green onion, stirring until fragrant. Stir in bamboo shoots, mushrooms, and water chestnuts for 30 seconds. Return chicken and add sauce, tossing vigorously to coat thoroughly.

To serve, spoon chicken mixture on top of rice sticks. Sprinkle with peanuts. Arrange lettuce rounds on another plate. Toss rice and chicken lightly at the table. Spoon 2 to 3 tablespoons mixture into each lettuce cup to eat out of hand.

• Notes •

1. Squab may be substituted for chicken.

2. Don't try to deep-fry the rice sticks all at one time; they need room to expand!

Chicken In Phoenix Nest   *Pictured on page 73*

The Phoenix, which represents beauty and grace, is properly remembered in the presentation of this dish. Cubes of plump chicken nestle in a lacy basket made of shredded potatoes. Green pepper, slices of carrot, and delicate quail eggs are a colorful and surprising addition.

Makes: 4 to 6 servings
Cooking time: 30 minutes

- 1 large russet potato
  Pinch salt
- 1 broiler-fryer chicken (about 2½ lbs.), boned, skinned, and cut into bite-size pieces

MARINADE

- 2 teaspoons light or regular soy sauce
- 2 teaspoons dry sherry
- 1 egg white
- 1 tablespoon cornstarch
- 1 tablespoon vegetable oil

- ½ teaspoon cornstarch

  Vegetable oil, for deep-frying

- 2 green onions (white part), finely chopped
- 1 clove garlic, sliced

SAUCE

- 2 tablespoons soy sauce
- 2 tablespoons Hoisin sauce
- 1 tablespoon dry sherry

VEGETABLES

- 1 green pepper, seeded and cut into 1-inch squares
- ¼ white onion, cut into 1-inch squares
- 6 thin slices carrot

  Dash sesame oil
- 5 or 6 quail eggs
  Shredded lettuce or bok choy

- 2 medium-size wire strainers

Peel potato and shred; place in a bowl of water, add salt and let stand until ready to use.

Combine chicken with MARINADE ingredients in the order listed and let stand for 10 minutes; set aside.

Drain potatoes thoroughly and toss with the ½ teaspoon cornstarch. Heat 2 quarts oil in a wok to 350°.

To shape, dip the 2 identical strainers into the oil to prevent sticking. Distribute half the potatoes evenly around the sides and bottom of one strainer. Press the other strainer down into the potato-lined one.

To deep-fry, holding the strainers tightly together, carefully lower them into the oil and rotate so that oil touches all the sides. Deep-fry for 3 to 4 minutes, basting if necessary, until potato nest becomes slightly brown. Remove from oil, gently separate strainers and tap nest out onto a paper towel to drain. Repeat, using remaining potatoes.

To oil-blanch, remove 1 quart oil (reserve for future use) and heat remaining oil to 300°. Add chicken, stirring to separate, and blanch for 2 to 3 minutes. Remove and drain.

Combine SAUCE ingredients and set aside.

To stir-fry, remove all but 3 tablespoons oil from the wok and when hot, add onion and garlic. Stir-fry until fragrant and then add VEGETABLES and chicken. Cook for 1 minute; stir in SAUCE. Continue cooking and stirring for 1 minute longer, then stir in sesame oil and drained quail eggs.

To serve, position potato nests on top of platter lined with lettuce. Fill each nest with half the chicken mixture, carefully keeping quail egg on top.

Show-stopping chicken in phoenix nest features quail eggs and stir-fried chicken and vegetables in hoisin sauce, nesting in edible basket of fried shredded potatoes. Seasonal asparagus, tossed with oyster sauce, and boiled rice complete the menu.

Snow White Chicken

Plump chicken breasts are sliced paper thin and then lightly marinated before being stir-fried with snow peas and black mushrooms. I recommend it to my customers who prefer a mildly-flavored chicken dish.

Makes: 6 servings
Cooking time: 10 minutes

4 dried black mushrooms

1 whole chicken breast, split, boned, and skinned

MARINADE

¼ teaspoon salt
Pinch white pepper
3 tablespoons water
1 egg white
1 tablespoon cornstarch
1 tablespoon vegetable oil

SAUCE

1 green onion (white part), finely chopped
¼ teaspoon minced fresh ginger
1 cup Rich Chicken Broth (page 52), or chicken bouillon
1½ tablespoons dry sherry
¼ teaspoon salt
Pinch white pepper
¼ teaspoon sugar
1 tablespoon cornstarch paste

Vegetable oil, for blanching
5 or 6 snow peas, ends trimmed and cut in half

Soak mushrooms in warm water for 20 minutes; drain, remove stems, and cut in half.

Partially freeze chicken breast, then slice paper thin (about ⅛-inch thick). Combine MARINADE ingredients with chicken in the order listed. Let stand for about 10 minutes.

Combine SAUCE ingredients thoroughly; set aside.

To oil-blanch, set wok over high heat for about 1 minute. Add 4 cups oil and heat to 300°. Add chicken, stirring to separate pieces. Turn off heat and add snow peas and mushrooms; blanch for about 15 seconds, then remove and drain.

To stir-fry, remove all but 2 tablespoons oil from wok. Turn heat on high, add sauce and cook until thickened. Add chicken mixture, lightly stir-fry to coat thoroughly for about 30 seconds.

• *Note* •

A good rich chicken broth is required for this dish. If you don't have any Rich Chicken Broth (page 52), dissolve an additional bouillon cube in the broth you're using to increase the flavor.

Kung Pao Chicken

As the story goes, the chef of a provincial viceroy, a *kung pao,* made a mistake whilst cooking dinner—he overbrowned the chili in the hot oil before adding the chicken; however, in so doing, he created an aroma which was spicy and smoky. To his good fortune, his viceroy loved it, and both the dish and the story became widespread. The number of dried chili pods in this recipe indicates that this dish is fiery hot.

Makes: 8 servings
Cooking time: 15 minutes

1 whole chicken breast, split, boned, and skinned

MARINADE

2 teaspoons soy sauce
2 teaspoons dry sherry
1 teaspoon cornstarch
1 tablespoon vegetable oil

Vegetable oil, for blanching

SEASONINGS

3 tablespoons soy sauce
1 tablespoon dry sherry
2 tablespoons red rice vinegar
1 teaspoon sugar
½ teaspoon cornstarch paste

10 dried red chili pods

VEGETABLES

6 to 8 water chestnuts, cut in fourths
¼ cup diced bamboo shoots
2 green onions (white part), cut in ½-inch pieces
1 clove garlic, minced or pressed

¼ teaspoon sesame oil
1 teaspoon hot chili oil
¼ cup roasted peanuts

Bone chicken, remove skin and cut meat into ¾-inch cubes. Combine with MARINADE ingredients in the order listed; set aside.

To oil-blanch, set wok over high heat for about 1 minute. Add 2 cups oil and heat to 300°. Add chicken, stirring to separate pieces. Remove and drain.

Combine SEASONINGS thoroughly; set aside.

To stir-fry, remove all but 2 tablespoons oil from wok. Reheat, swirling pan to coat sides. Add chili pods, breaking only one in half. Stir for about 45 seconds or until browned (but not burned). Return chicken and cook for 1 to 2 minutes until browned. Add VEGETABLES, stir-frying for 1 minute. Add SEASONINGS, mixing thoroughly, and cook until thickened. Sprinkle with sesame and hot chili oils and finally with roasted peanuts to serve.

• *Notes* •

1. Chili seeds, not pods, determine just how hot a dish will be. I suggest breaking open only one the first time; if you want it hotter, open more next time.

2. Try a delicious variation using squid instead of chicken. It's listed as Hunan Lichee Squid, page 109.

Cutting a Duck

After applying skill and patience to the preparation of Peking duck, take some care with the presentation, too. The aim is to remove the bones, then reassemble the skin and meat to recreate the duck's original shape. 1, 2) Carve off the duck's legs and wings, and then 3) remove skin from the back and 4) breasts. 5) Cut meat and place bite-size pieces on serving platter; cover with skin and 6) arrange legs, wings, and head to create original shape. Served with steamed Mandarin pancakes, Peking sauce, and onion slivers. (A dish containing shredded pieces of duck and celery—for extra nibbling—is in the foreground.)

Classic Peking Duck   *Pictured on page 76*

This truly grand duck will challenge the best of cooks but the secret is patience; pay careful attention to this recipe, and results will earn you the chef's hat.

Makes: 8 servings
Cooking time: 2 hours

- 1 fresh duck (5 lbs. or larger), cleaned with head attached
- 2 quarts water
- ½ teaspoon baking soda

COATING
- 1 quart water
- 1 tablespoon maltose or honey

- 12 to 18 Mandarin Pancakes (page 187)
- 8 Onion Brushes (page 217)

PEKING SAUCE
- 2 tablespoons Hoisin sauce
- ¼ teaspoon sesame oil
- ¼ teaspoon sugar

This first procedure is an optional but authentic step in making Peking duck.

Seal tail opening with a skewer. Using a pump, force air in between skin and meat by inserting it at neck opening. When inflated, seal off at neck with a piece of string. (The air will escape naturally during cooking.)

To water-blanch, bring water and soda to a boil. Drop in duck, ladling water over it as necessary, and blanch for about 30 seconds. Remove duck, discarding water.

To coat, bring water and maltose to a boil in a wok. Holding duck over wok, ladle coating syrup evenly all over surface; repeat about 6 times.

Hang duck in a cool place (preferably near a fan) with circulating air for at least 4 hours or longer until skin is dry to the touch.

To roast, preheat oven to 400°. Place duck, breast side up, on a V-shaped rack in a roasting pan. Cover loosely with a tent of aluminum foil (avoid touching skin), and roast for 30 minutes.

Meanwhile, make pancakes as directed on page 187; set aside to be steamed just before serving. Carve onion brushes as directed on page 217; set aside.

Combine SAUCE ingredients and set aside

To continue roasting, turn duck over on rack, cover with foil, and continue roasting for 30 minutes longer. Then turn duck over, breast side up, and remove foil. Roast for 5 to 10 minutes more or until golden brown (watch carefully to prevent burning).

Place pancakes wrapped in damp towel inside steamer. Cover and steam for about 3 minutes; keep warm.

To carve, transfer duck to a cutting board. Carefully, remove skin in large pieces; cut meat from carcass into bite-size pieces and arrange on serving platter. Cover with skin pieces and position wings and legs properly, recreating its original shape (see page 77). Garnish plate with onion brushes.

To serve, brush warm pancake with Peking Sauce, add onion and a few pieces of duck and skin. Roll up and eat out of hand.

Canton West Lake Duck

This simple-to-prepare duck entrée, served on a bed of crispy blanched lettuce, simmers slowly in a spicy master sauce until very tender. So tender, in fact, that guests help themselves to small pieces right from the plump bird itself, using chopsticks or a small seafood fork.

2 quarts Master Sauce (recipe on page 86)

1 fresh duck (4½ to 5 lbs.), cleaned

Boiling water

2 tablespoons soy sauce

½ large head Iceberg lettuce, leaves separated slightly

Chicken broth (or water), for blanching

Cornstarch paste

Prepare MASTER SAUCE as directed on page 86 and simmer for 30 minutes. Measure out 2 quarts (reserve remaining sauce for other uses) and set aside in large pot.

To par-boil, place whole duck in enough boiling water to cover and par-boil for 3 minutes. Remove and drain; let cool slightly.

To simmer, rub duck with soy sauce and place in pot with master sauce. Bring to a boil, reduce heat, and simmer for about 1 hour or until duck is very tender.

To water-blanch, bring broth (or water) to a boil, drop in lettuce sections, and blanch for 30 seconds. Quickly drain and arrange on serving platter.

To serve, remove duck from sauce, drain slightly and place on bed of lettuce. Measure 2 cups of the sauce and place in small pot. Stir in 2 tablespoons cornstarch paste and continue cooking until sauce thickens. Ladle sauce over entire duck at the table.

American tradition with a Chinese twist, on grandmother's English china, features roast turkey, homemade giblet gravy, and all the trimmings. Eight treasure stuffing (page 81), a mélange of rice, black mushrooms, onions, shrimp, ham, raisins, gingko nuts, and dates, is tucked inside. Garden fresh snow peas with water chestnuts (page 146) and sesame-topped glazed apples (page 188) complete the holiday fare.

Turkey With Eight Treasure Stuffing   *Pictured on facing page*

At holiday-time try this Chinese stuffing. It is easy to make and a surprise to serve. To depart from the ordinary completely, let your next festive occasion follow a Chinese turkey dinner menu commencing with Wonton Soup and concluding with Glazed Apples.

Makes: 16 to 20 servings
Cooking time: 5 hours

1   turkey (14 to 15 lbs.)

MARINADE
4   green onions
1   thumb-size chunk fresh ginger, smashed
3   tablespoons dry sherry
1   tablespoon roasted Szechuan peppercorns
2   tablespoons salt

1½   cups sweet rice

STUFFING
4   dried black mushrooms
2   tablespoons dried shrimp
1   small piece (about 2 ounces) Virginia ham or Chinese sausage, chopped (optional)
5   tablespoons dried red dates, seeds removed and chopped
2   tablespoons raisins
1   green onion (white part), chopped
2   preserved candied kumquats, chopped
10   canned gingko nuts, chopped

2   tablespoons vegetable oil

SEASONINGS
2   tablespoons soy sauce
½   teaspoon sugar
1   teaspoon salt
¼   teaspoon white pepper

COATING
3   tablespoons honey
½   cup hot water

Curly endive
Plum sauce (purchased)

Remove giblets and set aside; reserve other innards for other uses. Combine MARINADE ingredients and rub on turkey, inside and out. Let stand for 2 hours (or overnight in refrigerator).

Soak rice in warm water for 1 hour. Then line the inside of a steamer with wet cheesecloth. Place rice on cheesecloth, cover, and steam over boiling water for 25 minutes. Remove and set aside.

Soak mushrooms in warm water for 30 minutes; drain, remove stems, and chop. Soak shrimp in warm water for 30 minutes; remove, drain, and chop.

In a large bowl, combine STUFFING ingredients and cooked rice; add oil and SEASONINGS and mix well.

To stuff, remove seasonings clinging to turkey. Spoon stuffing into turkey. (Take care not to overstuff and allow room for expansion.) Close openings with skewers.

Combine COATING ingredients and brush evenly over turkey. Let stand for 10 minutes.

To roast, preheat oven to 350°. Place turkey, breast side up, on V-shaped rack in roasting pan. Arrange giblets around edges of pan. Cover with a tent of aluminum foil. Allowing 20 minutes per pound, roast turkey brushing occasionally with honey glaze until juices run clear when thigh is pierced. Remove cooked giblets and chop; set aside. Remove foil and increase temperature to 375° to 400° to brown just before serving, if desired.

To serve, make favorite gravy and add chopped giblets; keep warm. Border a large serving platter with curly endive. Slice turkey and arrange on platter. Remove stuffing and mound into center. Offer plum sauce.

Crisp Spicy Duck

The spicy marinade permeates and flavors the meat to make this crispy delicacy a mouth-watering family dish. Serve with steamed buns, slivers of onion, and spicy Hoisin sauce.

Makes: 6 to 8 servings
Cooking time: 75 minutes

- 1 large fresh duck (4½ to 5 lbs.), cleaned

MARINADE

- 2 green onions, cut in half
- 2 thumb-size chunks fresh ginger, crushed
- 1 tablespoon Szechuan peppercorns
- 3 tablespoons dry sherry
- 3 tablespoons salt

- 2 tablespoons soy sauce
- 3 tablespoons flour

- 1 dozen Butterfly Steamed Buns (page 176)

    Vegetable oil, for deep-frying

    Slivers of green onion
    Hoisin sauce

Rub duck inside and out with MARINADE ingredients; let stand for 8 hours or overnight in refrigerator.

To steam, place duck on rack in steamer. Cover and steam over boiling water for 1 hour. Remove, discarding spices clinging to duck. Brush duck with soy sauce and dust with flour, shaking off excess. (The above procedure may be done in advance.)

Prepare buns following directions on page 176; set aside until ready for steaming.

To deep-fry, heat 4 cups oil in wok (or electric deep-fat fryer) to 350°. Fry duck for 10 to 12 minutes, turning occasionally with a spatula to prevent skin from sticking to the bottom. Remove when duck is golden brown.

Meanwhile, place buns on rack in bamboo steamer. Cover and steam over boiling water for about 5 minutes.

To serve, cut duck into major parts, then slice ½-inch thick including the bone. Reassemble on platter recreating the original shape as illustrated on page 85. Offer steamed buns, onion slivers, and Hoisin sauce at the table.

• *Note* •

If you find it more comfortable, cut the duck in half before the deep-frying process.

Sautéed Ginger Duck

Unlike most Chinese duck recipes calling for roasting, steaming, or braising, this one specifies sautéeing. It's one of my favorites because preparing duck this way creates such a unique texture and flavor.

Makes: 8 servings
Cooking time: 10 minutes

1 fresh duck (3 to 4 lbs.), cleaned

MARINADE

1 teaspoon soy sauce
Pinch white pepper
1 egg white
1 teaspoon cornstarch
1 tablespoon vegetable oil

SAUCE

2 teaspoons soy sauce
1 teaspoon dry sherry
1 teaspoon white vinegar
½ teaspoon cornstarch paste
¼ teaspoon sugar
¼ teaspoon sesame oil

Vegetable oil, for blanching

VEGETABLES

20 thin slices fresh ginger
10 snow peas, ends trimmed and diagonally cut in half
10 to 15 canned straw mushrooms
1 green onion (white part), diagonally sliced ½-inch thick
2 cloves garlic, sliced

Pinch salt

Bone duck; cutting with the grain, slice meat about ⅛-inch thick.

Combine MARINADE ingredients with duck in the order listed, mixing well. Let stand for 10 minutes.

Combine SAUCE ingredients thoroughly; set aside.

To oil-blanch, heat wok over high heat for about 1 minute. Add 2 cups oil and heat to 350°. Add duck slices, stirring for 15 seconds to separate. Remove and drain.

To stir-fry, remove all but 3 tablespoons oil from wok. Reheat, swirling pan to coat sides. Add VEGETABLES and salt; stir-fry for about 15 seconds and then return duck to wok. Quickly stir in sauce, tossing to coat duck pieces thoroughly. Transfer to a serving platter.

• *Notes* •

1. It's easier to slice meat—especially when the recipe calls for paper-thin slices—if you partially freeze it first.

2. You may have noticed that we call for a higher blanching temperature in this recipe. It's needed to quickly seal in the juices, thus creating a more tender texture in the duck.

Tea-smoked Duck   *Pictured on page 33*

Tea-smoked duck, often served in Szechuan-style Chinese restaurants, takes a little more time to prepare but it's worth it. The meat is tender and juicy with a hint of smoky flavor that's irresistible.

Makes: 8 servings
Cooking time: 1½ hours

1   large fresh duck (4½ to 5 lbs.), cleaned

MARINADE

2   green onions, cut in half
2   thumb-size chunks fresh ginger, crushed
5   star anise seeds, broken
3   tablespoons dry sherry
1   tablespoon Szechuan peppercorns
3   tablespoons salt
¼   teaspoon curing salt (optional)

1   dozen Butterfly Steamed Buns (page 176)

3   tablespoons black tea leaves
2   tablespoons brown sugar
2   tablespoons rice

Vegetable oil, for deep-frying

Slivers of green onion

Rub duck inside and out with MARINADE ingredients. Let stand for 8 hours or overnight in the refrigerator.

Prepare buns following directions on page 176; set aside until ready for steaming.

To steam, place duck on rack inside steamer. Cover and steam over boiling water for 1 hour. Remove, discarding spices clinging to duck.

To smoke, line a 14-inch wok and its cover with aluminum foil. Sprinkle tea leaves over foil, then sugar and then rice. Place duck, breast side up, on a V-shaped rack in wok. Cover and cook on high heat for 2 minutes. Turn heat off for 5 minutes; then back on for 2 minutes and off again for 5 minutes. (Don't take the lid off during the smoking process.) Remove duck and hang up to cool; discard smoking material. (The above procedure may be done in advance.)

To deep-fry, heat 4 cups oil in wok (or electric deep-fat fryer) to 350°. Fry duck, turning over once, for 10 to 12 minutes or until coffee brown. Watch closely to prevent duck from getting too dark. Remove and drain.

Meanwhile, steam buns in steamer over boiling water for 5 minutes until hot; keep warm.

To serve, cut duck into major parts; then slice ½-inch thick including the bone. Reassemble on platter recreating the original shape (see illustrations on facing page). Offer steamed buns and onion slivers at the table.

• *Notes* •

1. In some parts of China, cooks prefer wood shavings or pine needles instead of tea leaves for smoking. The type of wood shavings used determines the flavor produced by the fragrance of the smoke.

2. Lining the wok with aluminum foil first prevents the carmelized sugar from sticking to the bottom.

3. If you wish, offer Hoisin sauce as a condiment, too. But go easy—you don't want to overpower the subtle tea-smoked flavor.

Carving a Duck

1) Cut duck in half along backbone. 2) Carefully, remove wings and thigh sections; then 3) separate breasts from back sections. 4) Chop entire back section into bite-size pieces and place in center of platter. Separate legs from thighs and 5) chop thighs into bite-size pieces. Place at one end of platter. 6) Cut breasts into pieces and arrange nicely on top of backbone pieces. Cut legs into pieces and arrange with wings on platter 7) recreating duck's original shape. To serve, 8) open steamed butterfly bun, spread with little sauce, add onion sliver and piece of duck; eat just like sandwich.

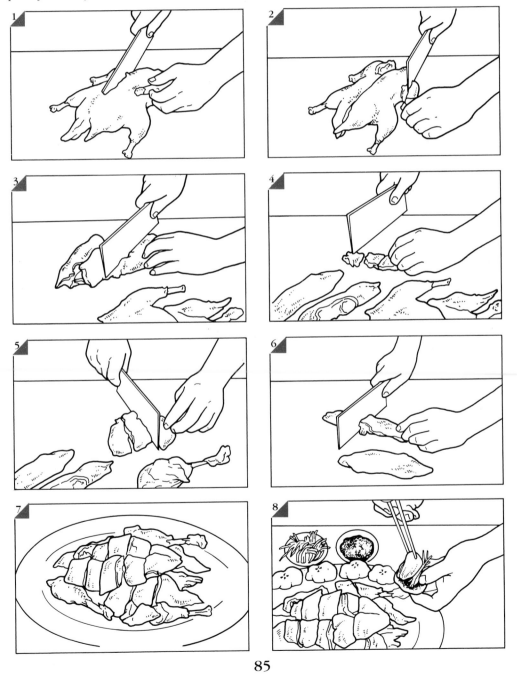

Mandarin Pressed Duck

Crunchy on the outside, tender on the inside, this carefully prepared deboned duck dish was devised by early Chinese cooks in this country for American diners.

Makes: 8 to 10 servings
Cooking time: 2 hours

MASTER SAUCE

    4 quarts water
    2 knobs fresh ginger, crushed
    4 green onions, tied in knots

In a cheesecloth bag put:

    6 star anise
    1 teaspoon Szechuan peppercorns
    1 teaspoon fennel seed
    2 pieces preserved tangerine peel
    5 cardamom seeds
    ½ teaspoon whole cloves

    ¾ cup soy sauce
    4 teaspoons sugar

    1 fresh duck (4½ to 5 lbs.), cleaned
    1 tablespoon soy sauce

    Vegetable oil, for blanching

    2 ounces ground pork
    4 tablespoons water chestnut starch or cornstarch

    1 cup Sweet & Sour Sauce (page 213) or canned plum sauce
    Cornstarch paste

    Vegetable oil, for deep-frying

    Shredded lettuce
    2 tablespoons roasted almonds, crushed

In a deep pot, bring water to a boil; add remaining MASTER SAUCE ingredients including the cheesecloth bag. Reduce heat and simmer for about 30 minutes. Stir in soy sauce and sugar; continue to simmer.

Trim fat around neck and tail of duck; split in half and brush skin with soy sauce.

To oil-blanch, set wok over high heat for about 1 minute. Add 4 cups oil and heat to 350°. Immerse duck in oil (watch out for splattering) and blanch for about 2 minutes or until skin is browned. Remove and drain.

To simmer, place duck in simmering master sauce and continue to simmer for about 45 minutes. Remove (discarding spices that cling to sides) and drain. (Reserve master sauce for other uses.)

To assemble, cut off legs and wings from duck. Peel off skin from breasts without tearing and place right side down on platter. Tear meat off duck, including off legs and wings; finely shred and place in a mixing bowl. Add pork, water chestnut starch or cornstarch, and 4 tablespoons of the master sauce. Spoon mixture out onto both duck skins, pressing down tightly against skin.

To steam, place bowls (or pie tins) filled with duck into steamer. Cover and steam over boiling water for 15 minutes. Remove from steam, pat meat down slightly, and allow to cool. Invert bowls to turn out both duck sections. Cut into wedges like a pie.

In a small saucepan, heat Sweet & Sour sauce and thicken with about 1 tablespoon cornstarch paste; keep warm.

To deep-fry, heat 4 cups oil in a wok (or electric deep-fat fryer) to 350°. Carefully, deep-fry pressed duck wedges, a few at a time, for 6 to 8 minutes or until brown. Remove and drain.

To serve, arrange shredded lettuce on serving platter. Place duck wedges attractively on lettuce, and spoon warm sauce over duck. Garnish with almonds.

Squab Cantonese

Fresh squab goes through two cooking processes to achieve its barbecue-like flavor. After marinating for about 2 hours, it's steamed and then deep-fried. The result is a tender, tasty bird beneath a crisp and golden brown skin.

Makes: 6 to 8 servings
Cooking time: 30 minutes

MARINADE

- 2 green onions, cut in half and crushed to bring out juices
- 1 thumb-size chunk fresh ginger, sliced
- 2 star anise seed, crushed
- 4 tablespoons soy sauce
- 2 tablespoons dry sherry
- ½ teaspoon sugar
- ¼ teaspoon salt

- 2 large squab (1 lb. each), cleaned

Vegetable oil, for deep-frying

Shredded lettuce
Chinese Five-spice Salt (page 212)

Combine MARINADE ingredients together; rub squabs inside and out and let stand for 2 hours.

To steam, place squab on plate (or pie tin) inside steamer. Cover and steam over boiling water for 10 minutes. Remove, discarding spices that may be clinging to sides of squab.

To deep-fry, heat 4 cups oil in a wok (or electric deep-fat fryer) to 350°. Fry squabs, one at a time, for about 1 minute. Lift out of oil for 30 seconds, then return to fry for about 1 minute longer or until golden brown.

To serve, cut squabs into 2 sections lengthwise; then cut each section into 3 parts, including the bone. Reassemble on bed of lettuce to recreate original shape. Offer a small dish of five-spice salt for dipping.

• Notes •

1. If you prefer to use quail, you'll need four of them. Remember to cut the steaming time in half.

2. If you use chicken, you'll need one weighing about 2½ pounds.

▪ SEAFOOD ▪

China has more than 8,500 miles of coastline fronting on the Pacific Ocean, with its northernmost region of Shandong embracing the Yellow Sea, with Shanghai and the eastern region facing the East China Sea, and with Canton, an active trading region, boldly exposed to the South China Sea. Two very lengthy rivers, the Yangtse and Yellow, twist and wind through the vast countryside, and thousands of lakes add to the variety of marine life. It is no wonder that this abundance finds its way into many dishes and conversations among Chinese chefs.

The recipes that follow are among the best from the four major regional schools of cooking: Sole Fillets in Wine Sauce from Peking, Prawns in Lobster Sauce from Canton, Spicy Hot Braised Fish from Szechuan, and Crab in Bean Sauce from Shanghai.

American seafood markets offer a great variety of fish. I recommend rock cod and red snapper often because they are easy to handle, good sized, and have a modest number of bones.

When selecting a *whole fish,* check the eyes to see that they are clear, shiny, and

Knowing how to select fresh seafood is critical. Here, faced with so many choices, the suggestions in the text come in handy.

protruding. Gills should be pinkish-red; the body should be firm and shiny. Rub your finger along the fish's body to make sure it bounces back and feels sleek, not sticky. It should have a fish smell, but not a strong one. When selecting fillets of sole, look for those with a shiny glaze.

Prawns generally come fresh-frozen in 5-pound block boxes. If you have a sizeable freezer, this is the most economical way to buy them. When partially thawed, break them into smaller blocks and then refreeze to have them readily available. When buying loose prawns, look for those with a greyish-blue tinge to the shell and a translucent color to the flesh. Do not buy raw prawns already peeled and deveined because chemicals have been added to prolong their shelf life. Prawns that have been cooked and peeled should be light pink in color.

When buying *clams,* check that their shells are tightly shut; if they are open, even slightly, they are dead and should not be purchased. Put live clams in clear cold water for them to breathe and spew sand trapped inside. Clams should open after blanching in boiling water; discard those that don't!

Crab season is from November to mid-spring, so that is the time to cook crab dishes. Buy them live and prepare them according to the recipes. If you want to offer crab in the off-season, buy them fresh-frozen and cook immediately.

Canton Salt-baked Prawns

Succulent prawns are cooked in such a way that the natural juice is sealed in the shell. My Chinese countrymen enjoy this dish by sucking the prawns out of their shell believing that the shell adds flavor to the meat. Not really baked, the prawns are dusted in flour before deep-frying for a brief minute.

Makes: 8 to 10 servings
Cooking time: 10 minutes

1 pound medium-size prawns (26 to 30 count)

MARINADE
1 clove garlic, minced or pressed
1 tablespoon dry sherry
½ teaspoon salt
Pinch black pepper
Pinch roasted Szechuan peppercorns

2 tablespoons flour

Vegetable oil, for deep-frying

Shredded lettuce
Chinese Five Spice Salt (page 212)

Cut prawns along back with small scissors, leaving shell on. Devein and snip off legs and hard pointed tips on tails as illustrated. Rinse and drain well.

Combine prawns with MARINADE ingredients; mix well and set aside for 30 minutes. Dust with flour just before deep-frying.

To deep-fry, heat 2 cups oil in wok (or electric deep-fat fryer) to 375°. Carefully, add prawns, stirring to separate. Deep-fry for 1½ minutes; then remove and drain on paper towels.

To serve, line serving platter with lettuce. Arrange prawns decoratively on top and sprinkle with five-spice salt.

• Notes •

1. Dusting prawns with flour right before deep-frying prevents flavor and moisture loss.

2. Sometime, try serving these prawns perched in a bird's nest. See directions for Chicken in Phoenix Nest, page 72.

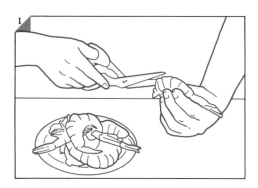
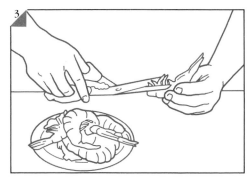
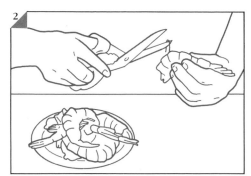

1) Cut along back of prawns with small scissors, leaving shell on. 2) Carefully, lift out black vein and then 3) snip off legs and hard pointed tips of tail.

Prawns In Lobster Sauce

This isn't as decadent as it sounds! Actually, there isn't any lobster in this Cantonese dish at all. It's just that the color and the taste will fool anyone.

Makes: 6 servings
Cooking time: 10 minutes

1 pound medium-size prawns (26 to 30 count)

MARINADE

Pinch salt
Pinch white pepper
1 egg white
1 teaspoon cornstarch
1 tablespoon vegetable oil

Vegetable oil, for blanching

1 ounce ground pork
1 tablespoon fermented black beans, smashed
1 clove garlic, minced or pressed

VEGETABLES

1 green pepper, cut into ½-inch squares
½ small white onion, cut into ½-inch squares
4 or 5 slices water chestnuts

1 tablespoon dry sherry

SEASONINGS

½ cup chicken broth
¼ teaspoon salt
¼ teaspoon sugar
1 tablespoon soy sauce

Cornstarch paste

2 eggs, lightly beaten
Dash sesame oil

Shell, devein, and rinse prawns. Pat dry and combine with MARINADE ingredients in the order listed; set aside for 10 minutes.

To oil-blanch, set wok over high heat for about 1 minute. Add 3 cups oil and heat to 300°. Add prawns stirring to separate. Blanch for 1 minute; then remove and drain.

To stir-fry, remove all but 3 tablespoons oil from wok. Add pork and fry until separated. Stir in black beans and garlic; cook until fragrant. Add VEGETABLES and sherry, stirring for about 15 seconds. Return prawns and add SEASONINGS. Bring to a boil and thicken with about 2 teaspoons cornstarch paste. Gently stir eggs in one direction and fold into mixture but don't overcook. Add dash sesame oil and remove from heat. Serve immediately.

Crystal Prawns

Sautéed prawns like these never fail to win approval from my family. They are simple to make, with just a hint of fresh ginger and green onion, and a dash of vinegar.

Makes: 6 servings
Cooking time: 10 minutes

1 pound medium-size prawns (26 to 30 count)

MARINADE
Pinch salt
Pinch white pepper
1 egg white
2 teaspoons cornstarch
1 tablespoon vegetable oil

Vegetable oil, for blanching

SAUCE
¼ cup chicken broth
¼ teaspoon minced fresh ginger
1 teaspoon dry sherry
½ teaspoon salt
¼ teaspoon sugar

2 green onions (white part), diagonally sliced ¼-inch thick
Dash white vinegar
Cornstarch paste

Shell, devein, and rinse prawns; pat dry and split in half lengthwise. Combine MARINADE ingredients with prawns in the order listed. Mix well and let stand for 10 minutes.

To oil-blanch, set wok over high heat for about 1 minute. Add 3 cups oil and heat to 300°. Add prawns, stirring gently to separate. Blanch for 1 minute, remove, and drain.

Combine SAUCE ingredients and set aside.

To stir-fry, remove all but 2 tablespoons oil from wok. Add green onion and stir-fry for 15 seconds. Return prawns and stir-fry for 10 seconds. Sprinkle with vinegar, pour in sauce, and bring to a boil. Thicken with 1 teaspoon cornstarch paste. Remove immediately and transfer to serving plate.

• Notes •

1. Vinegar brings out the flavor and aroma of seafood.

2. There shouldn't be too much sauce; it's only supposed to coat the prawns.

3. Blanched green vegetables (snow peas, broccoli) may be added during the stir-frying or you might want to add sliced carrots or cashews.

Chef Chu's Lovers' Prawns

Here's a doubly delicious recipe serving red hot, spicy dry-braised prawns with delicate, crystal light prawns in white wine sauce. Both are presented on the same plate, suggesting that a pair of lovers might have different tastes. (Timing is critical so make sure your serving platter is ready for presentation before you start cooking.)

Makes: 8 servings
Cooking time: 15 minutes

1 pound medium-size prawns (26 to 30 count)

MARINADE

¼ teaspoon salt
Pinch white pepper
1 egg white
3 teaspoons cornstarch
1 tablespoon vegetable oil

1 green onion

Vegetable oil, for blanching

SAUCE #1

¼ cup chicken broth
1 tablespoon dry sherry
¼ teaspoon salt
¼ teaspoon sugar
½ teaspoon cornstarch paste

SAUCE #2

2 tablespoons catsup
1 tablespoon dry sherry
1 teaspoon sugar
Pinch salt
1 teaspoon soy sauce

1 tablespoon cooked peas
2 tablespoons minced white onion

½ teaspoon minced fresh ginger
1 clove garlic, minced or pressed
1 teaspoon chili paste

Cornstarch paste

¼ teaspoon sesame oil
Sliced tomato
Chinese parsley (cilantro)

Shell, devein, and rinse prawns. Pat dry and split in half. Combine MARINADE ingredients with prawns in the order listed. Let stand for 10 minutes.

Cut lower white part of green onions into ½-inch pieces; coarsely chop upper green part. Set aside.

To oil-blanch, set wok over high heat for about 1 minute. Add 4 cups oil and heat to 300°. Add prawns, stir to separate, and blanch until pink; remove and drain. Combine ingredients for SAUCE #1, then SAUCE #2 in separate bowls.

To stir-fry, remove all but 1 tablespoon oil from wok. Heat oil and add peas, lower part of green onion, half the prawns, and sauce #1. Mix well until hot and thickened; transfer to one side of serving platter.

Quickly, wipe wok clean and heat 2 tablespoons oil. Add white onion, ginger, garlic, and chili paste; stir-fry for 15 seconds. Add remaining prawns, upper part of green onion, and sauce #2. Bring to a boil, mix well, and thicken with about 1 teaspoon cornstarch paste. Sprinkle with sesame oil and transfer to other half of platter. Use tomato slices as divider between prawns and garnish with parsley.

• Note •

Timing is crucial! Have everything ready—including your serving platter with tomato slices—so that the dish can be served hot.

Szechuan Dry-braised Prawns   *Pictured on page 36*

Presenting one of my most requested "four-star" menu items! Plump, succulent prawns are quickly braised in a hot-and-spicy sauce and then sprinkled with green onion and a little sesame oil.

Makes: 6 to 8 servings
Cooking time: 5 minutes

- 1 pound medium-size prawns (26 to 30 count)

MARINADE
- Pinch salt
- Pinch white pepper
- 1 egg white
- 1 tablespoon cornstarch
- 2 tablespoons oil

- Vegetable oil, for blanching

SPICES
- ½ small white onion, minced
- 2 teaspoons minced fresh ginger
- 2 cloves garlic, minced or pressed
- 1 teaspoon chili paste

SEASONINGS
- ½ cup catsup
- 2 tablespoons dry sherry
- 1 tablespoon sugar
- ½ teaspoon salt
- ½ tablespoon soy sauce

- 1 green onion, chopped
- 1 teaspoon sesame oil

Shell and devein prawns, leaving tails attached. Rinse and pat dry. Combine MARINADE ingredients with prawns in the order listed. Let stand 10 minutes.

To oil-blanch, set wok over high heat for about 1 minute. Add 3 cups oil and heat to 300°. Add prawns, stirring gently to separate. Blanch until pink, remove, and drain.

To braise, remove all but 3 tablespoons oil from wok. Add onion and brown slightly; stir in remaining SPICES and cook until fragrant. Add SEASONINGS and prawns and braise over high heat until sauce is reduced. Stir in green onion and sesame oil. Transfer to platter to serve.

• *Notes* •

1. You can adjust the chili paste according to your own taste.

2. Substitute the meat from 2 lobster tails to make dry-braised lobster.

3. Using smaller prawns and less sauce makes this dish suitable for an appetizer.

Velvet Prawns

Try this recipe if you want to prepare prawns a little differently! First they're marinated in a frothy-like batter of seasoned egg whites, then blanched in oil. Straw mushrooms, baby corn, and snow peas are stir-fried with tiny bits of ham before the prawns go back in the pan.

Makes: 6 servings
Cooking time: 10 minutes

1 pound medium-size prawns (26 to 30 count)

MARINADE
¼ teaspoon salt
Pinch white pepper
1 egg white
1 tablespoon cornstarch paste
1 tablespoon vegetable oil

4 egg whites
1 tablespoon cornstarch paste

SAUCE
1 cup Rich Chicken Broth (page 52), or chicken bouillon
1 green onion, finely chopped
¼ teaspoon minced fresh ginger
2 tablespoons dry sherry
½ teaspoon salt
¼ teaspoon sugar
White pepper

Vegetable oil, for blanching

VEGETABLES
5 or 6 snow peas, trimmed and cut in half
8 to 10 canned straw mushrooms
5 or 6 canned baby corn, cut in half lengthwise

1 thin slice Virginia ham, cut into ½-inch squares
Cornstarch paste
1 tablespoon vegetable oil

Shell, devein, and rinse prawns; pat dry and combine with MARINADE ingredients in the order listed; mix thoroughly; let stand for 10 minutes. In a bowl, mix together egg whites and cornstarch paste; set aside.

Combine SAUCE ingredients; set aside.

To oil-blanch, set wok over high heat for about 1 minute. Add 4 cups oil and heat to 300°. Add prawns, stirring to separate completely; remove and drain. Pour egg white mixture into oil and stir slightly for 30 seconds until mixture expands and floats. Remove and drain, keeping oil in wok. Reheat oil and blanch vegetables for 10 seconds. Remove and drain.

To stir-fry, remove all but 1 tablespoon oil from wok. Stir in sauce, vegetables, and ham. Return egg whites; bring to a boil for 30 seconds, stirring to separate. Add prawns, stir, and then thicken sauce with 1 tablespoon cornstarch paste. Stir in oil and serve.

Variation: Velvet Chicken. Prepare chicken following directions for Snow White Chicken on page 74. Cook as instructed above substituting chicken for prawns.

• *Note* •

Straw mushrooms might be new to you. See page 205, for more information.

Sole Fillets In Wine Sauce

This classic Peking-style of preparing fillets of sole in sweet rice wine will make the delicate fish melt in your mouth.

Makes: 6 servings
Cooking time: 10 minutes

5 or 6 tree mushrooms (cloud ears)

1 pound fillet of sole or rock cod

MARINADE

¼ teaspoon salt
Dash white pepper
1 egg white
1 tablespoon cornstarch
1 tablespoon vegetable oil

Vegetable oil, for blanching

SAUCE

1 cup Rich Chicken Broth (page 52), or chicken bouillon
2 tablespoons wine sauce (see page 207), or rice wine
1 teaspoon sugar
½ teaspoon salt
¼ teaspoon minced fresh ginger
1 tablespoon cornstarch paste

2 tablespoons vegetable oil
1 green onion (white part), diagonally sliced ¼-inch thick
10 snow peas, trimmed

Soak mushrooms in warm water for 20 minutes; drain, and cut large ones into 1-inch squares.

Cut fish in half lengthwise; then diagonally slice, cutting pieces about 1½-inches wide. Pat dry. Combine fish with MARINADE ingredients in the order listed. Mix well after each addition. Let stand for 10 minutes.

To oil-blanch, set wok over high heat for about 1 minute. Add 4 cups oil and heat to 300°. Immerse fish, piece by piece, into oil. Turn off heat, stir gently for about 1 minute, and remove carefully (don't break pieces) to drain. Remove oil and clean wok.

Combine SAUCE ingredients and set aside.

To associate, heat wok over high heat for 1 minute. Add 2 tablespoons oil and then green onion; stir-fry for 10 seconds until fragrant. Stir in mushrooms, snow peas, and sauce. Bring to a boil, return fish and mix gently. Transfer to a rimmed serving platter to serve.

• *Notes* •

1. For a better presentation, it's important to try to avoid breaking fish during the cooking process.

2. To the Chinese, the real soul in this recipe is the sweet rice wine sauce.

Spicy Hot Braised Fish

I describe this as very Szechuan. That translates as very spicy, very flavorful!

Makes: 6 to 8 servings
Cooking time: 20 minutes

1 red snapper or rock cod (2 to 3 lbs.), cleaned
1 tablespoon soy sauce

6 tablespoons vegetable oil
1 thumb-size slice fresh ginger

SPICES

¼ cup vegetable oil
1 tablespoon hot chili oil
2 tablespoons chili paste
½ small white onion, coarsely chopped
1 tablespoon minced fresh ginger
2 cloves garlic, minced or pressed

SEASONINGS

¼ cup soy sauce
2 tablespoons dry sherry
3 cups chicken broth
2 tablespoons catsup
2 teaspoons sugar

1½ tablespoons chopped green onion
Cornstarch paste

Make a crisscross pattern on both sides of fish by making cuts 1-inch apart and all the way through to the bone. Rub with soy sauce and let stand for 5 minutes.

To pan-fry, heat wok (or wide frying pan) over high heat for 1 minute. Add oil and swirl to coat sides. Rub wok with slice of ginger. Add fish and fry for about 3 minutes, turning fish once and tipping wok occasionally so that oil touches entire fish. Remove and drain; discard oil and ginger.

To braise, heat clean wok for about 1 minute until hot. Add SPICES and cook until fragrant. Stir in SEASONINGS and bring to a boil. Return fish, cover, reduce heat, and simmer for about 15 minutes, turning fish over once and basting occasionally. Carefully, remove fish to a serving platter, reserving sauce. To the sauce, add green onion; bring to a boil and thicken with 1½ tablespoons cornstarch paste until a syrupy consistency is reached. Spoon over fish to serve.

• *Note* •

Remember to use hot chili oil to suit your own taste. You may not like it as "hot" as I do.

Shanghai Braised Whole Fish

The artful combination of pork, black mushrooms, ginger, garlic, onion, bamboo shoots, spices, and a fresh plump fish made this dish very popular in cosmopolitan Shanghai.

Makes: 6 to 8 servings
Cooking time: 20 minutes

- 5 dried black mushrooms
- 1 rock cod or red snapper (2 to 3 lbs.), cleaned
- 6 tablespoons vegetable oil
- 1 thumb-size slice fresh ginger
- 2 tablespoons vegetable oil
- 1 ounce pork butt, thinly sliced

SPICES

- ¼ small white onion, thinly sliced
- 10 thumb-size slices fresh ginger
- 4 cloves garlic, minced or pressed
- ⅓ cup sliced bamboo shoots

SEASONINGS

- ¼ cup soy sauce
- 3 tablespoons dry sherry
- 1 tablespoon sugar
  Pinch white pepper
- 3 cups water
- 2 green onions, cut into 1½-inch pieces
  Cornstarch paste

Soak mushrooms in warm water for 20 minutes; drain, remove stems, and cut in half. Make several slashes on both sides of fish about ½-inch deep. Rinse and pat dry.

To pan-fry, heat wok (or wide frying pan) over high heat for 1 minute. Add 6 tablespoons oil and swirl to coat sides. Rub wok with slice of ginger. Add fish and fry for 3 to 4 minutes, turning fish once and tipping wok occasionally so that oil touches entire fish. Remove and drain; discard oil and ginger.

To braise, heat clean wok over high heat for about 1 minute. Add 2 tablespoons oil and swirl to coat sides. When oil is hot, add pork, stirring to separate. Add SPICES and cook until fragrant. Stir in bamboo, mushrooms, and SEASONING ingredients. Return fish, cover, reduce heat, and simmer for 7 to 8 minutes. Turn fish over, cover, and simmer for 5 minutes longer. Remove fish to serving platter.

To the sauce, add green onion; thicken with 1½ tablespoons cornstarch paste.

To serve, pour sauce over fish and offer immediately.

• Notes •

1. I prefer snapper or cod because the bones are larger and therefore easier to remove.

2. I never mind repeating my instructions for selecting fresh fish: look for clear eyes, pink gills, a firm touch, and a fresh smell.

3. Lightly pan-frying a whole fish makes it more manageable or slightly firmer; that's important so it won't fall apart during the braising process.

4. Sometimes I add bean cake—it absorbs the flavor of the fish beautifully.

Steamed Hunan-style Fish

In China, especially near the Lake Dong-Ting region in Hunan, fresh fish is regularly served. This is an authentic Hunan family-style recipe for fish, spicy and aromatic.

Makes: 8 to 10 servings
Cooking time: 20 minutes

- 1 dried black mushroom
- 1 rock cod or red snapper (about 3 lbs.), or 1 piece Ling cod

SEASONINGS

- 2 pieces dried red chili peppers, crushed
- 2 tablespoons fermented black beans, smashed
- 1 green onion (white part), slivered
- 2 teaspoons salt
- 3 thumb-size slices fresh ginger, slivered
- 1 strip bacon, chopped

- 1 piece caul fat (optional)

Soak mushroom in warm water for 20 minutes; remove stem and cut into slivers.

Remove head from fish (if desired) and trim off tail. Make one lengthwise slash along backbone, cutting all the way down to the bone. Pat dry and place on a footed plate suitable for steaming.

Combine SEASONINGS and distribute over top of fish. Drape caul fat over fish, tucking excess under at edges.

To steam, place plate in steamer. Cover and steam over boiling water for 20 minutes. Remove plate and place on top of serving platter for easier handling. Discard caul fat before serving.

• *Notes* •

1. Caul fat, sold in sheets resembling netting, is optional but it does help preserve the flavor and tenderness of the fish. For more information, see page 203.

2. Make sure you choose a footed plate for steaming that is deep enough to hold all the fish juices.

Hangchow Poached Fish   *Pictured on page 17*

Delicately poached fresh rock cod topped with slivers of green onion and ginger whose flavors are quickly released just before serving is a memorable dish reminiscent of great restaurants on the shores of West Lake in the resort town of Hangchow.

Makes: 6 to 8 servings
Cooking time: 25 minutes

1 whole fish, such as rock cod or red snapper (2 to 3 lbs.), cleaned
2 green onions, cut into fourths
4 thumb-size slices fresh ginger

SEASONINGS

¼ cup soy sauce
3 green onions (white part), slivered
3 thumb-size slices fresh ginger, slivered
   Pinch white pepper

½ cup vegetable oil
1 tablespoon sesame oil
   Chinese parsley (cilantro)

Remove fins from fish, if necessary. From head to tail, cut a slash on both sides of fish about 1 inch below the backbone.

To poach, heat wok over moderate heat and when hot, add onion and ginger. Stir-fry until fragrant. Pour about 2 quarts water into wok, bring to a boil, then immerse fish (add more boiling water, if necessary). Return to a boil, reduce heat, cover, and simmer for 10 minutes. Turn fish over and boil for about 5 minutes longer. Remove carefully with a spatula and drain well. Place fish on serving platter.

To serve, sprinkle SEASONINGS all over fish. Heat oils in a small saucepan until hot and just smoking. Quickly pour over fish and garnish with parsley. Lightly mix pieces of fish with sauce at the table and serve.

• Notes •

1. Only the best ingredients—good quality fresh fish and seasonings—should be used in any simple poaching recipe such as this.

2. Poaching time for fish needs to be accurate. I check for doneness this way: the meat is still slightly rare near the bone yet flaky and easy to remove on the outside.

Steamed Kirin Fish   *Pictured on page 6*

Kirin was a mythical creature said to be half dragon and half lion. Our presentation of Steamed Kirin Fish is a colorful one: thin slices of ham, black mushroom, and ginger are tucked into pockets cut along the sides of a whole fish.

Makes: 8 to 10 servings
Cooking time: 30 minutes

- 5 or 6 dried black mushrooms
- 1 rock cod or red snapper (about 3 lbs.), or 1 piece of Ling cod
- 10 to 12 pieces Virginia ham (sliced ⅛-inch by 1-inch)
- 10 to 12 slices fresh ginger
- 1 tablespoon dry sherry
- 1½ teaspoons salt
- 1 green onion, crushed slightly
- 1 piece caul fat

Soak mushrooms in warm water for 20 minutes; drain, remove stems, and cut in half.

Remove head of fish (if desired) and trim off tail. Starting at the head, make 10 to 12 slashes about 1-inch apart the length of the fish. Only do this on one side and make sure you don't cut through the backbone. Rinse and pat dry.

To assemble, tuck 1 slice ham, 1 slice ginger, and 1 piece mushroom into each slash. Sprinkle entire fish with sherry and salt. Place on a footed plate suitable for steaming. Lay green onion on fish and drape caul fat over top, tucking excess under the edges.

To steam, place plate in steamer; cover and steam over boiling water for 20 minutes. Remove and place plate on top of serving platter for easier handling. Discard onion and caul fat before serving. Offer juices to spoon over.

• *Notes* •

1. Caul fat is optional but I strongly recommend it. (See page 203, for more information.) You may have to order it in advance from your butcher.

2. I like to specify Rock or Ling cod or red snapper for this dish because they have fewer bones than other varieties.

3. For a different presentation, cut the fish in the pattern pictured on page 103.

Dragon Fish *Pictured on facing page*

Dragon Fish, symbolizing prosperity and happiness, is a speciality dish usually reserved for banquets or other festive occasions. It is garnished with red cherries suggesting good luck to Chinese people, and is an item that I gladly prepare.

Makes: 6 to 8 servings
Cooking time: 20 minutes

1 whole red snapper or rock cod (4 to 5 lbs.), cleaned
Dash salt

BATTER
1 cup flour
1 cup cornstarch
1½ cups water
1 tablespoon vegetable oil

Vegetable oil, for deep-frying

1½ cups Sweet & Sour Sauce (page 213)
Cornstarch paste

2 olives
1 lemon, sliced
2 cherries
1 can (10 oz.) preserved cucumber slices, drained OR a combination of 2 tablespoons green peas, 2 diced black mushrooms, ¼ diced white onion, ½ chopped tomato, and some diced carrot.

Remove fish head and reserve. Prepare fish according to illustrations on facing page. After cutting, hold fish by tail and immerse in lukewarm water until pattern shows up. Pat dry and sprinkle with salt.

Combine BATTER ingredients in a bowl until the consistency of heavy cream is reached.

To deep-fry, heat 4 cups oil in a wok to 350°. Coat fish head in batter and deep-fry in oil until golden brown. Remove, drain, and place on serving plate. Return oil temperature to 350°. Turn fish inside out and hold by its tail to dip into batter. Make sure all the scored (patterned) flesh is covered with batter. Let excess drip off.

With fish still inside out, grasp both ends and slowly immerse fish in oil. Deep-fry, basting occasionally and turning so that oil reaches all sides, for about 8 minutes or until golden brown. With a spatula or strainer, carefully remove and set aside. (The above procedure may be done in advance.)

Prepare Sweet & Sour Sauce, thicken with about 3 tablespoons cornstarch paste.

To deep-fry again, reheat oil in wok to 350°. Add fish and fry for about 3 minutes, basting occasionally. Carefully, remove with spatula or strainer and place on serving platter. Arrange fish head to recreate original shape.

To serve, place olives in the eyes and place lemon slices topped with cherries around edge of plate. Ladle sauce over fish; sprinkle with preserved cucumber. Serve immediately.

• *Notes* •

1. The fish is immersed in water before coated with batter to slightly shrink the flesh and cause the scored diamond pattern to show up.

2. Make sure that the fish is completely pat dry before deep-frying; just a little bit of water can cause splattering.

3. A spatula or strainer used for removing the fish from the oil is important since the fish will be flaky and could fall apart.

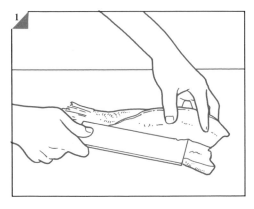

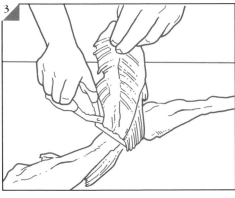

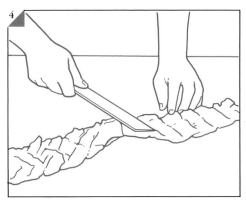

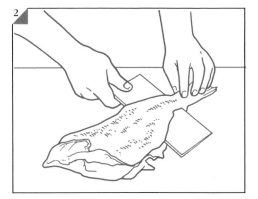

1) Fillet fish by cutting along backbone. 2) Cut down spine, sliding over the ribs on both sides, stopping just before reaching tail. 3) Remove entire bony skeleton using shears or scissors. Open fish and place, skin side down, on cutting board. 4) Lightly score meat in crisscross (diamond) pattern going just to (but not through) the skin. Holding fish by tail, turn inside out and 5) immerse in lukewarm water until pattern becomes prominent. Pat dry, sprinkle with salt, and dip into batter, using same inside-out procedure. Deep-fry as directed and 6) arrange on platter, with patterned, meaty side out. Decorate and ladle sauce over fish to serve.

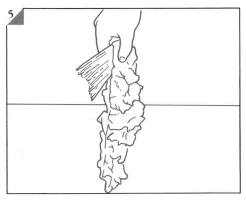

Scallops In Cream Sauce

Unlike rich French cream sauces, this North China-style cream sauce is thin, light, but delicious. Served with scallops, this dish offers a beautiful contrast of color, texture, and taste. It exemplifies and captures the essence of good Chinese cuisine—the marriage of flavors.

Makes: 4 to 6 servings
Cooking time: 10 minutes

MARINADE

- 1 thumb-size chunk fresh ginger
- 2 teaspoons dry sherry
  Pinch salt

- 1 pound large scallops
- 1 head (about 1 lb.) broccoli

  Vegetable oil, for blanching

SAUCE

- 1 cup Rich Chicken Broth (page 52), or chicken bouillon
- 1 tablespoon dry sherry
- ½ teaspoon sugar
- ½ teaspoon salt
- ⅛ teaspoon white pepper

- 2 tablespoons milk
  Cornstarch paste

- 1 thin slice Virginia ham, cut in julienne strips
- 1 green onion (white part), slivered

Crush and squeeze juice from ginger and combine with remaining MARINADE ingredients. Split scallops in half lengthwise, mix in marinade, and let stand for 20 minutes.

Trim off ends of broccoli; cut and separate buds and stalks. Slice stalks into bite-size pieces.

To water-blanch, cook broccoli in boiling water for 1 minute. Remove, drain, and arrange on serving platter with buds circling edge and stalks in center.

To oil-blanch, set wok over high heat for 1 minute. Add 2 cups oil and heat to 275° to 300°. Add scallops, blanch for 1 minute until they turn white, remove.

To associate, remove all but 2 tablespoons oil from wok. Stir in SAUCE ingredients, return to a boil, and add scallops. Stir in milk and thicken with 1½ tablespoons cornstarch paste until the consistency of cream sauce. Spoon over broccoli and garnish with ham and onion.

• Note •

For an easy variation, after oil-blanching scallops, add a few colorful vegetables such as blanched broccoli or carrots. Stir-fry with less sauce.

Foochow Steamed Clams   *Pictured on page 17*

Here is a seacoast delicacy: freshly caught clams smothered in black beans, garlic, ginger, green onion, and sherry. Aromatic and delicious.

Makes: 6 to 8 servings
Cooking time: 10 minutes

2 pounds fresh clams (24 to 26 count)
½ teaspoon oil
3 tablespoons vegetable oil

SEASONINGS
1 tablespoon dry sherry
1 tablespoon soy sauce
½ cup chicken broth
1 teaspoon sugar
 Pinch white pepper

SPICES
1 tablespoon fermented black beans, smashed
2 cloves garlic, sliced
4 thumb-size slices fresh ginger, shredded
½ teaspoon chili paste (optional)

1 green onion, chopped
 Cornstarch paste
¼ teaspoon sesame oil

In a large bowl, cover clams with cold water mixed with ½ teaspoon oil. Soak for 2 hours in order for clams to spew out the sand.

To water-blanch, drop clams in boiling water and blanch for 2 minutes. Remove and drain, discarding those clams that did not open.

Combine SEASONINGS and set aside.

To stir-fry, heat wok (or wide frying pan) over high heat for 1 minute until hot. Add oil and swirl pan to coat sides. When oil is hot, add SPICES and stir-fry for about 30 seconds until fragrant. Return clams to wok, add SEASON-INGS, stir gently and cover for about 1 minute or until all clam shells are more widely opened. Add onion and stir for 1 minute. Without causing meat to pop out of clams, thicken slightly with 1 to 2 teaspoons cornstarch paste until the consistency of cream soup is reached. Sprinkle with sesame oil.

To serve, place clams and sauce in a wide serving bowl deep enough to hold all the sauce.

• *Notes* •

1. Eliminate the chili paste if you prefer a dish with less spice.

2. When buying fresh clams, choose only the freshest ones that are closed shut. Ones that have opened—even slightly—are dead!

Canton Ginger Sherry Crab

Though not actually baked, this crab is so succulent and flavorful you'll think it's been cooked in the oven.

Makes: 4 servings
Cooking time: 20 minutes

1 fresh crab (1½ to 2 lbs.), cleaned and cracked

2 thumb-size pieces fresh ginger

1 tablespoon dry sherry

3 tablespoons flour

Vegetable oil, for deep-frying

SAUCE

1 cup Rich Chicken Broth (page 52), or chicken bouillon

2 tablespoons dry sherry

2 tablespoons soy sauce

1 teaspoon sugar

5 thumb-size pieces fresh ginger

1 green onion, cut into 1-inch pieces

Cornstarch paste

Combine crab, ginger, and sherry together; let stand for 10 minutes. Remove crab, discarding any ginger clinging to sides. Dust lightly with flour.

To deep-fry, heat 3 cups oil in a wok (or electric deep-fat fryer) to 350°. Add crab and fry, stirring occasionally, for about 5 minutes or until browned. Remove and drain.

Combine SAUCE ingredients in a small bowl; set aside.

To stir-fry, remove all but 4 tablespoons oil from wok. Heat, swirling wok to coat sides. Add ginger and green onion; cook until fragrant. Return crab to wok. Pour in sauce, cover, and cook over high heat for about 5 to 7 minutes or until sauce is reduced by one-fourth. Thicken with 1 tablespoon cornstarch paste to serve.

• *Note* •

This dish calls for fresh *live* crab. If you don't like to remove the shell of a live crab, ask your fish market to do so. Or, drop it into boiling water for 30 seconds and then clean.

Shanghai Crab in Bean Sauce

A light dusting of flour is the secret to sealing in the succulence of this fresh, marinated crab. Try this recipe when crab season opens and you'll wish the season wasn't so short.

Makes: 4 servings
Cooking time: 10 minutes

- 1 fresh crab (1½ to 2 lbs.), cleaned and cracked
- 2 thumb-size pieces of fresh ginger
- 1 tablespoon dry sherry

- 3 tablespoons flour

  Vegetable oil, for deep-frying

SAUCE
- 2 tablespoons dry sherry
- 2 tablespoons catsup
- 2 tablespoons sugar
- 2 tablespoons white vinegar
- 1 tablespoon minced green onion (white part)
- 1 tablespoon minced fresh ginger
- 1 tablespoon bean sauce
- 1 tablespoon cornstarch paste

Combine crab, ginger, and sherry together; let stand for 10 minutes. Remove crab, discarding any ginger clinging to sides. Dust lightly with flour.

To deep-fry, heat 3 cups oil in wok (or deep-fat fryer) to 350°. Add crab and fry, stirring occasionally, for about 5 minutes or until browned. Remove and drain.

Combine SAUCE ingredients thoroughly; set aside.

To stir-fry, remove all but 3 tablespoons oil from wok. Heat and swirl wok to coat sides. Return crab to wok. Pour in sauce; mix thoroughly for about 1½ minutes or until thickened. Remove and serve immediately, offering seafood forks and moist towels at the table.

• *Note* •

This dish calls for fresh *live* crab. If you don't like to remove the shell of your live crab, ask your fish market to do so. Or, drop the crab into boiling water for half a minute, then clean.

Cantonese Sautéed Fresh Squid

I've included this recipe because it's a basic one for preparing fresh squid. Other recipes with a combination of ingredients such as Chow Mein, benefit deliciously with the addition of sautéed squid.

Makes: 6 to 8 servings
Cooking time: 10 minutes

- 2 pounds fresh squid (about 10 to 12)
- 1 quart chicken broth
- 3 tablespoons vegetable oil
- 3 thumb-size slices fresh ginger, shredded
- 1 green onion (white part), diagonally sliced ½-inch thick
- 1 stalk celery, diagonally sliced ¼-inch thick
- 6 to 8 slices carrot, decoratively sliced
- 1 teaspoon salt

  Dipping sauce (see Notes)

Remove head and tentacles. (See Notes for Hunan Lichee Squid, facing page.) Slit squid open to flatten and rinse thoroughly. Remove plastic-like partition and scrape membrane off both sides of squid. Lightly score in small criss-cross pattern on inside of squid.

To blanch, heat chicken broth to boiling. Blanch squid for about 30 seconds until it curls. Then remove and drain.

To stir-fry, heat wok (or wide frying pan) over high heat for 1 minute. Add oil and swirl to coat sides. Add ginger and green onion; stir-fry until fragrant. Add celery and carrots, cooking for about 30 seconds. Sprinkle with salt and then add squid; quickly stir-fry until oil and salt thoroughly coat all the squid.

To serve, transfer to a serving platter and serve with your choice of dipping sauce.

• *Notes* •

1. I like to serve shrimp paste as a dipping sauce. It's a Cantonese specialty that's grayish colored and very salty.

2. When selecting squid, search for ones that are large and thick.

Hunan Lichee Squid

Fresh squid might make this delicious dish more accessible, but the Chinese love the crunchy texture of dehydrated squid which is reconstituted for cooking. The taste is different, but you may become a convert.

Makes: 6 to 8 servings
Cooking time: 5 minutes

1 package (8 oz.) dehydrated squid
About 1 quart water
1 tablespoon baking soda

1 teaspoon white vinegar

SAUCE

1 tablespoon dry sherry
2 teaspoons white vinegar
1 teaspoon sugar
1½ teaspoons cornstarch paste
½ teaspoon salt
1 teaspoon sesame oil
1 teaspoon hot chili oil (optional)

5 tablespoons vegetable oil
Pinch salt

2 green onions (white part), sliced ½-inch thick
2 cloves garlic, sliced
2 thumb-size pieces fresh ginger, cut in half

Remove squid eyes and discard; remove tentacles (save for other uses, if desired). Combine water and baking soda. Add squid and let stand for 24 hours. Drain, discarding water.

Put squid in a large pot, cover with water, and let soak for 30 minutes. Repeat this procedure 5 times for a total of 2½ hours. Remove. (This procedure may be done in advance.)

Remove cartilage and membrane from squid. Cut in half lengthwise. Score by cutting crisscross incisions in a diamond pattern. Cut into three sections (if large) or in half.

To water-blanch, cook squid in 2 quarts boiling water mixed with vinegar for 1 minute or until it curls. Remove and drain.

Combine SAUCE ingredients; set aside.

To stir-fry, heat wok (or wide frying pan) over high heat for 1 minute until hot. Add 2 tablespoons oil and salt and swirl to coat sides. Add squid and stir-fry for 30 seconds. Remove and drain; wipe wok clean. Add remaining 3 tablespoons oil and when hot, add green onions, garlic, and ginger. Stir until fragrant. Add squid to reheat (about 10 seconds) and then sauce. When mixture thickens, remove and serve immediately.

• *Notes* •

1. Some cooks like to save the tentacles. You can boil them or deep-fry them and serve with a dipping sauce as an appetizer.

2. Substitute Oyster Sauce (page 212) for the sauce in this recipe if you want a delicious variation.

·PORK·

Without question, pork is the meat most favored by Chinese. It is flavorful and very cooperative—since it can be cooked in a great many ways, and even assumes a disguise when cooked with other ingredients, such as fish, crab, or lobster.

The recipes in this section include the great American favorite, Sweet & Sour Pork. I have added my "mark" to this dish, so follow the instructions carefully. I have also included the recipe ranked number one by patrons of my restaurant—Mu Shu Pork. If you are of a vegetarian bent, the notes following the recipe tell you how to make a tasty variation without meat. In fact, a number of meat dishes in this book can be served to suit vegetarian standards.

When buying pork, choose meat that is deep pink with very white fat and skin. The marble grain should be firm and bounce back when touched. If the fat is wet and the meat has a dull or dark color, it has been frozen too long; if the meat appears somewhat brackish and feels sticky, it is beginning to spoil.

For overall versatility, I recommend buying *pork shoulder butt.* It can be cut

Mu Shu Pork is the unanimous favorite among patrons of Chef Chu's restaurant. To serve, spoon some filling inside pancake, add green onion and plum sauce, fold in half,—then cast your own vote!

into slices, shredded or cubed, as in Sweet & Sour Pork, cut into long strips for Mu Shu Pork or Barbecued Pork, or purchased in a 3- to 4-pound block and ground up.

Ground pork is used as stuffing in Won-ton, Cucumber Cups, Shanghai Braised Fish, Lion's Head in a Clay Pot, and many more dishes. To keep your cooking options open, I suggest buying 3 to 4 pounds of pork at a time. Ask your butcher to grind it for you, then bag it in 2-inch-square blocks and freeze it until you need it. (This is far preferable to buying pork which has already been ground.) The ratio of fat to lean in ground pork is up to you so instruct your butcher accordingly.

Spareribs generally come in large strips ranging from 4 to 5 pounds. Your butcher can help you find smaller, meatier ribs in strips weighing around 3 pounds if you ask.

I didn't include a recipe for *roast pig,* which the Cantonese do so well. If there is a Chinatown within driving distance, stop and visit a market where you will no doubt see a whole pig freshly roasted. Ask for a strip of the meat. These pigs are roasted daily, as they are quite popular in Chinese communities, and the likelihood of the pig still being warm is great. A side of roast pork, purchased from San Francisco's Chinatown, appears in the Chinese New Year's picture on page 6.

Mongolian Firepot *Pictured on facing page*

Excellent to serve at your next dinner party, this meal is cooked right at the table and by your guests! The fiery brass kettle adds a touch of drama to the presentation, and the array of thinly-sliced meat and fish, shrimp, and many vegetables fill the table and promise a delectable feast.

Makes: 8 to 12 servings
Cooking time: 30 minutes

4 quarts Rich Chicken Broth (page 52), or chicken bouillon

INGREDIENTS
(Allow 2 to 4 ounces of each per person)
   Slices of fish filet such as snapper or rock cod
   Slices of leg of lamb
   Slices of shelled, deveined, and butterflied prawns
   Slices of sirloin beef and lean pork
   Bite-size pieces of fresh spinach
   Bite-size pieces of bean cake (tofu)
   Presoaked pieces of bean thread
   Bite-size wedges of Chinese cabbage

SAUCES
   Soy sauce
   Chinese barbecue sauce
   Hot Chili Paste (page 212)
   Rice vinegar

Arrange fish and meat attractively on individual serving plates. Arrange vegetables together on one large serving platter.

To assemble, start charcoal in firepot braiser outdoors. When red hot, bring braiser indoors and place on wet towel on top of heat-resistant platter. Heat chicken broth on stove and when hot, pour about 2 quarts into firepot.

To cook, provide individual strainers for each guest to use. Blanch food by immersing into boiling broth until desired doneness is reached. Offer SAUCES for dipping at the table as well. Towards end of meal, offer broth in individual bowls for sipping.

• *Notes* •

1. The nice feature about cooking with a firepot is that the quantity of ingredients can be changed depending on how many people you're serving.

2. I enjoy offering other ingredients suchas fresh squid, oysters, shrimp balls, bite-size wedges of romaine lettuce, or any other type of food available.

Brass Mongolian firepot transforms into bubbling centerpiece for this cook-your-own Chinese dinner. Guests select from platters displaying paper-thin slices of meat and fish, vegetables, and bite-size pieces of bean curd and bean thread. When all is cooked, guests ladle out flavorful cooking broth into soup bowls.

Sweet & Sour Pork

Sweet, sour, pungent, and crunchy—an unbeatable combination. The secret to preparing this correctly is in the double-frying.

Makes: 6 to 8 servings
Cooking time: 20 minutes

1½ cups Sweet & Sour Sauce (page 213)

1 pound pork shoulder butt, boned, trimmed, and cut into ¾-inch cubes

MARINADE

1 teaspoon dry sherry
1 teaspoon garlic powder
½ teaspoon salt
Pinch Chinese five-spice

BATTER

½ cup flour
½ cup cornstarch
¼ teaspoon baking powder
1 cup water
1 teaspoon oil

Vegetable oil, for deep-frying

3 tablespoons vegetable oil

VEGETABLES

1 bell pepper, seeded and cut into bite-size squares
¼ small white onion, cut in bite-size squares
5 to 6 thin slices carrot

½ cup pineapple chunks
Cornstarch paste

Prepare Sweet & Sour Sauce as directed.

Combine pork and MARINADE ingredients; let stand for 30 minutes. Mix together BATTER ingredients until the consistency of heavy cream; let stand for 15 minutes. Just before using, stir to mix; pour enough batter over pork to coat.

To deep-fry, heat 4 cups oil in a wok (or electric deep-fat fryer) to 325°. Add half the pork and cook for about 3 minutes or until a crust is formed. Repeat with remaining pork. Remove and drain. (You can do the above procedure ahead of time, if desired.)

To deep-fry again, remove any pieces of batter left in oil and raise temperature in wok to 350° to 375°. Return pork and agitate (carefully shake) to separate. Deep-fry until golden brown; remove and drain oil in wok.

To hot mix, heat wok over high heat for 1 minute. Add 3 tablespoons oil and then sauce, VEGETABLES, and pineapple. Bring to a boil and thicken with 2 tablespoons cornstarch paste. Add pork, mix well, and serve.

• Notes •

1. For variety, you can add lichee nuts, loquats, cherries, tomatoes, or other fresh fruits or vegetables to this recipe.

2. To retain the crunchy texture of the deep-fried pork, it's important to "hot mix" quickly. You're trying to coat the pork, not cook it.

Mu Shu Pork   *Pictured on page 116*

Mu Shu is the name of a tree found in Northern China that bears beautiful yellow flowers. When the eggs in this dish are quickly cooked in a preheated wok, they puff up and blossom, resembling the Mu Shu flower. Vegetarians can leave out the pork and still have a flavorful dish.

Makes: 6 to 8 servings
Cooking time: 15 minutes

 1 large tree mushroom
¼ cup tiger lily buds

½ pound pork shoulder butt, cut into ⅛- by ⅛- by 1½-inch strips

MARINADE
 1 teaspoon soy sauce
¼ teaspoon cornstarch
 1 tablespoon vegetable oil

12 Mandarin Pancakes (page 187) or paper-thin pancakes made with flour

½ cup vegetable oil
 3 eggs, slightly beaten
½ cup shredded bamboo shoots
½ head regular cabbage, shredded
 2 green onions, white parts slivered and green tops cut in 1-inch sections

SEASONINGS
 2 tablespoons soy sauce
½ teaspoon sugar
¼ teaspoon salt
¼ teaspoon white pepper
    Dash sesame oil

 4 tablespoons Hoisin sauce
½ teaspoon sesame oil

Soak mushroom in warm water for 20 minutes; drain, remove stem, and shred. Soak tiger lily buds in warm water for 20 minutes; drain.

Combine pork with MARINADE ingredients in the order listed; mix well and set aside.

To steam, separate pancakes and fold them in half. Arrange inside a cloth napkin. Place napkin on rack in steamer (or in double boiler) and steam for 3 or 4 minutes. Remove from heat and keep warm and moist in steamer.

To stir-fry, heat wok (or wide frying pan) over high heat for 1 minute until hot. Add oil, swirling to coat sides. When oil is smoking hot, pour in eggs and scramble until golden; remove and drain. Add pork, stir vigorously to separate, and cook until well done. Remove and drain.

Remove all but 3 tablespoons oil. Return pork to wok and add mushrooms, lily buds, and bamboo shoots. Stir-fry for 2 minutes. Add cabbage, green onion, eggs, and SEASONINGS. Mix well and add dash sesame oil. Transfer to platter.

To serve, place green onion slivers on a small plate. Combine Hoisin sauce and sesame oil; place on another small plate. Open wrapper, spread center lightly with sauce mixture and a few slivers green onion. Spoon about 2 tablespoons pork into center of wrapper and fold up, jelly-roll fashion, to eat.

• *Notes* •

1. Time and time again I've found that my guests don't know how to assemble Mu Shu Pork correctly. Since this is a do-it-yourself dish, show them how to make the first one.

2. It's often difficult to keep the pancakes warm so I recommend using a candle (coffee warmer) holder similar to the bottom of a fondue pot. Place a flat pan on top. When your turn comes, quickly reheat your pancake by placing it on top of hot pan for 5 seconds.

3. If you wish, shrimp, chicken, or beef can be substituted for pork.

4. Oil must be smoking hot in order to achieve the correct texture for the scrambled eggs.

Mu Shu Pork, the most requested dish at Chef Chu's restaurant, is easily prepared at home. 1, 2) Scramble eggs in a heated wok, then 3) remove and drain off the oil. 4, 5) Stir-fry strips of marinated pork and then 6) remove and drain. 7) Add shredded cabbage, mushrooms, lily buds, bamboo shoots and green onion, 8) stir-frying as you go. 9) Return cooked eggs and pork; toss gently. Offer steamed Mandarin pancakes to serve.

Pork With Imperial Sauce

This East-meets-West sauce is of my own creation. Highly seasoned, it's sure to satisfy all senses, especially when you hear "delicious"!

Makes: 6 to 8 servings
Cooking time: 1 hour

1 pound pork shoulder butt, boned, trimmed, and cut into ¾-inch cubes

MARINADE
1 teaspoon dry sherry
1 teaspoon garlic powder
½ teaspoon salt
Pinch Chinese five-spice

BATTER
½ cup flour
½ cup cornstarch
¼ teaspoon baking powder
1 cup water
1 teaspoon vegetable oil

Vegetable oil, for deep-frying

SAUCE
5 tablespoons chicken broth
3 tablespoons catsup
2 tablespoons sugar
1 tablespoon Worcestershire
1 tablespoon soy sauce
1 tablespoon A-1 sauce
Pinch Chinese five-spice

2 tablespoons vegetable oil
Cornstarch paste
1 teaspoon sesame oil

Thin slices tomato
Chinese Parsley (cilantro)

Combine pork and MARINADE ingredients thoroughly; let stand for 30 minutes.

Mix together BATTER ingredients until the consistency of heavy cream is reached; let stand 15 minutes. Just before using, stir batter to mix. Pour over pork just to coat pieces.

To deep-fry, heat 4 cups oil in a wok (or electric deep-fat fryer) to 325°. Add half the pork and cook for about 3 minutes or until a crust is formed. Repeat with remaining pork. Remove and drain. (You can do the above procedure ahead of time, if desired.)

Combine SAUCE ingredients in a saucepan; bring to a boil, remove, and set aside.

To deep-fry again, remove any pieces of batter left in oil and then raise temperature in wok to 350° to 375°. Return pork and agitate (carefully shake) to separate. Deep-fry until golden brown; remove and drain off oil in wok.

To hot mix, heat wok over high heat for 1 minute. Add 2 tablespoons oil and then sauce. Bring to a boil and thicken with 1½ tablespoons cornstarch paste to a consistency of syrup. Mix in pork until well coated; stir in sesame oil.

To serve, transfer pork to a serving platter and decorate with tomato slices and parsley.

• *Note* •
To retain the crunchy texture of the deep-fried pork, it's important to "hot mix" quickly. You're trying to coat the pork with sauce, not cook it further.

Chef Chu's Pork Chops

I adapted this recipe from one I discovered in an international settlement near Shanghai. There it's served as an afternoon snack without the sauce and usually over boiled noodles. However, I prefer it as an entrée complete with its tangy sauce.

Makes: 6 to 8 servings
Cooking time: 15 minutes

1 pound thin center-cut pork chops with bone (6 to 8 pieces)

MARINADE

1 tablespoon dry sherry
1 tablespoon soy sauce
Pinch Chinese five-spice
Pinch ground roasted Szechuan peppercorns
Pinch white pepper

SAUCE

½ cup chicken broth
2 tablespoons catsup
2 tablespoons soy sauce
2 tablespoons Worcestershire
2 teaspoons dry sherry
1 teaspoon sugar
Pinch salt

Vegetable oil, for deep-frying

1 medium-size onion, cut in julienne strips
Cornstarch paste

Lightly pound meat with mallet to tenderize.

Combine MARINADE ingredients with pork and let stand for 10 minutes.

Combine SAUCE ingredients and set aside.

To deep-fry, heat 4 cups oil in a wok (or electric deep-fat fryer) to 350°. Add pork chops, stir occasionally, and cook for 3 to 4 minutes or until dark golden brown. (Don't allow heat to drop lower than 325°.) Remove and drain.

To stir-fry, remove all but 3 tablespoons oil from wok. Add onion and brown for 3 minutes. Stir in sauce, return pork chops, and bring to a boil; continue cooking for about 3 more minutes. Thicken with 2 tablespoons cornstarch paste and serve.

• Note •

Perfect for picnics!

*Tender slices of cured Virginia ham,
sweetened with lotus seeds and
fragrant* kuei-hua *blossoms, are
tucked inside slices of steamed
bread in this classic Hunan
banquet dish.*

Hunan Honey-glazed Ham   *Pictured on page 6 and on facing page*

Popular in Hunan restaurants, this succulent, thinly sliced, steamed ham is actually served with bread like finger sandwiches. Lotus seeds, a little sugar, and a dried ingredient called *kuei-hua* combine their flavors during the steaming process to create a wonderful syrup.

Makes: 6 servings
Cooking time: 45 minutes

- ½ cup lotus seeds
- ¾ pound boneless fresh Smithfield (Virginia) ham
- 12 slices white bread
- 3 tablespoons sugar
- ¼ teaspoon dried kuei-hua (cassia blossom)

Soak lotus seeds in warm water for 1 hour; then steam over boiling water for about 30 minutes or until soft. Set aside.

If outer skin remains on ham, steam ham over boiling water in steamer for about 30 minutes to soften. Then trim off and discard skin and fat to make pieces of ham measuring 1½ by 2 by 4 inches. Carefully slice pieces ⅛-inch thick.

Slightly freeze bread for easier handling. Trim off crust and cut in half. Split each half almost all the way through lengthwise, forming a pocket. Cover bread with towel to prevent drying and set aside.

To assemble, line the inside of a 6-inch bowl with rows of overlapping slices of ham. Add remaining ham slices and any meat trimmings.

To steam, place ½ cup water in bowl with ham. Put bowl on rack in steamer, cover, and steam over boiling water for 30 minutes. Remove and carefully pour off water. Sprinkle lotus seeds, 2 tablespoons sugar, and kuei-hua over ham.

To steam again, place bowl on rack in steamer and steam for 15 to 20 minutes longer. Remove (keeping steamer available for bread), and carefully tip bowl, pouring off juices into a saucepan. Soften bread in steamer for about 1 minute; keep warm.

To serve, quickly bring juices to a boil, add 3 tablespoons water and 2 tablespoons sugar, and cook until syrupy. Invert ham mixture onto serving plate; then spoon syrup over ham. Offer bread slices on the side.

• *Notes* •

1. Smoked ham may be substituted but there is a definite flavor difference.

2. To prepare ahead, cook ham as directed; then reheat at serving time by steaming for 20 to 30 minutes.

3. You can serve Butterfly Steamed Bread (page 176) instead of white bread.

121

Szechuan Ginger-flavored Pork

This dish is also called "fish flavored" but there is no fish in this recipe. The unique flavor of the spicy sauce is quite similar to one used with hot-braised fish, hence the association and name. Many ingredients go into this dish to make it sumptuous.

Makes: 6 to 8 servings
Cooking time: 2 hours

- 1 large tree mushroom
- 1 pound pork shoulder butt, boned and cut ⅛- by ⅛- by 1½-inches

MARINADE

- 1 tablespoon soy sauce
- 2 teaspoons dry sherry
- 2 teaspoons cornstarch
- 1 tablespoon oil

SAUCE

- 3 tablespoons soy sauce
- 1 tablespoon dry sherry
- 2 teaspoons sugar
- ½ cup chicken broth
- 1 tablespoon red rice vinegar
- 1 tablespoon cornstarch paste

  Vegetable oil, for blanching

- 2 cloves garlic, minced or pressed
- 1 teaspoon minced fresh ginger
- 1 tablespoon chili paste
- ½ cup shredded bamboo shoots
- 1 green onion, split lengthwise and cut in 1-inch pieces
- 5 water chestnuts, coarsely chopped
- ½ teaspoon sesame oil

Soak mushroom in warm water for 20 minutes; drain, remove stem, and chop.

In a bowl, combine pork with MARINADE ingredients in order listed; set aside.

Combine SAUCE ingredients and set aside.

To oil blanch, set wok over high heat for about 1 minute until hot. Add 3 to 4 cups vegetable oil and heat to 300°. Stir in pork and blanch for about 1½ minutes until redness is gone. Remove and drain.

To stir-fry, remove all but 2 tablespoons oil from wok. Stir in garlic, ginger, and chili paste; cook until fragrant. Add pork and bamboo shoots and continue stir-frying for 2 minutes. Add mushroom, green onion, and water chestnuts; stir for 30 seconds. Stir in sauce until thick. Sprinkle with sesame oil and serve.

• *Notes* •

1. Jicama, available in most supermarket produce sections may be substituted for water chestnuts; the flavor of both vegetables is quite similar.

2. Ginger, garlic, and green onions are very important ingredients to this dish. Make sure you cook them long enough to bring out their fragrance during stir-frying.

North China Pork

This recipe comes from a region where garlic is plentiful and even eaten as a snack, so be forewarned!

Makes: 8 servings
Cooking time: 30 minutes

1 -pound section of pork leg or butt, boned

SAUCE

5 cloves garlic, minced or pressed
1 teaspoon minced fresh ginger
1 green onion (white part), minced
1 tablespoon hot Chili Oil, page 212 or purchased
¼ cup soy sauce
2 teaspoons red rice vinegar
1 teaspoon sugar
1 teaspoon sesame oil
Salt to taste

Chinese parsley (cilantro)

To boil, place pork in enough boiling water to cover and simmer for about 20 minutes or until done. Remove, cover, and refrigerate until cool. Slice ⅛-inch thick and refrigerate until serving. Combine SAUCE ingredients well.

To serve, arrange cold pork in overlapping slices on serving platter. Pour sauce over all to serve. Garnish with parsley.

• Notes •

1. North China Pork can be served both hot and cold. If serving hot, steam slices of pork first and then top with sauce.

2. It's much easier to slice meat—especially when the recipe calls for ⅛-inch-thick slices—if it's been refrigerated or partially frozen first.

Cantonese Country Spareribs

Young and old alike enjoy these tasty pork ribs. They're perfect for a family-style dinner accompanied by a bowl of hot, steamed rice. In China, especially in Canton, you'll see them offered as dim sum in the teahouses.

Makes: 6 servings
Cooking time: 45 minutes

1 pound meaty spareribs, cut into bite-size pieces

MARINADE

1 clove garlic, minced or pressed
1 tablespoon fermented black beans, crushed
2 tablespoons soy sauce
1 tablespoon dry sherry
1 tablespoon vegetable oil
1 teaspoon sugar
1 tablespoon cornstarch
¼ teaspoon salt
1 dried red chili pod, crushed (optional)

Combine pork with MARINADE ingredients in a large bowl; mix thoroughly. Transfer to a deep footed bowl suitable for steaming.

To steam, place bowl on rack in steamer and steam over boiling water for 45 minutes. Remove and place on top of a serving platter for easier handling. Offer with rice, if desired.

• Notes •

1. Make sure the steaming bowl or plate is deep enough to hold the juices that develop during cooking.

2. You can increase the amount of chili pods for a hotter-style marinade.

3. The meatiest ribs are found on slabs weighing no more than 3 pounds.

4. If you don't have a heavy cleaver, ask your butcher to cut the ribs into pieces.

Lion's Head In Clay Pot

Yangchow, a gathering place where government officials met merchants, was a center where business was conducted over eating so some of the most elaborate dishes were created in this environment as you can well imagine. One of the most famous dishes which originated in Yangchow is Lion's Head, a delicious, succulent, and large meat patty.

Makes: 8 to 10 servings
Cooking time: 1 hour

5 to 6 dried black mushrooms

FILLING

1½ pounds lean ground pork
10 to 12 water chestnuts, minced
¼ package (4 oz.) bean curd (tofu)
1 green onion (white part), minced
2 eggs
1 teaspoon salt
1½ tablespoons cornstarch
¼ teaspoon white pepper

½ cup vegetable oil
1 head Chinese cabbage, cut into fourths lengthwise

SEASONINGS

2 quarts Rich Chicken Broth (page 52), or chicken bouillon
2 thumb-size slices fresh ginger
2 tablespoons dry sherry
Salt and white pepper to taste

Soak mushrooms in warm water for 20 minutes; drain, remove stems, and slice.

In a large bowl, combine FILLING ingredients. Using your hands, "slap" the meat mixture against the sides of the bowl (or on a chopping block) to break down the meat. Shape into 4 large balls.

To pan-fry, set wok over medium-high heat for 1 minute. Add oil and when hot, add meatballs. Cook, for about 4 minutes or until meatballs are brown on all sides. Remove and drain.

To water-blanch, blanch cabbage sections in enough boiling water to cover for 1 minute; remove and drain. Line an 8-inch-wide earthenware clay casserole, suitable for stovetop cooking, with layers of cabbage leaves.

To cook, place meatballs on cabbage in casserole. Add enough broth to cover, mushrooms, and remaining SEASONINGS. Cover and simmer over moderate heat for 1 hour.

To serve, skim off fat and adjust seasonings. Serve in soup bowls.

• Notes •

1. Instead of "slapping" the meat to break down the tissues, you can use a food processor.

2. Instead of simmering on the stove, you can bake the casserole in a 350° oven for 1 hour.

Cucumber Cups

Cucumber cups are rarely served in restaurants because they are considered too common. This is unfortunate because they make a delicious, family-style dish—one yours will surely enjoy. By removing pork, it's an excellent vegetarian dish.

Makes: 6 servings
Cooking time: 25 minutes

2 dried black mushrooms

3 large cucumbers, all the same length

FILLING

½ pound ground pork

2 green onions (white part), minced

½ teaspoon minced fresh ginger

1 egg

½ teaspoon salt

1 teaspoon cornstarch
Dash white pepper

Soak mushroom in warm water for 20 minutes; drain, remove stem, and mince.

Lightly scrape (but do not peel) cucumbers. Cut off ends and then make decorative cuts around cucumber as illustrated below. Then cut each one into fourths. Hollow out most of the center of each section, leaving a base to form a cup. Invert on paper towels to drain. Turn back over and arrange on a wide, footed plate suitable for steaming.

Combine FILLING ingredients thoroughly. Spoon about 1 heaping tablespoon of filling in each cucumber cup.

To steam, place plate on rack in steamer and steam for 20 minutes. Remove and place on top of a serving plate for easier handling.

To serve, spoon juices over cucumber cups.

• *Note* •

Turn this into a vegetarian dish by substituting 2 minced black mushrooms, 1 block of bean curd (smashed), and 1 tablespoon chopped Szechuan turnips for pork in the filling.

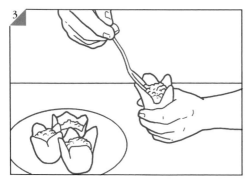

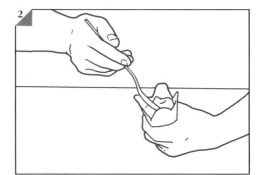

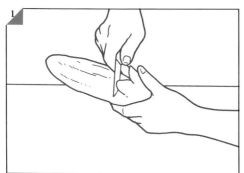

1) Decoratively cut around edge of cucumber, about ¼ of the way up from bottom. When all the way around, cut section off. (Repeat procedure 3 more times, until cucumber yields 4 decorative cups.) Cut thin, straight slice off bottom of cups to make level. 2) Hollow out center of each cup and 3) fill with 1 heaping tablespoon filling; steam.

Soochow Pearl Meatballs

These delicate pork balls are rolled in pearly sweet rice and steamed atop bok choy leaves. They are very versatile and can be served as an appetizer, with a main meal, or as a midday snack.

Makes: 16 meatballs
Cooking time: 15 minutes

- 1 cup sweet rice (glutinous rice)
- 2 dried black mushrooms

MIXTURE
- ½ pound lean ground pork
- 2 or 3 water chestnuts, coarsely chopped
- 1 green onion (white part), minced
- ½ teaspoon minced fresh ginger
- 1 tablespoon dry sherry
- ½ teaspoon sugar
- ½ teaspoon salt
- ¼ teaspoon white pepper
- 1 egg
- 1 tablespoon cornstarch

  Bok choy leaves (or other greens)
  Large bamboo steamer

Soak rice in warm water for 4 hours or overnight. Drain well and spread out on a plate. Soak mushrooms in warm water for 20 minutes; drain, remove stems, and mince.

Combine mushrooms and MIXTURE ingredients thoroughly in a large bowl.

To shape, grab a handful of mixture (about 4 tablespoons) and squeeze out 1-inch balls from top of fist as illustrated on page 30.

To steam, line bamboo steamer with leaves to prevent sticking. Roll meatballs in rice and place on leaves. Cover and steam over boiling water for 10 minutes. Remove and place on top of serving platter for easier handling. Bring steamer to the table to serve.

• *Notes* •

1. If possible, grind your own pork using pork butt. If you have a food processor, you can process the meat mixture at one time.

2. A bamboo steamer simplifies the serving process because you cook and serve in the same container. It's difficult to transfer hot meatballs from a conventional steamer onto a serving platter.

Peking Meat Sauce Over Noodles

What could be more versatile than an all-purpose tasty meat sauce? Use it just like spaghetti sauce!

Makes: 8 servings
Cooking time: 15 minutes

1 cucumber

8 cups Fresh Noodles (page 162) or purchased noodles

5 dried black mushrooms

2 tablespoons vegetable oil
1 pound ground pork
1 clove garlic, minced or pressed
½ cup shredded bamboo shoots; coarsely chopped
2 pieces pressed bean curd (about 2 inches by 2 inches), diced

SEASONINGS

3 tablespoons soy sauce
1 tablespoon dry sherry
2 tablespoons bean sauce
5 tablespoons Hoisin sauce
¼ teaspoon white pepper
2 cups Rich Chicken Broth (page 52), or chicken bouillon

Cornstarch paste
1 green onion, chopped
1 teaspoon sesame oil

Remove core from cucumber and cut into julienne strips. Refrigerate until ready to use.

Prepare noodles following directions on page 162. Soak mushrooms in warm water for 20 minutes; remove, drain, and mince.

To stir-fry, heat wok (or wide frying pan) over high heat for 1 minute until hot. Add oil and swirl pan to coat sides. When hot, add pork, stirring to separate. Add garlic and cook until fragrant. Add mushrooms, bamboo shoots, bean cake, and SEASONINGS. Cook, stirring occasionally, for about 2 minutes; then thicken with 2 tablespoons cornstarch paste until a spaghetti sauce consistency is reached. Stir in green onion and sesame oil.

Meanwhile, reheat noodles in enough boiling water to cover for about 1 minute; drain and divide into 8 individual serving bowls.

To serve, divide cucumbers and arrange over noodles on one side of each bowl. Spoon sauce over noodles on the other side.

Hunan Harvest Sauté

In Hunan province, once the harvest is over, farmers start smoking and curing meat. Smoked pork is a local speciality and a consistent ingredient in many of the provincial dishes. Here's a simple stir-fry recipe that exemplifies such a dish.

Makes: 8 servings
Cooking time: 5 minutes

- 1 pound smoked picnic-style ham, trimmed and sliced ¼-inch thick
- 2 cloves garlic, peeled and sliced
- 1 tablespoon fermented black beans, smashed and mixed with 1 teaspoon oil
- 2 leeks, washed and diagonally sliced ¼-inch thick

SAUCE

- 1 tablespoon soy sauce
- 1 teaspoon dry sherry
- ½ teaspoon sugar
- ¼ teaspoon salt

  Cornstarch paste
- 1 teaspoon hot chili oil

To stir-fry, heat wok (or wide frying pan) over high heat for 1 minute until hot. Add ham, stir to separate, and cook for 1½ minutes. Drain off any fat. Add garlic and black bean mixture and cook until fragrant. Stir in leeks and SAUCE and toss gently. Before leeks become soggy (1½ to 2 minutes), thicken with 1 teaspoon cornstarch paste. Add hot chili oil and serve immediately.

• *Note* •

Lean, slab bacon that has been smoked could be substituted. Cut it into 1½-inch pieces for stir-frying.

·BEEF·

While pork is the most plentiful meat in China, beef is the most scarce. Vast though the country may be, China has relatively little land for grazing, and grains, in much demand as a food source for its large population, have not been ample enough to supply any significant amount of feed for raising cattle. If you travel in China today, you will find excellent cuisine, but few appearances of beef on the menu. What beef dishes are served might be somewhat disappointing because the quality of beef is not comparable to American beef.

Cattle, particularly the water buffalo, is first and foremost a laborer and has been for centuries. Milk cows are not found since dairy products are not included in the Chinese diet. Instead, Chinese drink delicious almond milk and moisten breads, not with butter, but with delectable sauces and fillings made from bean or meat mixtures.

Beef dishes tend to originate from the northern region where the popular Mongolian Beef was devevloped, or from traditionally cosmopolitan ports where dishes, such as Curry Beef and Tomato Beef, were concocted to please merchants from the West. To these and other excellent samplings of Szechuan cooking, I have added a few of my own creations, including something special for steak lovers.

Beef also appears as a main ingredient in Mongolian Firepot (found in the preceding section on pork).

Buying good beef takes a good eye. Look for meat with a nice red color. If it is purplish, it means the meat is old. If it has a yellow tinge, that should tell you the meat is on the tough side and has been frozen too long. The grain should be small, not open; and the texture should be firm to the touch so that when the knife is inserted and pulled out, the meat springs back in place.

Flank steak is excellent for all stir-fry dishes. It has less fat and gristle and is easy to trim and slice because the shape is already somewhat flat.

Stewing beef, though tougher, is excellent for braising. The gristle or fat is fine because it adds flavor.

Beef shank is also on the tough side but fine for stews, soups, or for simmering in a master sauce. Five-spice Beef, served as part of a cold plate, uses beef shank.

A sharp knife and a solid chopping block are a must in a Chef's arsenal of equipment. Much of the time spent cooking Chinese food is taken up in slicing, dicing, and chopping so it is worth having the right utensils. To better identify equipment needed, see photograph on page 210-211.

Chef Chu's Hot & Sour Beef

Two distinct textures—soft and crunchy—plus two distinct flavors—
spicy hot and mild—are created using this traditional Hunan recipe. For
color and yet another texture, it is served on top of jade green broccoli.

Makes: 6 servings
Cooking time: 15 minutes

1 pound flank steak,
trimmed

MARINADE

2 teaspoons light or regular
soy sauce
2 tablespoons water
1 egg white
2 teaspoons cornstarch
1 tablespoon vegetable oil

1 head broccoli, trimmed
and cut into bite-size
pieces
Chicken broth

Vegetable oil, for
blanching

SPICES

2 teaspoons chili paste
2 teaspoons minced fresh
ginger
2 large cloves garlic,
minced or pressed

SEASONINGS

3 tablespoons soy sauce
2 tablespoons dry sherry
2 teaspoons sugar

1 green onion, chopped
2 tablespoons red rice
vinegar
Cornstarch paste
½ teaspoon sesame oil

Cut flank steak against the grain into ⅛- by 1- by
1½-inch slices. Combine with MARINADE ingredients in the order listed, mixing well. Let stand
for 10 minutes.

To water-blanch, cook broccoli in enough
boiling chicken broth to cover for 2 minutes. Remove, drain, and keep warm.

To oil-blanch, set wok over high heat for
about 1 minute. Add 2 cups oil and heat to 300°
Add beef, stirring vigorously to blanch just until
redness is gone. Remove and drain.

To stir-fry, remove all but 5 tablespoons oil
from wok. Reheat, swirling wok to coat sides.
Add SPICES; stir-fry for 15 seconds until fragrant.
Return beef to wok, cooking for 30 seconds. Stir
in SEASONINGS, mixing well. Sprinkle with
green onion and red rice vinegar. Thicken with
1 teaspoon cornstarch paste; then stir in sesame
oil, mixing thoroughly.

To serve, arrange broccoli on a serving platter and spoon hot beef over all.

Szechuan Tangerine Peel Beef

Preserved tangerine peel, with its citrus-like, almost sweet aroma and distinctive taste, transforms an ordinary stir-fried beef dish into something spectacular. We receive many requests for it at Chef Chu's.

Makes: 6 to 8 servings
Cooking time: 10 minutes

10 to 12 broken pieces preserved tangerine peel

1 pound flank steak, trimmed

MARINADE

2 teaspoons soy sauce
Pinch white pepper
2 tablespoons water
2 teaspoons cornstarch
2 tablespoons vegetable oil

Vegetable oil, for deep-frying

½ teaspoons Szechuan peppercorns
6 dried red chili pods
2 cloves garlic, sliced
2 green onions (white part), diagonally sliced ½-inch thick

SAUCE

3 tablespoons soy sauce
2 tablespoons dry sherry
1 teaspoon sugar
¼ cup chicken broth

Soak tangerine peel in warm water for 20 minutes until soft. Slice flank steak against the grain into ⅛- by 1- by 1½-inches thick. Combine with MARINADE ingredients in the order listed, mixing well after each addition. Let stand for about 10 minutes. Combine SAUCE ingredients and set aside.

To oil-blanch, set wok over high heat for about 1 minute. Add 2 cups oil and heat to 350°. Blanch beef, stirring to separate, for 2 to 3 minutes or until well done but not overcooked.

To stir-fry, remove all but 2 tablespoons oil from wok, swirling pan to coat sides. Using medium heat, stir in peppercorns quickly; then remove wok from heat for 1 minute. Remove and discard peppercorns. Return wok to heat and brown chili pods for about 30 seconds or until dark but not burnt. Add garlic and green onion, stirring for 10 seconds. Return beef along with tangerine peel and SAUCE ingredients. Cook over high heat until liquid is reduced.

Canton Oyster Beef Strips

Originating from Canton, this unique and quickly prepared dish results from stir-frying strips of marinated beef, onion, and green pepper together before blending in an oyster-flavored sauce.

Makes: 6 servings
Cooking time: 10 minutes

1 pound flank steak, trimmed

MARINADE

2 teaspoons light or regular soy sauce
2 tablespoons water
1 egg white
2 teaspoons cornstarch
1 tablespoon vegetable oil

1 green pepper
½ small white onion

SAUCE

3 tablespoons oyster sauce
1 tablespoon soy sauce
1 tablespoon dry sherry
3 tablespoons chicken broth
½ teaspoon sugar

Vegetable oil, for blanching

Cornstarch paste

Cut flank steak against the grain into 1½-inch-wide pieces; then cut with the grain into ¼-inch pieces. Finally, cut into ¼- by ¼-inch strips and then combine with MARINADE ingredients in the order listed; set aside.

Remove core and ends from bell pepper; slice lengthwise into julienne strips. Cut onion in half and then finely slice with the grain.

Combine SAUCE ingredients thoroughly; set aside.

To oil-blanch, set wok over high heat for about 1 minute. Add 3 cups oil and heat to 300°. Stir in beef, cooking just until redness is gone. Remove and drain.

To stir-fry, remove all but 3 tablespoons oil from wok. Reheat, swirling pan to coat sides. Add pepper and onion, cooking for about 1 minute until onion browns. Stir in beef and sauce, then thicken with 1 teaspoon cornstarch paste and serve.

• *Note* •

Blanched broccoli or asparagus, or sautéed green onion and ginger make a flavorful substitute for the bell pepper and onion.

Curry Beef

Curry is popular in the southern part of China, a true stimulant to the appetite with a one-of-a-kind aroma.

Makes: 6 to 8 servings
Cooking time: 10 minutes

1 pound flank steak, trimmed

MARINADE

1 teaspoon light soy sauce or regular soy sauce
2 tablespoons water
1 egg white
2 teaspoons cornstarch
1 tablespoon vegetable oil

SAUCE

1 tablespoon curry powder
⅓ cup chicken broth
1 teaspoon soy sauce
1 tablespoon dry sherry
2 teaspoons sugar
¼ teaspoon salt

Vegetable oil, for blanching

1 clove garlic, minced or pressed

VEGETABLES

½ small white onion, cut into 1-inch squares
1 green pepper, cut into 1-inch squares
¼ cup sliced bamboo shoots

Cornstarch paste

Slice flank steak against the grain into pieces ⅛- by 1- by 1½-inches thick. Combine with MARINADE ingredients in the order listed, mixing well after each addition. Let stand for about 10 minutes.

Combine SAUCE ingredients thoroughly; set aside.

To oil-blanch, set wok over high heat for about 1 minute. Add 2 cups oil and heat to 300°. Add beef, stirring to separate, and blanch until redness is gone. Remove and drain.

To stir-fry, remove all but 3 tablespoons oil from wok. Heat, swirling pan to coat sides. Add garlic and stir-fry until fragrant. Add VEGETABLES, tossing for about 30 seconds. Return beef, stirring well, and then pour in sauce. Bring to a boil and mix well; thicken with 1 tablespoon cornstarch paste. Serve immediately.

• *Note* •

My students always ask me what brands I use in cooking. For curry powder, I prefer Schillings.

Dry-sautéed Beef Strips

There's no better way to demonstrate how wonderful this Chinese technique of cooking is than to offer this recipe. You'll think the beef was grilled when its only been sautéed Szechuan-style. Celery and carrots add zest and color to this spicy dish.

Makes: 6 to 8 servings
Cooking time: 10 minutes

- 1 pound flank steak, trimmed
- 1 tablespoon soy sauce

SAUCE
- 1 tablespoon soy sauce
- 1 teaspoon dry sherry
- 1 tablespoon white vinegar
- ½ teaspoon salt
- ¼ teaspoon sugar

- 6 tablespoons vegetable oil

- 2 thumb-size slices fresh ginger, shredded
- 2 cloves garlic, thinly sliced
- ½ carrot, peeled and cut into julienne strips
- 2 stalks celery, cut into julienne strips
- 1 green onion (white part), shredded

- Cornstarch paste
- 1 tablespoon hot chili oil
- 1 teaspoon sesame oil

Cut flank steak against the grain into 1½-inch-wide pieces. Then slice ¼-inch thick with the grain and cut into ¼- by ¼-inch strips. Mix with soy sauce and set aside. Combine SAUCE ingredients thoroughly; set aside.

To stir-fry, heat wok (or wide frying pan) over high heat for 1 minute until hot. Add 4 tablespoons oil and swirl to coat sides of pan. Add beef, stir-frying for about 3 minutes until seared and brown. (Add more oil if beef sticks.) Remove, drain, and wipe wok clean.

To stir-fry again, heat wok over high heat and add remaining 2 tablespoons oil, swirling pan to coat sides. Add ginger, garlic, and carrot, tossing lightly. Stir in celery and green onion, cooking for 30 seconds. Pour in sauce and return beef to wok, stirring until slightly reduced. Thicken with 1 teaspoon cornstarch paste and stir in chili oil and sesame oil to serve.

Tomato Beef

This popular Cantonese dish is most frequently found in the metropolitan cities of China, perhaps because the tomato was introduced into China many, many years ago by foreign visitors. In fact, the Chinese word for tomato identifies it as a "foreign" fruit.

Makes: 6 to 8 servings
Cooking time: 10 minutes

1 pound flank steak, trimmed

MARINADE

2 teaspoons light soy sauce or regular soy sauce
2 tablespoons water
1 egg white
2 teaspoons cornstarch
1 tablespoon vegetable oil

1 tablespoon fermented black beans, smashed
1 clove garlic, minced or pressed
2 teaspoons vegetable oil

Vegetable oil, for blanching

¼ small white onion, cut into 1-inch squares
1 small green pepper, cut into 1-inch squares
2 tomatoes, peeled and cut into wedges
2 green onions (white part), cut into 1-inch pieces

SEASONINGS

3 tablespoons soy sauce
2 tablespoons chicken broth
1 tablespoon dry sherry
1 teaspoon sugar

Cornstarch paste
½ teaspoon sesame oil

Slice flank steak against the grain ⅛- by 1- by 1½-inches thick. Combine with MARINADE ingredients in the order listed, mixing well. Let stand for 10 minutes.

Combine slightly smashed black beans with garlic and oil; set aside.

To oil-blanch, set wok over high heat for 1 minute. Add 2 cups oil and heat to 300°. Add beef, blanching until redness is gone. Remove and drain.

To stir-fry, remove all but 3 tablespoons oil from wok. Add black bean mixture and stir-fry for 30 seconds until fragrant. Add white onion and green pepper; stir-fry for 30 seconds. Return beef to wok along with tomatoes and green onions; stir-fry for 1 minute. Add SEASONINGS, mix well and bring to a boil. Thicken with 1 tablespoon cornstarch paste and sprinkle with sesame oil to serve.

• Note •

You can easily use this recipe as a meat sauce for Pan-fried Noodles (page 169). Just substitute catsup for the black bean mixture and add a little more sugar.

Szechuan Steamed Beef With Anise Rice

Here's a typical Szechuan dish which is served all over China. Since beef is bountiful and preferred in this country, I have suggested beef as the main ingredient; however pork or chicken are equally flavorful.

Makes: 6 to 8 servings
Cooking time: 40 minutes

SPICY RICE

- 1 cup long grain rice
- 1 star anise seed

- 1 pound flank steak (or stew beef), cut into 1½-inch cubes

MARINADE

- 1 green onion, chopped
- 1 tablespoon chili paste
- 3 tablespoons soy sauce
- 2 tablespoons dry sherry
- 3 tablespoons vegetable oil

Put rice in a bowl with enough water to cover; soak for 2 hours. Drain well and then crush (or process in food processor) with star anise. In a dry wok, toast until brown and fragrant.

Put beef in a bowl suitable for steaming. Stir in MARINADE ingredients, and rice and mix thoroughly; let stand for 10 minutes.

To steam, place bowl on rack in steamer; cover and steam over boiling water for 30 minutes. Remove and place on top of serving platter for easier handling.

• Notes •

1. If you substitute pork for beef, you'll need to steam it slightly longer to cook it completely.

2. Spicy rice mixture may be purchased at Oriental markets.

3. In China, this meat mixture is often wrapped in lotus leaves and then steamed.

4. Serves 2 if considered a single-dish meal.

Beef With Assorted Vegetables

Nothing could be simpler than combining a variety of blanched vegetables with sautéed beef. I serve it often at home as well as at Chef Chu's.

Makes: 8 to 10 servings
Cooking time: 10 minutes

- 4 or 5 dried black mushrooms
- 1 pound flank steak, trimmed

MARINADE

- 1 teaspoon light or regular soy sauce
- 2 tablespoons water
- 1 egg white
- 2 teaspoons cornstarch
- 1 tablespoon vegetable oil

- 3 or 4 stalks broccoli, trimmed
- 1 stalk bok choy, diagonally sliced ¼-inch thick
  Chicken broth or water

VEGETABLES

- ¼ cup sliced water chestnuts
- ¼ cup sliced bamboo shoots
- 12 snow peas, ends snipped
- 12 canned baby corn, split in half lengthwise
- 8 to 12 canned straw mushrooms

SAUCE

- 3 tablespoons soy sauce
- 1 tablespoon dry sherry
- ¼ teaspoon sugar
  Pinch white pepper

  Vegetable oil, for blanching

- 1 green onion (white part), minced
- ¼ teaspoon minced fresh ginger
  Cornstarch paste
- 1 teaspoon vegetable oil

Soak mushrooms in warm water for 20 minutes; drain, remove stems, and cut in half.

Cut flank steak against the grain into ⅛- by 1- by 1½-inch slices. Combine with MARINADE ingredients in the order listed; mix well and let stand for 10 minutes.

Separate broccoli flowerets and then diagonally slice stalks ⅛-inch thick.

To water-blanch, cook broccoli and bok choy in boiling broth (or water) for 1 minute; add remaining VEGETABLES and blanch for 30 seconds. Remove, drain, and set aside.

Combine SAUCE ingredients thoroughly; set aside.

To oil-blanch, set wok over high heat for about 1 minute. Add 2 cups oil and heat to 300°. Add beef, stirring to separate; blanch until redness is gone. Remove and drain.

To stir-fry, remove all but 3 tablespoons oil from wok. Stir in green onion and ginger; cook until fragrant. Return beef and vegetables, stirring for about 30 seconds. Add sauce, mix thoroughly, and thicken with 1 tablespoon cornstarch paste. Stir in 1 teaspoon oil and serve immediately.

• Notes •

1. You'll enrich the flavor of your vegetables if you blanch them in chicken broth rather than water.

2. Use this recipe as a guideline, substituting any assortment of vegetables you have on hand.

Chef Chu's Chinese Steak

If you are in the mood for steak but want to try something different, this original approach is tailored to the American taste without sacrificing the Chinese tradition of cooking. Served with snow peas and tomato, this delicious steak can be a meal-in-a-dish for two.

Makes: 6 servings
Cooking time: 10 minutes

1 pound flank steak or top sirloin

MARINADE

2 tablespoons soy sauce
2 teaspoons dry sherry
2 tablespoons water
1 green onion (white part), minced
2 teaspoons cornstarch
1 tablespoon vegetable oil

SAUCE

3 tablespoons catsup
1 tablespoon Worcestershire
1 tablespoon sugar
2 teaspoons soy sauce
2 tablespoons chicken broth
   Pinch Chinese five-spice
   Cornstarch paste

2 cups snow peas, ends trimmed and cut in half
   Chicken broth or water

6 to 8 tomato slices

Trim off and discard fat and gristle from meat. Cut meat into pieces 1 inch by 1½ inches (you should have about 16 pieces). Pound pieces with a mallet to flatten and tenderize.

Combine meat with MARINADE ingredients in the order listed and let stand for 10 minutes.

Combine SAUCE ingredients in a bowl; set aside.

To water-blanch, blanch snow peas in boiling broth (or water) for about 30 seconds; drain and arrange on serving platter (keep warm).

To pan-fry, heat wok (or wide frying pan) over high heat for 1 minute until hot. Add beef, stirring and browning on all sides until desired doneness is reached. Stir in sauce, mix well, and cook until thickened.

To serve, spoon meat over bed of snow peas and garnish platter with tomato slices. Serve immediately.

Mandarin Beef Stew

Here's home-style Chinese cooking at its best. It's one of the more popular items served at Chef Chu's—some customers ask for it over boiled noodles or rice, others prefer it just by itself.

Makes: 8 to 10 servings
Cooking time: 1 hour

- 2 pounds beef stew, cut into 1½-inch chunks
- 2 knobs fresh ginger, crushed
- 1 green onion, tied in a knot

In a cheesecloth bag put:
- 4 star anise seeds
- ½ teaspoon Szechuan peppercorns
- 2 pieces preserved tangerine peel
- ½ teaspoon whole cloves

- 2 tablespoons vegetable oil
- 6 to 10 whole red chili peppers
- 5 cloves garlic, slightly crushed

SEASONINGS

- ½ cup soy sauce
- 2 tablespoons dry sherry
- 2 tablespoons sugar
- 2 cups water

  Chinese parsley (cilantro)

To par-boil, place beef in enough boiling water to cover and cook for 3 minutes. Remove to colander and rinse under cold water.

In a 6-quart heavy stockpot (or earthenware pot), drop in ginger, onion, cheesecloth bag, and beef; set aside.

To stir-fry, heat wok (or wide frying pan) over high heat for 1 minute until hot. Add oil and swirl pan to coat sides. When oil is hot, add chili peppers and cook until brown. Add garlic and brown slightly. Stir in remaining SEASONINGS, and bring to a boil. Pour into stockpot and add just enough water to cover.

To stew, bring to a boil, cover, and reduce heat to medium. Cook for 45 minutes, stirring occasionally. Remove from heat and discard cheesecloth bag, ginger, and onion. Skim off any fat and garnish with Chinese parsley to serve.

• Notes •

1. I sometimes add chunks of bamboo shoots, tomato wedges, and a pinch of curry powder. Then I thicken with cornstarch paste and serve over hot boiled rice. It can also be served over boiled noodles. In either case, watch out for the chili peppers—they are hot!

2. Most Chinese prefer meat with some gristle remaining. A little gristle helps retain the shape of the meat during a long stewing time.

Szechuan Beef

Strips of marinated beef are deep-fried twice to create a light, crispy texture on the outside. Just before serving, the beef is hot-mixed in a tangy sauce made with garlic, ginger, soy sauce, and red rice vinegar then served on top of puffy rice noodles.

Makes: 6 to 8 servings
Cooking time: 15 minutes

1 pound flank steak, trimmed

MARINADE
2 teaspoons light or regular soy sauce
1 egg white
1 tablespoon cornstarch
1 tablespoon vegetable oil

BATTER
½ cup cornstarch
¼ cup water

Vegetable oil, for blanching
2 ounces rice sticks

SAUCE
5 tablespoons soy sauce
¼ cup water or chicken broth
1 tablespoon red rice vinegar
1 tablespoon sugar

½ teaspoon minced fresh ginger
1 large clove garlic, minced or pressed

Cornstarch paste
1½ teaspoons hot chili oil
½ teaspoon sesame oil
1 green onion (including top), chopped

Cut flank steak against the grain into ¼- by 1- by 1½-inch-thick slices. Combine with MARINADE ingredients in the order listed, mixing well. Let stand for 10 minutes.

Combine cornstarch and water to make a paste; set aside.

To deep-fry, heat 4 cups oil in a wok (or electric deep-fat fryer) to 350°. Add rice sticks and deep-fry for about 30 seconds until puffy. Remove, break into small pieces and arrange on serving platter. Remove any pieces left in oil and then return oil to 350°. Dip beef slices, a few at a time, into cornstarch paste and then deep-fry in oil until a hard crust is formed. Remove, drain, and keep oil warm. Skim oil for any leftover crust and discard.

Combine SAUCE ingredients thoroughly; set aside.

To deep-fry again, bring oil back to 350°. Add beef all at once and fry for about 1 minute until hard crust forms again. Remove and drain.

To hot mix, remove all but 3 tablespoons oil from wok. Add ginger and garlic, cooking until fragrant. Stir in sauce, bring to a boil, and thicken with 1 tablespoon cornstarch paste until the consistency of syrup is reached. Sprinkle with chili oil and sesame oil. Return beef to wok and toss with green onion. Mix well and serve on top of rice sticks.

To serve, toss beef with rice sticks at the table.

• Notes •

1. "Hot mixing" is just that—quickly mixing crisp, deep-fried or cooked ingredients with a sauce. It's intended to mix the ingredients not cook them any more.

2. This recipe is ideal for entertaining because everything, except for the hot mixing, can be done in advance.

Mongolian Beef

In Mongolia, cattle herders move with their cattle across the open range like American cowboys once did. They cook their meals over an open fire, using ingredients on hand or seasonings that transport easily. This beef dish, cooked the same way over hot, direct heat, uses just a few basic seasonings for flavor.

Makes: 4 to 6 servings
Cooking time: 10 minutes

1 pound flank steak, trimmed

MARINADE

2 teaspoons light or regular soy sauce
2 tablespoons water
Pinch white pepper
2 teaspoons cornstarch
2 tablespoons vegetable oil

1 bunch green onions

SAUCE

3 tablespoons soy sauce
1 tablespoons dry sherry
1 teaspoon sugar

¼ cup vegetable oil
10 thumb-size slices fresh ginger

Cornstarch paste

Cut flank steak against the grain into ⅛- by 1- by 1½-inch slices. Then combine with MARINADE ingredients in the order listed; mix well and set aside.

Cut onions into 1½-inch-long pieces, then separate outer layers from inner ones.

Combine SAUCE ingredients; set aside.

To stir-fry, set wok (or wide frying pan) over high heat for 1 minute until hot. Add oil and swirl pan to coat sides. When oil is very hot, add beef, stirring to distribute evenly in pan and to sear both sides. Add ginger, stirring until fragrant. Add green onion; mix well and stir for 30 seconds. Pour in sauce, stir-fry quickly until green onion starts to wilt. Slightly thicken with 1 teaspoon cornstarch paste and serve.

• Note •

This kind of stir-frying must be done over high heat for only a short period of time to bring out the flavor of the ingredients.

·VEGETABLES·

America is a bountiful country, rich in high quality meats and produce—but, sadly, the variety of vegetables do not begin to match the variety found in China. So, travelers, you have new tastes and textures to encounter just in vegetables when you make that gastronomic trip to the land of my birth.

Snow peas, certain cabbages, bean sprouts, Oriental eggplant, and bean curd (tofu) may be found in most supermarkets, so the supply is adequate, especially when supplemented with dried Chinese mushrooms, canned bamboo shoots, dried lily roots, and many other vegetables described in the glossary of Chinese ingredients (page 202).

As a rule, Chinese cooking brings out the flavor of a vegetable through very light cooking. However, in some cases, vegetables must be water-blanched first, so please read your notes carefully.

One vegetable which, by its appearance, doesn't make one think of typical vegetables, is bean curd (also called bean cake and tofu). Bean curd is made from puréed soybeans pressed into blocks about 3 inches square. It is a staple in Chinese diets, high in protein, inexpensive, and delicious because it absorbs all the flavors when cooked in a sauce. Anyone on a diet should consider incorporating bean curd into their menu—it is easy to digest and low in calories, too! For a simple, satisfying combination, just add several half-inch cubes or slices of bean curd to Rich Chicken Broth and you'll have a nutritious, light dish.

Vegetarians should be able to satisfy their taste buds thoroughly with Chinese cooking. Many of the dishes that appear in other sections of the book may be served without meat. And vegetable dishes that require a chicken broth will taste fine with a vegetable bouillon (broth) substitute, as will the soups in the soup section.

Buddhist and Taoist dishes are strictly vegetarian and do not even include milk or eggs. They are so delicious and popular that they are considered a highly-respected cuisine of China.

The virtuous philosophy of these religions are so well-regarded throughout the land that Chinese do not celebrate the New Year without saving one of their classic dishes.

Large, fresh Chinese or Napa cabbage and bok choy are plentiful in vegetable stalls of Chinatown, and they are readily available in most supermarkets as well. Though large-sized cabbages are appealing, smaller ones often are more tender.

Stir-fried Bean Sprouts

A simple dish with a simple taste, this is easy on the budget and quick to prepare. Timing is critical.

Makes: 6 to 8 servings
Cooking time: 5 minutes

---

3 tablespoons vegetable oil
6 to 8 dried chili pods (optional)
2 green onions, cut into 1½-inch pieces
3 thumb-size slices fresh ginger, slivered
4 cups bean sprouts
½ teaspoon salt
2 teaspoons sugar
1 teaspoon white vinegar

To stir-fry, heat wok (or wide frying pan) over high heat for 1 minute until hot. Add oil and swirl pan to coat sides. Stir in chili pods (if used), cooking just until brown. Add green onions and ginger, stir-frying for 10 seconds. Add bean sprouts, quickly stirring over maximum heat, for 30 seconds. Mix in salt, sugar, and vinegar. Toss vigorously about 45 seconds (to prevent bean sprouts from wilting). Quickly remove to serving platter.

• Notes •

1. To add hotness to this dish, break open one or more chili pods to expose seeds. Remember, the more you break open the hotter the dish will be!

2. Use maximum heat for stir-frying. You're trying to force the flavor out yet keep the texture crunchy.

Snow Peas With Water Chestnuts   *Pictured on page 80*

Jade green snow peas and coin-like slices of water chestnuts make this the most requested Chinese vegetable combination in America.

Makes: 6 to 8 servings
Cooking time: 5 minutes

---

1 can (8 oz.) sliced water chestnuts
2 cups snow peas, ends trimmed

SAUCE
½ cup Rich Chicken Broth (page 52), or chicken bouillon
½ cube chicken bouillon
2 tablespoons dry sherry
½ teaspoon sugar
Salt to taste
Pinch white pepper

3 tablespoons vegetable oil
1 green onion (white part), minced

Cornstarch paste

To water-blanch, cook water chestnuts and snow peas in boiling water for 30 seconds. Remove and drain.
Combine SAUCE ingredients; set aside.
To stir-fry, heat wok (or wide frying pan) over high heat for 1 minute until hot. Add oil and swirl pan to coat sides. When oil is hot, add onion and cook until fragrant. Stir in sauce and vegetables to coat. Thicken with 2 tablespoons cornstarch paste and transfer to serving platter.

Lettuce With Oyster Sauce

What can you serve on the spur of the moment when someone unexpected arrives for dinner? Try cooking lettuce. This is unusual, quick, and never fails to win approval. A variation using asparagus is shown on page 36.

Makes: 6 servings
Cooking time: 5 minutes

1 head Romaine lettuce

SAUCE
¼ cup oyster sauce
2 tablespoons vegetable oil
1 tablespoon sesame oil

Immerse lettuce in cold water for 5 minutes; then cut off stem end.

To water-blanch, cook lettuce in boiling water for 30 seconds. Remove and drain; cut into thirds crosswise and place on serving platter.

Combine SAUCE ingredients and spoon over lettuce. Toss gently at the table to serve.

• *Note* •

Why not use asparagus, broccoli, or another vegetable you have on hand instead of lettuce? You'll need to blanch them about 2 minutes.

Szechuan-style String Beans

Typically, this recipe is saved for the restaurant or professional kitchens in China because for maximum flavor you need intense heat. However, I've developed a technique for this "dry" stir-frying process that can be successfully duplicated at home.

Makes: 6 to 8 servings
Cooking time: 5 minutes

1 tablespoon dried shrimp

Vegetable oil, for blanching

1 pound string beans, trimmed and cut into 2-inch lengths
1 ounce ground pork
1 clove garlic, minced or pressed
1 teaspoon minced preserved Szechuan mustard green
1 teaspoon chili paste

SEASONINGS
1 tablespoon dry sherry
2 tablespoons soy sauce
3 tablespoons chicken broth
¼ teaspoon sugar

Soak shrimp in warm water for 5 to 10 minutes; drain and mince.

To oil-blanch, set wok over high heat for about 1 minute. Add 2 to 3 cups oil and heat to 350°. Blanch beans in batches for about 1½ minutes or until wrinkles form. Remove and drain.

To stir-fry, remove all but 3 tablespoons oil. Reheat wok until hot. Add pork, stirring to separate. Add garlic, mustard green, shrimp, and chili paste. Stir-fry for 30 seconds; return beans to wok and then stir in SEASONINGS. Toss gently until liquid coats string beans. Remove and serve immediately.

In China, a chef's skill is demonstrated in the speed, accuracy, and uniformity with which he cuts vegetables—admired talents that take practice and patience. Pictured above are (clockwise, from top): roll-cut turnip; diced onion; slant-cut asparagus; fan-cut Oriental eggplant; matchstick strips of celery; peeled, sliced ginger root (note "thumb-size knob," often referred to in recipes); shredded Chinese cabbage; bite-size pieces of bok choy; sliced lotus root, exposing decorative pattern; and in center, notched bamboo shoot that is thinly sliced.

Mixed Chinese Vegetables   *Pictured on page 6*

Just like any other dish that relies on the choicest ingredients, this recipe requires a little extra time when selecting the vegetables. Look for ones at their peak of freshness with good color and texture.

Makes: 8 servings
Cooking time: 10 minutes

4 or 5 dried black
mushrooms

VEGETABLES

½ small head broccoli
2 or 3 stalks bok choy, slant-cut into 1½-inch pieces
¼ cup sliced water chestnuts
¼ cup sliced bamboo shoots
12 snow peas, ends trimmed
12 canned baby corn
8 to 12 canned straw mushrooms

SEASONINGS

½ cup chicken broth
½ teaspoon dry sherry
1 teaspoon salt
½ teaspoon sugar
Pinch white pepper

3 tablespoons vegetable oil
1 green onion (white part), minced
1 thumb-size slice fresh ginger, minced

Cornstarch paste

Soak mushrooms in warm water for 20 minutes; drain, remove stems, and cut in half. Cut broccoli flowerets into bite-size pieces; slice stems ⅛-inch thick.

To water-blanch, cook broccoli, bok choy, and black mushrooms in boiling water for 1 minute; add remaining VEGETABLES and blanch for 30 seconds. Remove and drain.

Combine SEASONINGS together; set aside.

To stir-fry, heat wok (or wide frying pan) over high heat for 1 minute until hot. Add oil and swirl pan to coat sides. When oil is hot, add green onion and ginger, stirring until fragrant. Stir in seasonings, add vegetables, and stir-fry for 1½ minutes. Thicken with 2 teaspoons cornstarch paste and serve.

• Notes •

1. Rendered chicken fat is often used in China to enrich the flavor of this vegetable dish. Use a few drops after thickening sauce with cornstarch paste.

2. Almost any vegetable dish—snow peas with water chestnuts, black mushrooms, or Chinese greens—may be prepared in this manner.

3. Vegetarians can substitute vegetable bouillon for chicken broth.

Shanghai Braised Three Delicacies

Here's a tasty Shanghai-style dish that is perfect for vegetarians. The taste is wonderful because the deep-fried gluten puffs absorb all the other flavors during braising.

Makes: 6 to 8 servings
Cooking time: 30 minutes

- 5 to 7 dried black mushrooms
- 1 can (15 oz.) winter bamboo shoots
- 1 package (1 lb.) frozen gluten puff, thawed and torn into 1-inch pieces

  Vegetable oil, for deep-frying

- 1 tablespoon vegetable oil
- 1 thumb-size chunk fresh ginger, crushed
- 3 green onions (white part), diagonally sliced ½-inch thick

SEASONINGS

- 3 cups Rich Chicken Broth (page 52), or vegetable bouillon
- 5 tablespoons soy sauce
- 1 tablespoon dry sherry
- 2 tablespoons sugar
- ½ teaspoon salt

- 1 teaspoon sesame oil

Soak mushrooms in warm water for 20 minutes; drain, remove stems, and cut into bite-size pieces. Cut bamboo shoots into bite-size pieces using rolling-cut method (see page 195).

To boil, bring puffs to boil in 2 quarts water for 5 minutes. Remove and drain, squeezing out excess water. Let dry for about 5 minutes.

To deep-fry, heat 4 cups oil in a wok (or electric deep-fat fryer) to 350°. Add gluten puffs in two batches. Deep-fry for 8 to 10 minutes or until golden brown; outside should be firm and all the moisture should be gone. Remove and drain well. Add bamboo shoots to oil and fry for about 3 minutes; remove and drain.

To braise, remove all but 1 tablespoon oil and return wok to heat for 1 minute; swirl pan to coat sides. Stir in ginger and onion, cooking until fragrant. Add gluten puffs, bamboo shoots, mushrooms, and SEASONINGS. Braise over medium heat, stirring occasionally, for about 10 minutes or until most of the liquid is absorbed. Stir in sesame oil and discard ginger before serving.

• Notes •

1. Frozen gluten puff is available at Oriental markets.

2. We deep-fry them first to achieve a sponge-like texture outside; then we braise them to absorb all the flavor. (For more information, see page 204.)

3. This dish may be served hot or cold. It can be made ahead and refrigerated until serving; while reheating, add a few snow peas for color.

Sure you can do it! Each recipe, including Chef Chu's most requested one, Mu Shu pork, in preparation here, is written in a way that helps you visualize each step even before you begin. He encourages students to let senses of smell, touch, sight, hearing, and taste—plus Chinese sixth sense of good timing—take command. (Recipe on page 115.)

152

Four Seasons Vegetables

Presentation is the key to the success of this elegant dish. The vegetables star, so choose the very freshest.

Makes: 6 to 8 servings
Cooking time: 10 minutes

VEGETABLES

- 12 dried black mushrooms
- 4 firm red tomatoes
- 1 head broccoli
- 24 canned baby corn, drained

- 1 quart Rich Chicken Broth (page 52), or chicken bouillon

SEASONINGS

- ½ cube chicken bouillon
  Salt to taste
  Dash white pepper

  Cornstarch paste
- 1 tablespoon vegetable oil

Soak mushrooms in warm water for 20 minutes; drain, remove stems, and cut mushrooms in half. Cut 3 slices (½-inch wide) from sides of tomatoes, cutting from top to bottom. (You should have a triangular-shaped tomato "core" left; reserve for other uses.)

Remove broccoli stalks (save for other uses); slice flowerets in half lengthwise.

To water-blanch, bring broth to a boil. Add black mushrooms, cook for about 3 minutes, and remove. Add broccoli, cook for 3 minutes, remove, and drain. Blanch tomatoes, and baby corn separately in boiling broth for 1 minute; remove and drain. Plunge tomatoes in cold water to cool; then peel off skin. Pour 2 cups broth through strainer into a wok (discarding seeds).

To assemble, arrange vegetables attractively on a white serving platter.

To cook, bring broth to a boil with SEASONINGS. Thicken with 2 tablespoons cornstarch paste; then stir in oil. Ladle over vegetables to serve.

• Notes •

1. You can substitute other vegetables for those suggested above but retain the 4 different colors. (For example, substitute white asparagus for corn, bok choy or asparagus for broccoli.)

2. Save the chicken broth for other uses; first remove any leftover vegetable pieces using a strainer.

3. I use the reserved tomato cores in other dishes like Egg Flower Soup (page 59).

Tientsin Cabbage

The natural, light sweet flavor of cabbage makes this dish, enhanced by a shrimp topping. Most Chinese vegetables are cooked quickly to preserve their crunchy texture. This recipe results in very soft cabbage ready to melt in your mouth.

Makes: 6 to 8 servings
Cooking time: 25 minutes

10 dried shrimp

2 small heads Chinese cabbage

½ teaspoon salt

1 cup chicken broth

2 tablespoons vegetable oil
   Salt to taste
   Pinch white pepper
   Cornstarch paste

Soak shrimp in warm water for 30 minutes; remove, drain, and mince. Cut off tops and ends of cabbage; then cut into eighths lengthwise.

To par-boil, place cabbage in enough boiling water to cover and cook for 10 minutes or until soft. Remove, run under cold water, and drain.

To assemble, arrange cabbage sections decoratively in a medium-size bowl suitable for steaming. Sprinkle salt over cabbage; then sprinkle shrimp. Carefully pour in broth.

To steam, place bowl on rack in steamer. Cover and steam over boiling water for 10 minutes; carefully drain broth into another bowl and reserve. Invert cabbage onto serving platter, flattening down slightly.

To cook, heat wok over high heat; add oil, swirling pan to coat sides. Pour in reserved broth (including shrimp) and bring to a boil. Season to taste with salt and pepper; then thicken with 4 teaspoons cornstarch paste.

To serve, spoon sauce over cabbage sections.

• *Notes* •

1. Dried scallops—soaked in boiling water for 30 minutes and then slivered—can be used instead of shrimp, if desired.

2. Try assembling cabbage sections in overlapping rows similar to Hunan Honey-glazed Ham, pictured on page 120.

Braised Eggplant

Deep-purple Oriental eggplant, available at some supermarkets as well as most Oriental markets, are preferred for this recipe. Their skin is so tender, peeling isn't necessary. Besides eggplant, you'll discover an assortment of tasty ingredients: ground pork, water chestnuts, ginger, garlic, green onion, and chili paste.

Makes: 6 servings
Cooking time: 10 minutes

8 Oriental eggplant, cut in half lengthwise and then into two sections

SAUCE

3 tablespoons soy sauce
1 tablespoons sugar
1 cup Rich Chicken Broth (page 52), or chicken bouillon
1 tablespoon dry sherry
¼ teaspoon salt

Vegetable oil, for deep-frying

2 ounces ground pork

SPICES

2 cloves garlic, minced or pressed
1 teaspoon minced fresh ginger
1 tablespoon chili paste

2 tablespoons coarsely chopped water chestnuts (or jicama)
1 tablespoon red rice vinegar
1 green onion (including top), coarsely chopped

Cornstarch paste
1 teaspoon sesame oil

Score each section of eggplant, cutting into fan-shaped pieces as pictured on page 149.

Combine SAUCE ingredients; set aside.

To deep-fry, heat 2 cups oil in a wok to 350°. Drop in eggplant pieces, a few at a time, and deep-fry for about 3 minutes or until soft. Remove and drain well.

To braise, remove all but 1 tablespoon oil from wok. Reheat oil until hot and then add pork, stirring to separate. Add garlic, ginger, and chili paste; stir-fry until fragrant. Return eggplant to wok along with water chestnuts and sauce. Braise over medium heat until liquid is reduced; then add vinegar and green onion. Mix thoroughly and thicken slightly with 1 tablespoon cornstarch paste. Stir in sesame oil and serve.

• *Notes* •

1. You can leave the skin on the eggplant as directed, or you can score the skin making slashes ¹⁄₁₆-inch apart for a more decorative look.

2. Make sure to drain the eggplant well after deep-frying so that it won't taste greasy.

3. Vegetarians can enjoy this dish by simply deleting the pork.

Hunan Bean Curd

How can such a simple food answer to so many different names? Chinese usually call it bean curd while Japanese call it tofu. Americans call it bean cake but in supermarkets you also see it labeled soybean cake or even dofu. No matter what you call it, bean curd is really just the milk or juice left from puréed soybeans that has been compressed into soft blocks and then packaged.

Makes: 8 to 10 servings
Cooking time: 10 minutes

- 1 block (16 oz.) bean curd (tofu)

- 3 tablespoons vegetable oil
- 2 ounces pork shoulder butt, cut into julienne strips
- 2 cloves garlic, thinly sliced
- 1 tablespoon fermented black beans
- 1 teaspoon chili paste

SEASONINGS
- 1 cup Rich Chicken Broth (page 52), or chicken bouillon
- 2 tablespoons soy sauce
- 1 tablespoon dry sherry
- 1½ teaspoons sugar
  Salt to taste

- 1 green onion, cut into 1-inch pieces
  Cornstarch paste
- 1 teaspoon sesame oil

Cut bean curd into 1- by ½- by ½-inch pieces.

To water-blanch, cook bean curd in enough boiling water to cover for 1 minute; then remove.

To braise, set wok over high heat for 1 minute until hot. Add oil, swirling pan to coat sides. Add pork, stirring to separate, and fry for 1 minute. Add garlic, black beans, and chili paste; stir until fragrant. Add SEASONINGS, stirring well, and then bean curd. Bring to a boil and braise, stirring occasionally, for 5 to 6 minutes or until flavors penetrate. Add green onion; cook for 1 minute longer. Thicken with 1 tablespoon cornstarch paste and then stir in sesame oil to serve.

Ma Po's Hot Bean Curd *Pictured on page 61*

Chinese say that a long time ago a woman known as Lady "Pock-mark" made this dish famous throughout the Szechuan province. I'm not sure what her name has to do with it, but her recipe is typically Szechuan—hot enough to stimulate the palate and numb the tongue.

Makes: 6 to 8 servings
Cooking time: 10 minutes

1 block (16 oz.) soft bean curd (tofu)

SAUCE
1 cup Rich Chicken Broth (page 52), or chicken bouillon
3 tablespoons soy sauce
1 tablespoon dry sherry
2 teaspoons sugar
½ teaspoon salt

3 tablespoons vegetable oil
2 ounces ground pork (or beef)
1 clove garlic, minced or pressed
2 teaspoons chili paste

1 green onion, chopped
Cornstarch paste

1 teaspoon hot chili oil (optional)
½ teaspoon sesame oil
Pinch ground roasted Szechuan peppercorns

Cut soft bean curd into ½-inch cubes.

Combine SAUCE ingredients; set aside.

To braise, set wok over high heat for 1 minute until hot. Add oil and swirl pan to coat sides. Add pork, stirring to separate. Add garlic and chili paste, stirring for 30 seconds until fragrant. Pour in sauce and bean cake. Bring to a boil and braise for 5 minutes. Stir in green onion for 30 seconds, then thicken with 1½ tablespoons cornstarch paste. Mix in chili and sesame oil, remove to a serving plate, sprinkle with peppercorns, and mix to serve.

• *Notes* •

1. To make a vegetarian dish, substitute presoaked sliced black mushrooms for the pork.

2. Make sure the seasoning spices and the bean cake are blended together well. The bean cake should be hot (temperature-wise), saltier than normal, and spicy hot with an aromatic flavor.

3. It's nice to accompany with steamed rice.

EGGS, ·NOODLES· & RICE

Eggs, such simple things, have been converted by the Chinese into many tastes. I know of no ethnic treatment of eggs which covers quite the gamut—from thousand-year-old eggs (eggs preserved in a lime mixture), to salted duck eggs, to marbled chicken eggs, to popular quail eggs. Chinese also cook eggs by the more understandable method of shirring, steaming, pan-frying, and deep-frying. They also use them in puddings. Entire cookbooks have been devoted to eggs cooked Chinese-style, and I regret that we have space only for a few of my very favorites.

Noodles may be part of a family's daily diet, but they perform a ceremonial duty as well. Because they are cut in long strands, they have, for centuries, been symbolic of long life. Noodles are always served for birthdays, New Year's, and other festive occasions. It is believed that all who partake in eating these celebrated noodles share in the blessing.

Noodles may be eaten as a snack, as part of a meal (served as one of the last courses in a banquet), or as the meal itself. Three Delicacies Over Pan-fried Noodles is very hearty and a great combination of tastes and textures.

Green noddles have the surprising addition of spinach, and children as well as grown-ups love them. Fried noodles are a wonderful treat at birthday parties—try them with your youngsters. Using chopsticks may, at first, be a game for them, then a race to see who can master the technique first; it's surprising how simple these sticks are to manage. Children can do it!

Rice is a staple in China and is generally eaten three times a day, at all meals. It is often omitted in formal or banquet meals because such a "common" food is not called for. If it does appear at a banquet, it is served at the very end so that guests are made aware that they are not expected to "fill up" on rice but on the more elaborate dishes.

There are three basic types of rice. *Glutinous* (or sweet) *rice* is short grained, milky white, and becomes sticky when cooked. It is used for stuffings, pastries, and desserts such as Eight Treasure Rice Pudding. *Long-grain rice* is most commonly used in Chinese cooking and is fluffy when steamed. *Short-grain* rice is a bit starchy and preferred in Japanese cooking.

The Chinese expression for let's go and eat is: "let's go and eat rice!"

"Adjust seasonings to taste" is a common instruction in cookbooks—this Chef takes his own advice, adding a little salt to Fancy Fried Rice.

159

Marble Eggs *Pictured on facing page*

The unusual appearance of these eggs—fine dark lines in a pattern similar to marble—makes them an impressive addition to any appetizer or cold plate selection. Chinese also enjoy them as a simple accompaniment to rice porridge or *congee.*

Makes: 6 servings
Cooking time: 1½ hours

12 eggs
2 quarts water

SEASONINGS
3 bags black tea (or 3 tablespoons loose black tea leaves)
3 tablespoons soy sauce
2 teaspoons Chinese five-spice
2 star anise
1 green onion, tied in a knot
1 thumb-size slice fresh ginger

Shredded lettuce

Place eggs in a large pot, cover with cold water, and bring to a simmer. Simmer for about 15 minutes, rinse and drain, and let cool. Gently crack shells, but do not remove until a pattern of fine cracks appear all over.

To simmer, return cracked eggs to the pot, add the 2 quarts of water, and stir in SEASONINGS. Bring to a boil, reduce heat, and simmer for about 1 hour. Remove from heat and allow eggs to cool completely in the liquid.

To serve, shell eggs and slice or cut into quarters; or if you prefer, leave eggs whole. Place on a bed of lettuce to serve.

• *Notes* •

1. Chinese most often serve Marble Eggs in sections, presented as part of a cold plate.
2. Try bringing these fanciful eggs on your next picnic.

Simple homestyle breakfast features congee rice porridge (page 172), often accompanied by fish, meat, or other condiments such as cubes of preserved bean curd shown here. Eggs, a favorite breakfast item, are offered on antique porcelain dishes. Our selection includes (clockwise, from top): quartered, black 1000-year-old eggs; dish with whole marble egg (above) and halved preserved salty egg; bowl containing unpeeled marble eggs; whole black salty eggs, and whole 1000-year-old eggs with outer covering of dried rice husks.

Fresh Noodles & Wrappers

Here's an all-purpose noodle recipe that can easily be adapted to making fresh egg roll and won-ton wrappers, too.

Makes: 6 to 8 servings
Cooking time: 15 minutes

2 cups all-purpose flour
1 egg, lightly beaten
¼ cup water
  Pinch salt

1 cup cornstarch
1 cloth handkerchief (to wrap around cornstarch)

2 quarts water
3 cups cold water
2 tablespoons vegetable oil

Mound flour in a large mixing bowl or on a work surface. Make a deep well in the center and pour in egg, water, and salt. Using a chopstick or fork, mix ingredients well and then knead dough into a stiff ball. Cover with a damp cloth and let stand for 10 minutes.

Meanwhile, spoon cornstarch into the center of the handkerchief. Holding all 4 corners, shake cornstarch down into a "bag" and tie securely with string. Set aside.

To shape, knead dough by hand for 4 to 5 minutes, dusting the board and dough with cornstarch bag to prevent sticking. Using a rolling pin, roll dough out into a rectangle about ⅛-inch thick.

Roll up rectangle evenly onto the rolling pin as illustrated, pressing down firmly and evenly to further stretch the dough. Unroll the dough, dust with cornstarch on both sides, and roll up on rolling pin again (change the position so that all the dough remains about the same thickness). Repeat this procedure until the dough is 1/16-inch thick all over.

To cut, unroll the dough for the last time by unfolding it in such a way that pleats are created (see illustration). The pleats should be about 2 inches wide. Using a sharp cleaver or knife, slice straight across the folds, making strips 1/16-inch wide. Cut all the way through and cut the entire length of the dough. Carefully lift up the top layer (pleat) of noodles and unfold.

To cook, bring 2 quarts water to a boil in a large pot. Add noodles, stirring to separate, and return to a boil. Pour in cold water, then bring to a boil again. Remove and pour noodles through a colander; rinse under cold water and drain well. Mix with oil to serve.

Variation: Egg Roll Wrappers and **Won-ton Wrappers.** Follow the same procedure for making noodles and roll out as directed until a thickness of 1/16-inch is reached. Using a ruler and a sharp cleaver or knife, cut dough into 7-inch squares for egg roll wrappers or 3½-inch squares for won-ton wrappers. Dust with cornstarch and then stack them; wrap in plastic until ready to use.

162

Making & Cutting Fresh Noodles

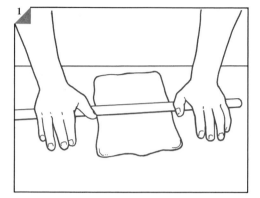

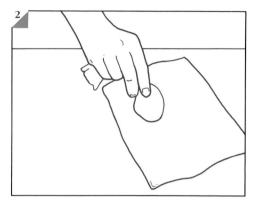

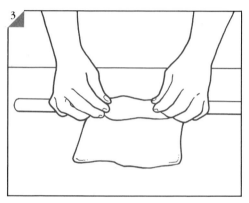

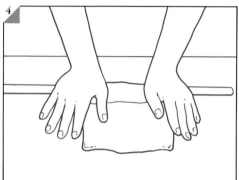

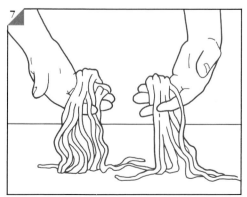

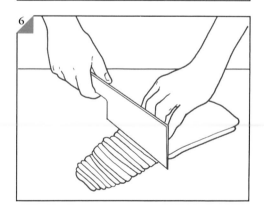

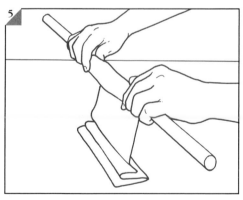

1) Roll out dough into a rectangle, 2) dusting dough with cornstarch bag. 3) Roll dough up evenly onto rolling pin, 4) pressing down firmly and evenly as you go to further stretch dough. Unroll dough, dust with cornstarch on both sides, and roll up again; repeat procedure until dough is 1/16-inch thick. 5) Unroll dough for the last time by unfolding it in pleats. Using a sharp knife, 6) slice across folds at one end, making strips about 1/16-inch wide. Cut entire length of dough this way and 7) lift up top layer (pleat) and unfold noodles.

Oodles and oodles of long-life noodles were eaten before everyone mastered the art of using chopsticks—well, almost everyone!

Long Life Spinach Noodles   *Pictured on page 164*

Every Chinese birthday is celebrated by serving noodles such as these because their extra length promises long life and happiness. In this recipe, the juice from the spinach rather than the spinach itself is used for flavoring the noodle dough.

Makes 8 to 10 servings
Cooking time: 15 minutes

⅓ bunch fresh spinach
⅓ cup water

4 cups all-purpose flour
2 eggs, lightly beaten
   Pinch salt

1 cup cornstarch
1 cloth handkerchief (to
   wrap around cornstarch)

2 quarts water
3 cups cold water
2 tablespoons vegetable oil

Wash spinach thoroughly, cut off and discard stems, and place in a food processor or blender. Add the ⅓ cup water and process until finely chopped. Pour spinach and juice into a bowl through a fine strainer. Further squeeze out excess juice by hand, extracting and saving as much juice as possible. Discard spinach pulp and set juice aside.

Mound flour in a large mixing bowl or on a work surface. Make a deep well in the center and pour in spinach juice, eggs, and salt. Using a chopstick or fork, mix ingredients well and then knead dough into a stiff ball. Cover with a damp cloth and let stand for 10 minutes.

To shape, cut, and cook, follow instructions for making cornstarch bag and for shaping, cutting, and cooking noodles as directed for Fresh Noodles & Wrappers (on page 163).

• *Notes* •

1. If you have a food processor, you can make the dough in seconds using the metal blade. Process until dough forms a stiff ball.
2. You can also use a manual or electrical pasta machine—it is a lot easier. However, Chinese cooks believe that the warmth of a hand is needed to bring out the best qualities of a dough.
3. Cornstarch is very important in noodle making. Dusting with it gives the dough a smooth feeling without changing the texture. This isn't true when you use additional flour.
4. If you prefer, dry the noodles on a rack and then store in plastic bags for later use.
5. To the Chinese, using the juice from fresh spinach makes much more sense than using the spinach pulp because all the nutrients leach out into the water during processing.
6. Adding cold water, rather than increasing or decreasing the heat, helps maintain a constant cooking temperature. The noodles should be cooked through but still be *al dente* or just tender to the bite like pasta.

Egg Foo Yung

Americans seem to love Egg Foo Yung—perhaps it's because they invented it! That's right, it's not a traditional Chinese dish, but I've included it in my book because it's so popular and because I like it, too. At Chef Chu's we try to vary the recipe to include diced barbecued pork or shrimp or whatever is on hand.

Makes: 4 servings
Cooking time: 20 minutes

MIXTURE

- 4 eggs
- 2 cups bean sprouts, broken into bite-size pieces
- ¼ small white onion, coarsely chopped
- 1 green onion, coarsely chopped
- 2 tablespoons flour
- ¼ teaspoon salt

- ¼ cup vegetable oil

GRAVY

- 2 tablespoons vegetable oil
- 2 tablespoons flour
- 1 cup Rich Chicken Broth (page 52), or chicken bouillon
- 1 tablespoon oyster sauce
- 1 teaspoon dry sherry
- ¼ teaspoon salt
- ¼ teaspoon white pepper

Combine MIXTURE ingredients thoroughly.

To pan-fry, heat wok (or heavy skillet) over moderate heat until hot. Add 2 tablespoons oil and when hot, ladle mixture into 4 mounds in wok. Using a spatula, gently flatten each mound. Cook until underside is brown, turn over, and add remaining 2 tablespoons oil. Continue cooking for 6 to 7 minutes. Remove and drain.

To make gravy, mix oil and flour in a pre-heated skillet; cook over medium heat to make a roux. Gradually stir in broth along with remaining GRAVY ingredients, cooking until a gravy consistency is reached.

To serve, lightly score top of each patty with an "X" and arrange on serving platter. Spoon sauce over all.

• *Note* •

Try your own variations with this recipe. Add diced pork, chicken, shrimp—whatever—to the gravy.

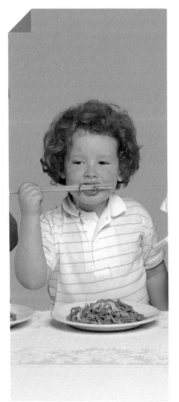

In China, you can't have a birthday party without noodles. White or green, "taffy-pulled" or hand-cut, noodles are served at every birthday for they represent long life. Birthdays only take on a truly special significance after one reaches 70, when the birthday is celebrated with a large gathering of family and friends and the meals are of banquet proportions. But children's birthdays are celebrated, too, and noodles are consumed by young guests with equal relish. Our friend here didn't wait for instructions on how to use chopsticks (see page 216), but learned through trial and error. He got the hang of it in a few minutes and the green noodles disappeared quickly. Consider serving noodles at your next birthday party. Grandparents love it and kids do, too.

Pan-fried Noodles

Made from simple boiled noodles, Pan-fried Noodles are the authentic Chinese way of preparing Chow Mein.

Makes: 6 servings
Cooking time: 15 minutes

1 recipe Fresh Noodles, page 162
¼ cup vegetable oil

Prepare noodles following directions on page 162.

To pan-fry, heat cast-iron or other heavy-bottom skillet over medium heat. When hot, add oil and swirl pan to coat sides. When oil is hot, add boiled noodles, spreading evenly over bottom of pan. Brown on the bottom without disturbing for 5 to 6 minutes or until golden brown; carefully turn over and brown other side. Remove to a paper towel to drain; serve immediately.

Chow Mein

Chow Mein, in Chinese, simply means fried noodles but I've discovered that in the United States it means something different to everyone. It can be sautéed ingredients in gravy served on top of pan-fried noodles; ingredients and pan-fried noodles that are then sautéed together; or sautéed ingredients served on top of crispy noodles. (The latter is not Chinese, rather, it is an American version.) Here is my version.

Makes: 6 to 8 servings
Cooking time: 15 minutes

2 dried black mushrooms
2 tablespoons vegetable oil
¼ small white onion, cut in slivers
½ cup shredded bamboo shoots
1 stalk celery, thinly sliced on diagonal
1 pound Pan-fried Noodles

SEASONINGS

½ cup chicken broth
2 teaspoons soy sauce
½ teaspoon sugar
½ teaspoon salt
Pinch white pepper

1 cup bean sprouts
1 green onion, split lengthwise and cut into 1-inch pieces
5 snow peas, trimmed and cut in half lengthwise

Soak mushrooms in warm water for 20 minutes; drain, remove stems, and cut into slivers.

To stir-fry, heat wok (or wide frying pan) over high heat for 1 minute until hot. Add oil, swirling pan to coat sides. When oil is hot, add white onion, bamboo shoots, and celery; stir-fry for 30 seconds. Then add noodles, stirring to separate. Stir in SEASONINGS, tossing for 1 minute; adjust taste, if necessary. Add bean sprouts, green onion, mushrooms, and snow peas. Stir-fry for about 1 minute or until bean sprouts are cooked through but not wilted. Serve immediately.

• Notes •

1. Barbecued pork strips, cooked shredded chicken, or cooked and peeled shrimp are tasty additions to this dish. Add any cooked meat or seafood along with the bean sprouts.

2. Crispy noodles are egg noodles, deep-fried without ever being boiled. They add crunch but have lost their pasta-like texture.

169

Three Delights Over Pan-fried Noodles

I like to think of this as Shanghai-style Chow Mein but it's more of an American version of traditional Chow Mein. Tasty ingredients such as prawns, black mushrooms, ham, water chestnuts, and more are sautéed and then served over my Pan-fried Noodles.

Makes: 8 servings
Cooking time: 20 minutes

- 4 or 5 dried black mushrooms
- 8 to 10 medium-size prawns, shelled, deveined, and split in half

MARINADE

- Pinch salt
- ¼ teaspoon cornstarch
- ¼ teaspoon vegetable oil

- 1 pound Pan-fried Noodles, page 169

SEASONINGS

- 1 teaspoon dry sherry
- ½ teaspoon soy sauce
- ½ teaspoon sugar
- 1 teaspoon salt
- Pinch white pepper

- ¼ cup vegetable oil
- 1 green onion, cut in 1-inch sections
- ¼ head Chinese cabbage, cut into bite-size pieces
- 1 slice ham, cut into ½-inch pieces
- 1 cup Rich Chicken Broth (page 52), or chicken bouillon

VEGETABLES

- 10 snow peas, trimmed and cut in half
- 8 to 10 slices water chestnuts
- 12 slices bamboo shoots
- 4 to 6 slices fancy-cut carrots (optional)

- Cornstarch paste

Soak mushrooms in warm water for 20 minutes; drain, remove stems, and cut in half. Combine prawns with MARINADE ingredients in the order given.

Prepare noodles as directed on page 169. Place on plate, pull apart slightly using your hands, then keep noodles warm.

Combine SEASONINGS and set aside.

To associate, heat wok (or wide frying pan) over high heat. Add 3 tablespoons oil, swirling pan to coat sides. When oil is hot, add prawns and green onion; stir-fry for 30 seconds and remove. Add cabbage and 1 more tablespoon oil; stir-fry for 1½ minutes. Stir in ham, broth, mushrooms, and VEGETABLES. Bring to a boil, mixing well. Add seasonings along with prawns and green onion. Thicken with 1 tablespoon cornstarch paste and serve over bed of Pan-fried Noodles.

Simple Boiled Rice

Whether it's boiled, steamed, or even fried, rice is the staple food throughout China. Perhaps the easiest way to prepare it is by boiling. Chinese prefer long-grain rice, simply cooked without even the addition of salt. Traditionally, a heavy-bottomed pot is used to promote an even cooking surface.

Makes: About 7 cups
Cooking time: 30 minutes

   3 cups long-grain rice
   3 cups water

Wash rice thoroughly by rinsing under cold water.

Combine rice with the 3 cups water in a heavy pot with a tight-fitting lid. Bring to a boil and reduce heat to medium. When water recedes to expose the top of the rice, cover pot and reduce heat to simmer for about 20 minutes. Turn off heat and let stand, without uncovering, for 10 minutes longer. Stir with fork to separate and fluff before serving.

• *Note* •

Judging the "age" of rice plays a factor in cooking it correctly. New rice softens easily, so use less water; older rice that's tough requires more water. Once you've become accustomed to a certain kind of rice, and have cooked it often enough, you'll be able to tell how "old" your rice is.

Rice Crust

In China, we purposely allow a crust to form on the bottom of the rice pot. After scooping out the boiled rice, we save the crust for deep-frying to be used in soups or other dishes. Or, for a sweet snack, we sprinkle fried rice crust with sugar and eat it like candy.

Makes: 4 servings
Cooking time: 5 minutes

   1 recipe Simple Boiled
      Rice, above

Follow directions for making rice. Remove most of the cooked rice (save for other uses), leaving a thin layer on bottom of pan.

To remove, heat rice pot, uncovered, over low heat until rice becomes dry and crust pulls away from sides of pot. Remove in chunks, let dry completely, and store in plastic bag in a dry place.

Variation: Golden Rice Crust. Follow directions for making rice crust above. Heat 2 cups oil in a wok (or electric deep-fat fryer) to 350°–375°. Carefully, drop chunks of rice into oil and fry for about 45 seconds or until popping and golden brown. Use in soups and other dishes; or sprinkle with sugar for a quick snack.

Congee Rice Porridge   *Pictured on page 161*

What chicken soup is to a Jewish mother, *congee* is to a Chinese cook.

Makes 8 to 10 servings
Cooking time: 30 minutes

1   cup long-grain rice
8   to 10 cups water

Rinse rice thoroughly under running cold water. Drain and place in a large, heavy cast iron or metal pot. Add water and stir.

To cook, bring mixture to a boil, reduce heat to medium, and cook for about 30 minutes or until mixture reaches the consistency of a thick, soup-like porridge.

• *Note* •

You can use leftover cooked rice to make *congee,* too. Reduce the amount of water to 7 or 8 cups but keep the cooking time the same. The result will be a porridge with less starch.

Egg Fried Rice

Egg Fried Rice starts with boiled rice so I use leftover rice that's cold and separates easily. Like so many other basic recipes, you can add just about anything to change the flavor to suit your own taste.

Makes: 8 to 10 servings
Cooking time: 10 minutes

3   tablespoons vegetable oil
2   eggs, lightly beaten
4   cups cold boiled rice

SEASONINGS

2   teaspoons soy sauce
½   teaspoon salt
    Pinch white pepper

1   green onion, chopped

To stir-fry, heat wok (or wide frying pan) over high heat. Add 2 tablespoons oil, swirling pan to coat sides. When oil is hot, add eggs and scramble. Remove and set aside. Add remaining 1 tablespoon oil and when hot, add rice. Stir-fry over medium heat for 3 to 4 minutes or until rice separates. Return eggs along with SEASONINGS and toss for about 1 minute until fluffy. Sprinkle with onion, mix well, and serve.

Variation: Pork Fried Rice. Follow directions for making fried rice except: just before stir-frying rice, add ¼ cup diced barbecued pork. After stir-frying rice, mix in 2 tablespoons cooked peas.

Fancy Fried Rice

The more you add the better this rice becomes. We really start with Egg Fried Rice, then stir in shrimp, pork, bean sprouts, peas, roasted peanuts, and a hint of curry powder.

Makes: 8 to 10 servings
Cooking time: 10 minutes

- 3 tablespoons vegetable oil
- 2 eggs, slightly beaten
- ¼ cup diced Chinese Barbecued Pork (page 39 or purchased)
- 2 tablespoons small cooked shrimp
- 1 tablespoon chopped white onion
- 4 cups cold boiled rice

SEASONINGS

- 2 teaspoons soy sauce
- 1 teaspoon curry powder (optional)
- ½ teaspoon salt
  Pinch white pepper

- 1 cup bean sprouts
- 2 tablespoons cooked peas
- 2 tablespoons roasted whole peanuts, skins removed

To stir-fry, set wok (or wide frying pan) over high heat. Add 2 tablespoons oil, swirling pan to coat sides. When oil is hot, add eggs and scramble. Remove and set aside. Add remaining oil and when hot, stir in pork, shrimp, and onion. Toss for 1 minute and then add rice. Stir-fry until rice is soft and separates, then add eggs along with SEASONINGS and bean sprouts. Toss to mix well and add peas quickly. Sprinkle with peanuts to serve.

• Notes •

1. Use medium heat to stir-fry rice; later when all ingredients are added, raise the temperature to high to bring out the flavor. Remember to stir constantly to prevent rice from sticking. I always pull the wok off the burner when adding ingredients, then return to heat to stir-fry.

3. You can add a little more oil if the rice begins to stick or a little water if it gets too dry.

4. I first tried serving fried rice with bean sprouts, curry, and peanuts some years ago. My customers always made it a special request so now I offer it to you.

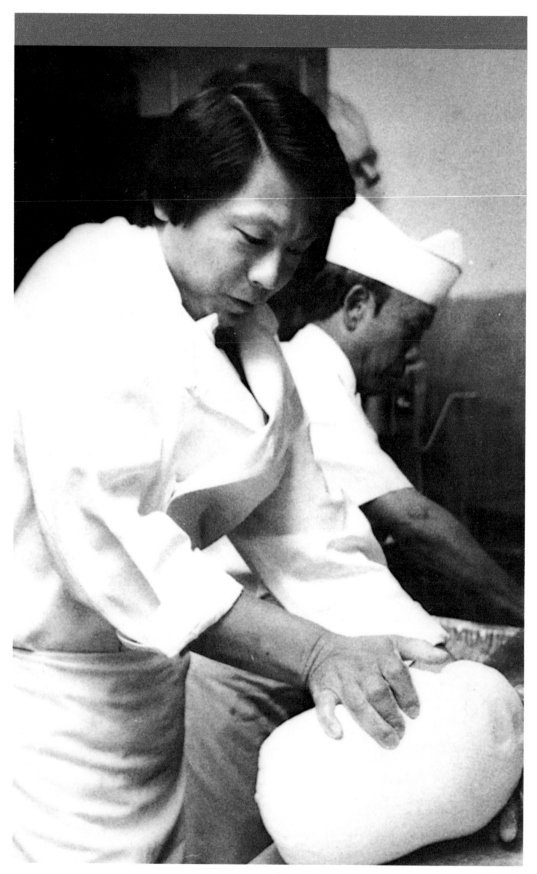

Rick Smolan

PASTRIES & DESSERTS

Pastries or snacks, such as the steam buns served in "dim sum"—which loosely translated, means sweet thing to please the heart—are consumed all day long, from breakfast to bedtime. (Won-ton soup is really a snack and is not served as a soup to accompany a meal in China.)

The pastry recipes that follow are wonderful as luncheon treats or tea-time morsels. And if there are any left over, place them in the refrigerator—your children will make them disappear.

The photograph on pages 180-181 shows a sampling of the wonderful snacks for which recipes appear in the following pages; snacks such as the popular Potsticker, so named because its base is cooked until it is browned and, in the process, adheres to the pan and must be gently pried away to be served (gently so that it's juices, sealed in the pastry, aren't lost—until *you* bite into it).

In China, street vendors sell many of these snacks in the early morning to be purchased by people as they hurry off to work. The vendors seem to disappear in the midday and reappear in the evening, again, with snacks for nibbling as one strolls in the street or park or socializes with friends. This practice may be seen in Hong Kong or Taiwan. Street vendors aren't common in America, but dim sum houses are thriving in cosmopolitan areas.

Chinese desserts are artful and tasty but sometimes don't meet the American craving for a rich finale to a meal. Nevertheless, I urge you to try them. Lichee Nut Blossoms are a delightful, cooling combination of fresh fruit, lichee nuts, and liqueur served over shaved ice. Almond Cream Squares taste like sponge cake but have the texture of jello or rich custard. Two elaborate desserts that take time to prepare are Glazed Apples—wedges of apple, dipped in batter and deep-fried, and then carmelized in a golden syrup—and Eight Treasure Rice Pudding. A photograph of this impressive fruit-studded pudding appears on page 177.

Chinese, as a rule, do not have a "sweet tooth" so our desserts have a lightly sweetened flavor rather than being richly sweet. We don't ever add sugar to our tea, either!

Or, you may want to forget a fancy dessert and relax and do what the Chinese do—bring out a basket of fresh fruit!

Kneading dough by hand is an important step in bread making. Chinese cooks believe the "warmth" of one's hands gives dough character.

Basic Bread Dough

What a rich chicken broth is to a soup, this basic bread dough is to many of my Chinese pastries or snacks. You're lost without it! Even in China, a cook's all-purpose steamed bread dough is the basis for any type of dumpling, cake, or bun.

Makes: 1 recipe dough
Cooking time: None

- ¾ cup warm water (about 110°F)
- 1 tablespoon sugar
- ½ cup warm milk (about 110°F)
- ½ package active dry yeast
- 4 cups all-purpose flour
- ½ teaspoon baking powder

Combine water and sugar well. Stir in milk and check temperature (it should be about 110°F). Add yeast, stirring to dissolve, and set aside until mixture begins to bubble. Gradually add flour, mixing as you go. Knead for 3 to 4 minutes and shape into a ball and cover with a damp cloth to rise in a warm, draft-free spot for about 1 hour or until doubled in size.

Turn dough out onto a floured board, flatten slightly, and sprinkle surface with baking powder. Knead for about 5 minutes until smooth. Set aside, covered, until ready to use.

Butterfly Steamed Bread   *Pictured on page 33*

The name gives away the festive shape of these simple buns. I usually serve them as an accompaniment to all types of duck, Five-spice Beef, or Chinese Barbecued Pork.

Makes: 24 snacks
Cooking time: 15 minutes

- 1 recipe Basic Bread Dough (above)
- 2 tablespoons vegetable oil Decorative stamp and red food coloring

Prepare dough as directed above.

To shape, roll dough into a cylinder about 1-inch in diameter. Cut cylinder into pieces 1½-inch wide. With cut side up, press dough down with palm to flatten. Brush upper edge of pancake with oil; fold pancake in half (oil side in) and press down lightly to seal. With thumb and index finger, pinch together along folded edge to seal tightly. Using a thick utensil such as a cleaver, make 3 indentations along curved edge. Place on a floured cookie sheet to rise in a warm place for 10 minutes.

To steam, line the inside of a bamboo steamer with wet cheesecloth to prevent sticking. Arrange buns on cheesecloth, cover, and steam over boiling water for about 12 minutes.

To decorate, remove buns and let cool slightly. Dip stamp into red food coloring and then onto surface of bun.

*Eight-treasure pudding (page 191)
is sophisticated in presentation yet
simple to prepare. Dried fruit and
seeds, intricately placed in mold of
sweetened rice, resemble a crown,
regal enough to top off the most
festive Chinese banquet.*

Steamed Pork Buns

Prepared bread dough is shaped into buns and then filled with a stuffing made of diced barbecued pork, green onion, and flavorful oyster sauce. When steamed, they become puffy and white. Pork buns are prepared all over China though they originated in Canton province.

Makes: 12 to 18 snacks
Cooking time: 25 minutes

- 1 recipe Basic Bread Dough (page 176)
- 1 tablespoon vegetable oil

FILLING

- ½ pound Chinese Barbecued Pork (page 39), diced
- 1 green onion (white part), minced
- ½ cup chicken broth
- 3 tablespoons oyster sauce
- 1 tablespoon dry sherry
- 1 tablespoon sugar
- ¼ teaspoon salt

  Cornstarch paste
- ½ teaspoon sesame oil

Prepare dough as directed on page 176.

To stir-fry, heat wok (or wide frying pan) over high heat for 1 minute until hot. Add oil and swirl pan to coat sides. When oil is hot, add pork and onion, stirring for 30 seconds. Mix in broth, oyster sauce, sherry, sugar, and salt. Bring to a boil, thicken with 1 tablespoon cornstarch paste, and sprinkle with sesame oil. Transfer to a bowl, cool, and refrigerate until thickened.

To assemble, roll dough into a cylinder about 2 inches in diameter. Cut cylinder into pieces 1½ inches wide. With a cut side up, press down with palm of hand to flatten. Place 1 tablespoon filling in center of dough. Gather up edges of dough around filling in loose folds. Bring folds together at top and twist securely to make a stem as illustrated. Let rise in a warm place for 10 minutes.

To steam, line the inside of a bamboo steamer with wet cheesecloth. Arrange buns on cheesecloth, cover, and steam over boiling water for 12 minutes.

1) Place 1 tablespoon filling in center of flattened dough. Gather up edges around filling in loose folds. Bring together at top and 2) twist securely to seal and make a small stem.

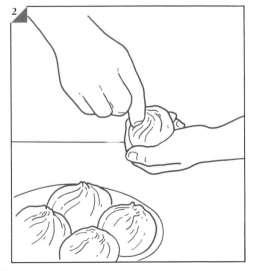

Shanghai Pan-fried Dumplings

Really a first cousin to Chinese potstickers, this dumpling differs slightly in the texture after cooking. The top is soft while the bottom is chewy and crunchy. Traditionally, pan-fried dumplings are eaten at breakfast or as a snack rather than during a meal.

Makes: 24 snacks
Cooking time: 15 minutes

- 1 recipe Basic Bread Dough (page 176)

FILLING
- ½ pound ground pork
- 1 head bok choy, cored and coarsely chopped
- 1 green onion, minced
- 2 thumb-size slices fresh ginger, minced
- 2 water chestnuts, chopped
- 1 teaspoon sesame oil
- ½ teaspoon sugar
- 1 teaspoon salt

  Black sesame seeds or sesame seeds
- 3 tablespoons vegetable oil
- ½ cup water

Prepare dough as directed on page 176.

Combine FILLING ingredients well and refrigerate until firm.

To assemble, roll dough into a cylinder about 1 inch in diameter. Cut cylinder into 24 pieces, each about 1½ inches wide. With cut side up, flatten pieces with palm of hand. Fill each center with 1 tablespoon filling. Pull edges of dough up over filling, twisting a small stem where drawn together as illustrated. Sprinkle tops with sesame seeds.

To pan-fry, heat a cast-iron or other heavy-bottom skillet over moderate heat. Add oil, swirling to coat bottom. Put buns in skillet, pour in water, and cover with a tight-fitting lid. Cook for about 8 minutes without removing cover. When water has evaporated, remove lid and let buns brown slightly for 2 to 3 minutes (watch carefully to prevent burning).

1) Spread 1 tablespoon filling in center of flattened dough. 2) Pull edges of dough up over filling, 3) pleating as you go, and 4) twist securely at top to seal and make a small stem.

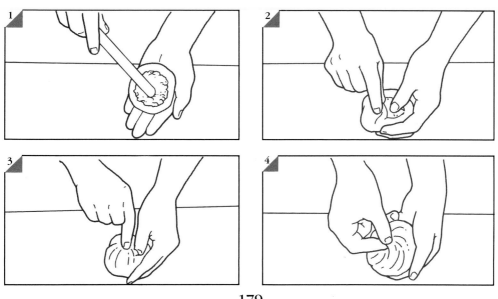

Savory dim sum, perfect for snacks and afternoon tea, including tempting array of dumplings and filled Chinese pastries. Arranged on decorative Chinese dishes are (clockwise, from top): pan-fried dumplings (page 179) and Shanghai onion cake (186); bamboo steamer and plate of butterfly steamed bread (176); four season dumplings, colorful pork and shrimp-filled pastries with toppings of minced black mushrooms, onion, carrot, and cilantro (page 183); crescent-shaped potstickers (page 185); and in center, silver thread buns (page 182).

Steamed Silver Thread Buns   *Pictured on page 180*

Because rice is rarely served at a banquet, Chinese often present dumplings or other pastries such as these fancy-shaped ones. Originating from Hunan, they have been adapted to be served as a snack as well.

Makes: 12 snacks
Cooking time: 20 minutes

- 1 recipe Basic Bread Dough (page 176)
- 5 tablespoons lard (or vegetable shortening)
- ¼ teaspoon salt
- 2 tablespoons sugar
- 2 tablespoons minced Virginia ham or other ham

Prepare dough as directed on page 176.

To shape, flatten dough slightly and put in 2 tablespoons lard and salt. Knead well for 5 minutes. Roll out into a rectangle about ¼-inch thick. Spread with remaining 3 tablespoons lard and sprinkle with sugar. Fold dough into thirds, like a letter, to make a rectangle.

Cut off 5 thin slivers from end of rectangle for each bun. Holding tops of slivers together, gently stretch dough until it reaches 6 inches long. Starting at one end and still holding slices together, roll dough into a ball. Tuck end into opening at top (or bottom) to secure as illustrated.

Sprinkle tops with just a little ham and let stand for about 10 minutes.

To steam, line the inside of a steamer with a wet towel to prevent sticking. Arrange buns in steamer, cover, and steam over boiling water for about 10 minutes.

1) Cut off 5 thin slivers of dough from end, making a piece. (Cut remaining dough in same way, making a total of 12 pieces.) Rotate piece of dough quarter-turn, and 2) holding ends of slivers together, gently stretch until dough reaches 6 inches long. 3) Starting at one end, wrap dough round and round in spiral shape and then 4) tuck end into opening at top to secure.

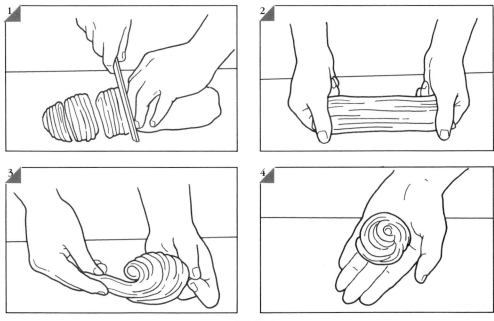

Four-season Dumplings   *Pictured on page 180*

Your guests will think you spent hours making these colorful gourmet snacks. After shaping bread dough around a spoonful of seasoned meat filling, you top the cloverleaf dumpling with four seasons' toppings: finely minced white onion, carrot, black mushroom, and Chinese parsley.

Makes: 24 snacks
Cooking time: 15 minutes

- 2 cups all-purpose flour
- ¼ cup boiling water
- ¼ cup cold water

FOUR SEASONS TOPPINGS

- 3 dried black mushrooms
- ¼ small white onion, minced
- 2 teaspoons minced carrot
- 10 stalks Chinese parsley (cilantro), minced

FILLING

- ½ pound ground pork
- 10 medium-size prawns, minced (optional)
- ¼ teaspoon minced fresh ginger
- 1 green onion (white part), minced
- 2 tablespoons bamboo shoots, minced
- ¾ teaspoon salt
  Pinch white pepper
- ¼ teaspoon sugar
- ¼ teaspoon sesame oil

  Bok choy or lettuce leaves

  Hot Chili Oil (page 212), or purchased
  Red rice vinegar
  Soy sauce

To make dough, combine flour and boiling water together in a mixing bowl, then stir in cold water. Shape into a ball and then turn out onto a floured board; knead for about 3 minutes. Cover with a damp towel and set aside for 10 minutes.

Meanwhile, soak mushrooms in warm water for 20 minutes; drain, remove stems, and mince. Set aside with remaining FOUR SEASONS TOPPINGS.

Combine FILLING ingredients thoroughly; refrigerate.

To assemble, knead dough again for 3 to 5 minutes until smooth. Roll into a cylinder 1-inch in diameter. Cut off ends, then cut into pieces ¾-inch wide. With a cut side up, press dough down with palm to flatten. Roll out with rolling pin into pancakes 2½-inches wide.

Place 1 teaspoon filling in center of pancake. Join opposite sides of pancake together by pinching at the top; then pinch remaining (opposite) sides at top to form a square with 4 holes—it should look like a 4-leaf clover. With a finger, spread open each hole slightly, pushing filling down to the bottom. Place dumplings on a cookie sheet and partially freeze.

To decorate, drop some white onion into the first hole, carrot in the second, black mushrooms in the third, and parsley into the fourth. Repeat for remaining dumplings.

To steam, line the inside of a steamer with bok choy leaves. Arrange dumplings in steamer, cover, and steam over boiling water for about 10 minutes.

To serve, without removing cover, bring steamer to the table on a large serving platter. Lift off lid to serve with dipping sauce made of chili oil, vinegar, and soy sauce in proportions to suit your taste.

• Notes •

1. You can chop the filling ingredients together in a food processor—just don't overprocess so that the ingredients lose their texture.

2. Partially freezing the dumplings before decorating helps to retain the shape and firmness.

Lichee Nut Blossoms

Lichee nuts come from the tropical regions of China and are used often when preparing simple Chinese desserts such as this one. A number of other fruits may be substituted or added depending on the season. We added kumquats, watermelon, and kiwi for the dessert pictured below.

Makes: 4 servings
Cooking time: None

- 4 champagne or other stemmed glasses
  Crushed ice
- 1 can (10 oz.) seedless lichee nuts, drained
- 4 maraschino cherries
- 1 ounce Cointreau

Fill each champagne glass half full of crushed ice. Distribute lichee nuts equally among glasses. Top each dessert with a cherry and a splash of Cointreau.

Variation: Rainbow Fruit Cups. Layer kumquats, loquats, and lichee nuts in regular or tall parfait glasses to create a rainbow effect. Use fewer kumquats since they are stronger in flavor than loquats and lichee nuts. Top with cherries and Cointreau as directed above, or with slices of kiwi.

• Note •

You can substitute Triple Sec or other fruity liquers for Cointreau if desired.

Potstickers *Pictured on page 180*

Here's a typical Northern Chinese pastry that's well-known and prepared throughout the world. Though eaten as a snack in China, I find that most Americans serve potstickers as an appetizer.

Makes: About 2 dozen
Cooking time: 15 minutes

DOUGH

2   cups all-purpose flour
½   cup water

FILLING

½   pound ground pork
½   small head Chinese (Napa) cabbage, cored and chopped
1   green onion, coarsely chopped
2   thumb-size slices fresh ginger, minced
2   water chestnuts, chopped
1   teaspoon salt
½   teaspoon sugar
    Pinch white pepper
1   teaspoon sesame oil

5   tablespoons vegetable oil
1   cup water

    Hot chili oil
    Red rice vinegar
    Soy Sauce

In a bowl, combine flour and water, mixing to form a ball. Remove to a floured board and knead with palm of hand for about 3 minutes. Shape into a ball, cover with damp towel, and let stand for about 10 minutes.

To make filling, combine FILLING ingredients well and refrigerate until ready to use.

To shape and assemble, knead dough for about 3 minutes. Roll into a cylinder that is about 1 inch in diameter. Cut off ends, then cut into about 24 pieces, each ¾-inch wide. With a cut side up, press dough down with palm to flatten. Roll out with a rolling pin to make pancakes about 2½ inches in diameter.

Spoon 1 tablespoon filling into center of each pancake. Fold dough over to make half circle and pleat edges firmly together.

To pan-fry, heat cast-iron or other heavy-bottom skillet over moderate heat. Add 3 tablespoons oil swirling to coat bottom. When oil is hot, place potstickers, seam side up, in skillet and agitate (shake) for 30 seconds. Pour in water, cover, and gently boil over moderate heat for 7 to 8 minutes. When oil and water start to sizzle, add remaining 2 tablespoons oil. Tip skillet to distribute oil evenly; watch carefully (uncovered)) to prevent sticking. When bottoms are brown, remove from heat and carefully lift out potstickers with spatula.

To serve, turn potstickers over (dark side up) and arrange on serving platter. Combine chili oil, vinegar, and soy sauce in proportions to suit your taste and offer sauce for dipping.

• Notes •

1. You can freeze uncooked potstickers for later use but remember to squeeze out the water from cabbage during preparation (in a colander or cheesecloth). Freeze potstickers separately on cookie sheets until firm, then put them in plastic bags.

2. When rolling out the pancakes, leave the centers slightly thicker than the edges. A thicker center will hold up better during the browning.

3. If you prefer, steam potstickers for about 12 minutes over boiling water instead of pan-frying.

Follow the many complex flavors of Chinese meal with simple, chilled dessert of sliced kiwi, kumquats, watermelon, and lichee nuts, offered in glass stemware filled with shaved ice and Cointreau. (Recipe on page 184.)

Shanghai Onion Cakes   *Pictured on page 181*

Cooked within the several layers of dough are concealed, aromatic green onions. A delicious snack.

Makes: 24 snacks
Cooking time: 25 minutes

- 2 cups all-purpose flour
- ½ cup boiling water
- ¼ cup cold water

  Vegetable oil
- 1 teaspoon salt
- 2 green onions,
  coarsely chopped

- 2 tablespoons lard,
  vegetable oil, or chopped
  bacon

To shape, mix flour and boiling water with chopsticks in a bowl; then add cold water. Remove to a board and knead with palm of hand for 3 minutes. Cover with a damp towel for 10 minutes. Then knead again for 3 to 5 minutes. Roll into a cylinder about 2 inches in diameter. Cut cylinder into 6 sections.

With either cut side up, press dough down with palm to flatten. Roll out into 7- or 8-inch pancakes.

To assemble, brush each surface of pancake with oil. Sprinkle evenly with a pinch of salt and chopped green onion. Roll up jellyroll fashion; then wind jellyroll in a spiral (it should look like a snail). Flatten slightly with heel of palm; then flatten more with rolling pin, making each "snail" about 5 inches in diameter.

To pan-fry, heat a cast-iron or other heavy-bottom skillet over moderate heat. Brush with oil. When hot, fry pancake on both sides for about 5 to 6 minutes total or until it turns brown and a crust is formed. Remove and wrap in a dry towel to keep warm. Cut into fourths to serve.

Mandarin Pancakes   *Pictured on page 116*

Simple-to-make pancakes that serve as "wrappers" for Peking Duck or Mu Shu Pork.

Makes: 1½ dozen
Cooking time: 40 minutes

- 2 cups all-purpose flour
- ½ cup boiling water
- ¼ cup cold water

  Vegetable oil

To shape, mix flour and boiling water with chopsticks in a bowl; then add cold water. Remove to a board and knead with palm of hand for 3 minutes. Cover with a damp towel for 10 minutes. Then knead again for 3 to 5 minutes. Roll into a cylinder about 1½-inches in diameter. Cut off ends, then cut cylinder into 1½-inch-thick pieces.

With either cut side up, press dough down with palm to flatten. Brush one pancake with oil, then place another pancake on top. Roll out into a 5- or 6-inch pancake.

To pan-fry, heat cast-iron or other heavy-bottom skillet over moderate heat. Brush with oil. When hot, cook pancake on both sides for about 1 minute on each side or until it starts to puff and turn lightly brown. Remove from pan, separating into 2 pancakes (they come apart easily). Wrap in dry towel to retain moisture.

To serve, reheat pancakes, wrapped in a damp towel, in steamer for about 5 minutes; keep warm.

Glazed Apples   *Pictured on page 80*

Originating in Northern China, this is a most prestigious dessert. Apple wedges are coated with batter and deep-fried; then they're carmelized to a golden brown in sugary syrup and sprinkled with black sesame seeds. Timing is very important so read through the recipe completely before starting.

Makes: 8 servings
Cooking time: 15 minutes

BATTER

- ¾ cup all-purpose flour
- ¼ cup cornstarch
- ½ cup water
    Pinch salt
- ¼ teaspoon baking powder
- 1 teaspoon vegetable oil

- 2 large firm apples

    Vegetable oil, for deep-frying

SYRUP

- 1 teaspoon vegetable oil
- 1¼ cups sugar
- ¼ cup water

- 1 tablespoon toasted black sesame seeds (or toasted regular sesame seeds)

    Ice water

Combine BATTER ingredients with a wire whip; mix well and let stand for 10 minutes.

Peel and core apples, cut into eighths, and immediately plunge into cold water to prevent discoloration. Just before using, drain and pat dry.

To deep-fry, heat 4 cups oil in a wok to 300°. Using a toothpick, coat apples with batter, shake off excess, and carefully drop into oil. Deep-fry for about 3 minutes or until a crust is formed. Remove, drain on paper towels, and trim off uneven parts of crust. (Remove any batter pieces left in oil.)

To deep-fry again, raise oil temperature to 350°. Return apples and deep-fry for about 1½ minutes or until golden brown. Remove and drain.

To make syrup, meanwhile, heat wok or wide frying pan over moderate heat. Add oil, swirling to coat sides. Add sugar and water, stirring constantly and vigorously to prevent burning. Continue stirring until bubbles disappear and syrup is clear. You may need to move wok off and on heat occasionally to prevent burning. When syrup carmelizes, add apples and sesame seeds; mix quickly until each apple is coated with syrup. Remove to a lightly oiled plate.

To serve, using tongs or chopsticks, gently pull apples apart to form a taffy-like effect. Immediately drop apples into bowl of ice water for 5 seconds—this changes the glaze to a crackling sugary crust. Remove and serve immediately.

• *Notes* •

1. Substitute 2 firm ripe bananas for the apples.

2. You may need to dust apples with a little cornstarch if the batter doesn't seem to stick well.

3. Timing is so critical!! Watch the syrup carefully as it starts to carmelize—it shouldn't be overcooked.

Banana Sesame

A typical Chinese dinner concludes with fresh fruit. Banana Sesame—bite-size pieces of fried banana sweetened with toasted sesame seeds and powdered sugar—is a tropical adaptation popular in Taiwan and South China.

Makes: 6 servings
Cooking time: 15 minutes

BATTER

- ¾ cup flour
- ½ cup cornstarch
- ½ teaspoon baking powder
  Pinch salt
  Pinch sugar
- ¾ cup water
- 1 teaspoon vegetable oil
  Few drops yellow food coloring (optional)

- 2 firm ripe bananas

  Vegetable oil, for deep-frying

- 2 tablespoons sesame seeds, lightly toasted
- 2 tablespoons powdered sugar

Combine BATTER ingredients using a wire whisk; let stand for 30 minutes.

Peel bananas and slice diagonally into pieces, dropping into batter; set aside.

To deep-fry, heat 4 cups oil in a wok (or electric deep-fat fryer) to 300°. Using a toothpick, pick up coated banana and let drain; carefully drop into oil and deep-fry for about 2 minutes or until a crust is formed. Remove, drain on paper towels, and trim off uneven parts of crust. Remove any batter particles in oil.

To deep-fry again, raise oil temperature to 350°. Return bananas and fry for about 2 minutes or until golden brown. Remove, drain on paper towels, and arrange on serving platter.

To serve, crush sesame seeds with rolling pin and combine with sugar. Sprinkle on bananas to serve.

• Note •

You can eliminate the sesame seed/sugar mixture and simply arrange fried bananas on a bed of fresh sweetened whipped cream.

Almond Cream Squares

I'd describe this refreshing almond-flavored dessert as a cross between jello, custard, and sponge cake. It tastes best when served cold.

Makes: 8 to 10 servings
Cooking time: 5 minutes

2 quarts water
1 ounce agar-agar
½ cup sugar
1½ cups milk
¾ to 1 ounce almond extract

Fruit cocktail or other fresh fruit in light syrup

Bring water to a boil in saucepan. Stir in agar-agar until completely dissolved. Add sugar and stir until dissolved. Remove from heat and add milk and almond extract. Pour into a shallow pan and chill until firm.

To serve, cut chilled mixture into ½-inch cubes; spoon into serving dishes and top with fruit.

• *Notes* •

1. Change the flavor to coconut by eliminating the almond extract and substituting coconut milk for regular milk. Add 1 ounce flaked coconut before chilling as well.

2. For a more dramatic presentation, chill almond mixture in a 2- to 2½-quart mold. To serve, invert mold onto platter and arrange fruit around base.

Eight Treasure Rice Pudding   *Pictured on page 177*

Probably the most impressive dessert in terms of presentation, this sweet dish resembles a jewel-studded crown and is served traditionally at banquets or on holidays.

Makes: 10 to 12 servings
Cooking time: 1½ hours

2 cups sweet rice
(glutinous rice)

FRUITS

10 preserved dragon eyes
(or any preserved fruit)
6 preserved red dates
2 tablespoons raisins
2 pieces preserved candied
kumquat, chopped
12 candied lotus seeds
1 maraschino cherry, halved
3 preserved green plums,
cut in fourths

¼ cup vegetable oil
½ cup sugar
½ can (10 oz.) red bean
paste

SYRUP

¼ cup sugar
1 cup cold water

Cornstarch paste

Soak rice in warm water for 2 hours or over-night; drain well.

To steam, line the inside of a steamer with wet cheesecloth. Place rice on cheesecloth, cover, and steam over boiling water for 25 minutes.

Meanwhile, soak dragon eyes in warm water for 10 minutes; drain and cut into small pieces. Also soak dates in warm water for 10 minutes; drain and cut into fourths.

To assemble, line 2 small bowls (about 1 quart each) that are suitable for steaming with plastic wrap. Combine rice, oil, and sugar together. Evenly divide half the rice (reserving other half) between both bowls; press rice up the sides of bowl to line, forming a well in the center.

Mix reserved half of rice with raisins, kumquats, dragon eyes, and some of the lotus seeds. Spoon all but 1 cup rice mixture into each well, still keeping a small well in the center. Fill each small well with half the bean paste, then cover entirely with remaining rice mixture.

Invert bowls on a plate and carefully remove (plastic lining should remain in bowls). Arrange plums, dates, cherries, and remaining lotus seeds decoratively on mounds as illustrated. Carefully put plastic-lined bowls back onto rice mounds and turn right side up.

To steam again, place bowls on rack in steamer, cover, and steam over boiling water for about 1 hour.

Meanwhile, combine SYRUP ingredients in a saucepan. Bring to a boil and then thicken with 1 tablespoon cornstarch paste until the consistency of syrup is reached.

To serve, invert bowls on serving plate and remove plastic wrap. Pour syrup over mounds.

• *Notes* •

1. Plastic wrap is essential—it keeps the rice mixture from sticking to the bowls.

2. The rice should be very soft; the longer you steam it, the more flavorful it becomes.

3. The "eight treasures" can be varied according to your taste. Choose any preserved candy or fruit.

THINGS TO KNOW

Just like any motion, cutting requires skill. I learned from experience that it takes years of practice to achieve good cutting skills. There is an old saying in China that suggests knowledgeable people can tell how accomplished the chef is by the appearance of his cuts. The real art of cutting, according to the Chinese, is to make the cuts perfectly even. When this is achieved, the results are appreciated even more.

Just how important is cutting correctly? Well, aside from the aesthetics of having a better looking dish, cutting is also important because *it affects the overall cooking time.* Many Chinese recipes, especially ones that specify only a short cooking time, rely on ingredients that are uniformly cut. If the ingredients start out the same size, there's a much better chance that they will cook evenly.

You may not become proficient at cutting uniformly right away. However, the information in this section plus the simple-to-follow directions and illustrations should help you to better understand just what to strive for. Keep in mind that practice does make perfect and in no time you'll be displaying abilities that rival a master chef's.

Here's a short description of cutting techniques used in Chinese cooking:

Slicing: to cut into thin pieces, $\frac{1}{16}$- to $\frac{1}{8}$-inch thick and 1 to $1\frac{1}{2}$ inches across

Slant cutting: to slice diagonally, usually $\frac{1}{4}$- to $\frac{1}{2}$-inch thick

Dicing: to cut into $\frac{1}{2}$-inch cubes

Cubing: to cut into $\frac{3}{4}$-inch cubes

Roll cutting: to cut into uniform triangular-shaped pieces

Shredding: to slice finely into matchstick-size pieces

Shaving: to cut into paper-thin slices

Chopping: to cut into pieces

Smashing: to flatten ingredient, using the side of a cleaver or large knife

Processing: to cut using different blades of a food processor

Saturday cooking classes in the studio at Chef Chu's restaurant are supplemented by occasional evening classes off-the-premises. Here, classes are conducted at Good Cooks & Company.

193

Cutting Techniques

1) Slicing and 2) dicing are most common cutting methods. 3) Roll cutting into triangular pieces is accomplished by rotating vegetable $1/3$ turn each time cut is made. 4) Shredding and 5) smashing (flattening) are other ways to prepare Chinese ingredients.

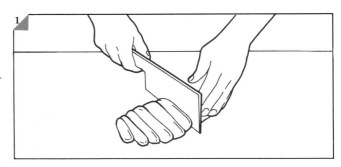

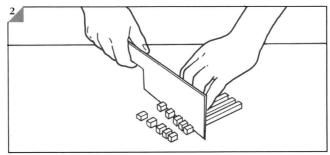

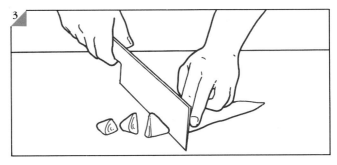

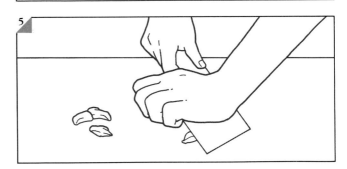

Slicing

Not everyone knows how to slice properly. Of course the shape of the slice depends on what ingredient you're cutting, but a good rule of thumb to remember is "no piece should be larger than bite-size nor thicker than ½-inch."

When slicing meat, cut against the grain to expose more surface. Slices are usually about ¼- by ½- by ½-inch in size. To make slicing easier, partially freeze meat or poultry just before cutting.

Fish should be sliced with the grain; you may have to cut the fish into sections first if it is too large to slice as is.

Slant Cutting

Slice most firm vegetables such as celery, bok choy, and asparagus on the diagonal to expose more of the surface and reduce cooking time. Slant cutting some meats such as flank steak also aids in tenderizing because it breaks down tissues or texture.

Dicing & Cubing

Any ingredient that has been cut into a small piece could be called a die, a cube, or a chunk. The difference between them is size.

Dicing usually produces a piece no longer than ½-inch square, while a cube can measure up to ¾-inch square. A chunk is larger still—up to 1-inch in diameter.

When cutting an ingredient with unstable sides or an uneven size, such as ginger root, cut a thin slice off the top, turn it over, cut-side down, until balanced, and then continue cutting.

Roll Cutting

Cutting a cylindrical vegetable such as a carrot or turnip so that it cooks evenly is tricky. Roll cutting—slicing into triangular pieces—is accomplished while rotating the vegetable. Once the pieces are cut, two sides or surfaces are exposed, thus creating a greater area for absorbing seasoning during cooking.

Make a diagonal cut near one end of the vegetable, rotate it ⅓ of a turn and make a second diagonal cut so that the new cut meets the first one. You've now created a new surface. Now, continue to roll and cut until you reach the end of the vegetable.

Shredding

Shredding is really just slicing and slicing, again and again, until thread-like pieces about 2 inches long are produced. Depending on the purpose, you'll have pieces varying in thickness from ⅛- to ¼-inch thick. Slivers, julienne strips, matchsticks, and french fries are terms used to describe different sizes of shredded ingredients.

Shredding can be done with a knife, cleaver, two forks, a shredder or grater, or even clean bare hands (provided the food has a definite grain running through it). Meat should be shredded with the grain, as should poultry. Both should be cut into sections first, to achieve the proper size.

Shaving

The only way to cut paper-thin slices of raw meat or poultry is to shave it. And the easiest way to do that is to partially freeze it first. You'll need a sharp knife or cleaver and a steady hand.

Chopping

Chopping—this can mean anything from finely diced pieces to coarsely cut chunks—is best accomplished with a cleaver or wide-bladed chef's knife.

Most cooks prefer wooden chopping boards or blocks (see Utensils & Equipment, page 208). The Chinese often use chopping blocks cut from a cross section of a tree limb.

It's a good idea to remember which side of a chopping block is used for onions and which side is used for cutting mild-flavored ingredients. Often enough, the flavors don't compliment each other.

Smashing

Although smashing isn't a cutting technique per se, I've included it here because it's so common in Chinese cooking. Used most often for preparing garlic or ginger, smashing involves placing a piece of food on the chopping board and hitting it with the broad side of the blade of a cleaver or wide knife. After it is crushed, it's usually minced finely and then combined with other ingredients.

Processing

Food processors can be used for slicing or dicing firm ingredients such as cabbage, celery, and carrots. When time is at a premium, you may be willing to sacrifice the appearance of some dishes for the convenience of a food processor. Many jobs such as fine chopping and shredding are accomplished readily—just use common sense when it comes to selecting ingredients.

Cooking Methods & Preconditioning

Each method used in Chinese cooking is different. The descriptions that follow should help you understand them and give you a clear picture of Chinese cuisine and just how diverse it can be.

I often tell my students that when they master the techniques, they can cook Chinese food without using Chinese ingredients. The same applies to you. Once you understand the principles, you've got it made.

Preconditioning

Preconditioning is often the necessary first step required in Chinese cooking, whether it be a simple marinade used to preseason meat or an actual cooking process, such as oil-blanching, used to partially cook food.

Marinating

Marinating is used to season an ingredient and to bring out its natural flavor, to tenderize (usually by adding a liquid), and to change the texture of an ingredient. Most marinades used in Chinese cooking are a simple combination of flavors.

Oil-blanching

Oil-blanching—really a form of deep-frying but at a lower temperature and for a shorter time—helps to separate ingredients as well as form a light crust to seal in the flavor. It also acts to shorten the overall cooking time and helps create a uniform texture.

Most professional chefs use some form of oil-blanching but rarely do you see it described in cookbooks. I always mention it to my students because I firmly believe you can broaden your Chinese cooking expertise if you know some of the "trade secrets" such as oil-blanching.

Unlike deep-fat frying that is actually a complete cooking process, oil-blanching is just a quick frying that always is followed by some other cooking method, such as stir-frying or steaming.

When estimating just how much oil to use, I suggest about 2 cups oil for each cup of food to be blanched at one time. Remember, oil used for blanching and deep-frying is reusable. You can recycle it, once it's cooled, by pouring it through a fine strainer directly into a jar or bottle fitted with a tight-sealing lid. Refrigerate for up to 1 month.

The oil temperature is usually low during blanching, although 3 different levels are mentioned in our recipes:

Lukewarm (275°–300°) is the most com-

monly used. Ingredients are cooked evenly and this is a good temperature for preconditioning large quantities.

Low (200°) is nicknamed "hot wok and cold oil" and is used for blanching delicate ingredients such as sole and scallops. Its main purpose to prevent discoloration and to help retain the shape of the ingredients.

High (350°) is used to seal in flavor, preserve tenderness, and create an outside texture or light crunch.

Oil temperature is determined by the ingredients you plan to blanch as well as the texture you want to achieve. Some recipes suggest that you recheck the oil temperature from time to time, especially when doing large quantities over a long period of time. The easiest way to determine oil temperature is to use a thermometer; any small thermometer (one with a disc-like face that reads from 200° to 450°) that can rest or be attached to the side of the wok is fine.

Water-blanching

Water-blanching, used primarily for vegetables, is a simple process where ingredients are immersed in boiling water for just a few minutes. The vegetables are partially cooked and have been "sealed," locking in vital nutrients and flavor.

I usually recommend blanching in chicken broth, if available, because its rich flavor is absorbed readily, especially by bland tasting vegetables. Just like oil, chicken broth can be recycled for future use, too. Allow it to cool and then pour through a fine strainer into a jar or bottle. Refrigerate up to 2 weeks.

Some Chinese dishes combine vegetables. Firmer ones, such as broccoli and carrots, need to be blanched slightly longer than softer ones like snow peas. If you skip water-blanching and simply try to stir-fry 4 or 5 different vegetables, you would never be able to cook them evenly in a wok or skillet.

Vegetables that are preconditioned by

water-blanching, retain their crunchy taste and fresh color, cook more evenly, and most important, retain much of their nutrients.

Par-boiling
Par-boiling is just that—boiling. It is helpful (and often necessary) when preconditioning tougher cuts of meat, root vegetables such as potatoes, and other firm ingredients. Quite often, ingredients used in stewing or braising have been par-boiled first.

Cooking
Stir-frying
Its name conveys the motion—keeping the ingredient in constant motion by stirring with a spatula. It could also be called toss-frying or sautéing.

Most stir-fried recipes follow this sequence: preheat the wok, add oil to prevent sticking, add spices (or enhancers such as ginger and garlic) to create an aroma, combine main ingredients while quickly cooking, stir in a seasoning sauce, and finally thicken the sauce just before serving.

I like to cook over a fairly high heat because it produces a "wok aroma" or fragrance that is produced from spices added just before the main ingredients. Ginger and green onion and perhaps garlic are good examples. As they start to brown slightly in a hot wok, they create an aroma that signals you to move on to the next step. Practice is the best way to perfect your ability to smell a wok's aroma.

When vegetables are stir-fried, it takes only a few minutes, especially if they have been preconditioned or water-blanched first. You want them to be *al dente* or slightly crunchy when removed from the heat because they continue to cook a little longer, just by using the heat they've acquired.

There are some instances where an intensive heat, almost to the point of smoking, is needed. Vegetables that have lots of water, such as bean sprouts, and other tender ingredients such as liver and squid, require just a few seconds in a hot wok to force out their flavor. You want to preserve their tenderness and texture and avoid overcooking.

Cook in batches, if you need to. Overloading a wok can cause burning because not enough oil remains in the bottom. And overloading can also result in soggy food; the temperature never gets high enough so the food is cooked longer.

Deep-frying
Before we get into deep-frying, let me offer an observation about Chinese cooking and the use of oils. Despite the great amount of oil used, Chinese food isn't greasy in the least bit, or it shouldn't be. That's because ingredients are cooked so quickly they don't "sit" in oil for long periods of time. Proper use of oil as well as correct temperature, results in greaseless, flavorful cooking.

Deep-frying does require more oil than stir-frying. I usually suggest 3 cups of oil for each cup of food. As I mentioned, proper temperature—and that includes maintaining the proper temperature—is essential. Unless otherwise noted, 350° to 375° is the normal temperature range for deep-frying.

I've discovered that an electric deep-fat fryer with a reliable thermostat (one that tells the actual temperature in degrees, rather than just "Low" or "Medium") can be very helpful. If you do a fair amount of cooking, you may want to invest in one.

Although I always recommend using a thermometer, at least when beginning Chinese cooking, you can learn to judge the approximate temperature of oil in a wok this way.

Drop a small amount of batter into the oil. If the temperature is:

Under 300°	Batter will drop to the bottom
300°–325°	Batter will drop down and rise slowly
325°–350°	Batter will come up immediately
350°–375°	Batter will not reach the bottom at all
Over 375°	Batter will splatter on the surface

You can deep-fry many different ways, depending on the ingredients used and the texture you want to create.

Dry deep-fry. No batter is used, just dry flour or powder. Deep-fry until the surface reaches a golden brown. Using a higher temperature prevents the flour from separating from the food during frying. Canton Salt-baked Prawns is an example.

Soft deep-fry. Marinated ingredients are coated with batter and then deep-fried until a golden brown is reached. Phoenix Tail Fried Prawns and Sweet & Sour Pork are good examples.

Crispy deep-fry. Ingredients are marinated, then steamed (or sometimes hung to dry) before being deep-fried. Many classic duck dishes are prepared this way.

Seasoned deep-fry. The ingredients are seasoned before being deep-fried. Chef Chu's Pork Chops exemplifies this method.

Double-fry. Either with or without batter, this process is designed for large pieces that often cannot cook completely at just one time. First the food is fried at a low temperature, to partially cook it; then the temperature is raised, and it is deep-fried again to create a crispy texture on the outside. Lemon Chicken is a good example.

Steaming
Steaming is done over boiling water but never in it. Ingredients are usually placed on a footed dish or in a bowl and then placed on a perforated tray in the steamer or wok.

Steaming is used to cook food in its own natural juices; to help flavors penetrate all the ingredients; to cook large pieces of meat, especially when another cooking method follows; and to maintain the food's original shape.

Most dishes can be steamed in a metal steamer or wok fitted with a tight lid and a steamer rack. However, for soft items such as Chinese pastries and buns, it's best to use a bamboo steamer. Because the baskets stack, you can steam several different dishes at once. For an impressive display, bring the steaming basket to the table for serving.

Some recipes use a dry-steaming process where food is placed in a bowl, covered, and then set in the steamer. Other recipes require a mold (or bowl). Slices or bite-size pieces of food are decoratively arranged inside the mold; the mold is then placed in the steamer to cook. When ready to serve, invert the mold onto a serving platter.

Braising
In braising, meat, fish or firm vegetables are browned in a little oil. Then they're cooked in a small amount of liquid over low heat until the liquid is reduced to a sauce and the spices have penetrated the food. A good example of this process can be found in the recipe for Szechuan Dry-braised Prawns.

Red Cooking
Red cooking, or *hung tsau,* is a Chinese term referring to a slow-cooking process similar to stewing. Meat is browned first and then cooked in plenty of liquid—usually dark soy sauce and other seasonings—until tender. Cooking time ranges from 1 to 4 hours and the result is a succulent piece of meat with a robust, reddish-brown color.

Associating
Associating means combining assorted ingredients that are precooked and preconditioned. They have either been oil-blanched, deep-fried, or boiled. After combining the ingredients, the dish is cooked for a short time over high heat to bring out the various kinds of flavors.

Pan-frying
Since a wok can act like a grill, you can pan-fry or brown ingredients with just the slightest amount of oil over a moderate heat. After browning, the food is usually dipped into a sauce or combined with another ingredient.

Poaching
A good definition of poaching is "gradual cooking in a liquid over moderate heat." Oftentimes, spices such as ginger and green onion are added to the poaching liquid for flavor.

Smoking
Normally, meat is cured or partially cooked before being slowly smoked. Traditionally, Chinese do their smoke-cooking in a large oven (often outdoors) that contains tea leaves, pine needles, or sawdust from aromatic pieces of wood. During the slow process, the smoky taste permeates the meat. However, a similar smoky taste can be achieved in a shorter time, using a large wok lined with foil. Tea leaves are scattered at the bottom along with a little uncooked rice and sugar. The wok is quickly heated and the smoke penetrates the meat. (See Tea-smoked Duck, on page 84.)

Simmering in Master Sauce
A master sauce is a concentrated spice sauce that may be used over and over—(see recipe, page 42). Larger pieces of food that have been par-boiled or oil-blanched are left to simmer in the master sauce, absorbing all the

wonderful flavors.

The master sauce can be refrigerated and used again and again. After each use, replenish it by adding more spices and water to bring it back to its original flavor. Chinese cooks know that the longer you keep it, the smoother the aroma and flavor become.

Hot Mixing
Here's a relatively new cooking term to describe combining deep-fried ingredients with a ready-made, preheated sauce. You quickly mix the two together and serve. The perfect example of hot mixing is Sweet & Sour Pork.

Cold Mixing
Most Chinese salads are prepared this way. First you salt pieces of firm vegetables such as cucumbers or radishes to leach out the excess water and to keep the vegetables crisp. Just before serving, seasonings and a small amount of sesame oil are added.

Baking/Roasting
In China, roasting means something different than it does here. Meat hangs in the middle of an oven instead of being placed on a rack, and the heat source is wood. As the heat circulates evenly around the meat, you're guaranteed the most even kind of cooking. Most restaurants and Chinese speciality stores roast their ducks or suckling pigs this way. Special racks are now available out of the pan and thus allow heat to circulate evenly. In the American kitchen, the oven can accomplish much the same thing; instructions are given with the individual recipes.

Diet Information

Many of Chef Chu's recipes are appropriate for persons on low-fat, low-carbohydrate, or low calorie diets. The recipes outlined in this section were selected because the foods used are relatively low in fat and carbohydrate and are prepared either by stir-frying, roasting, or steaming.

Most ingredients are chopped into bite-size pieces in Chinese dishes. More surface area is then available to absorb fat during cooking. For this reason, no recipes requiring deep-fat frying were selected. Instead, we have chosen stir-fried dishes that call for a small amount of oil. If you prefer a poly-unsaturated oil, such as safflower, corn, or sunflower, it may be readily substituted for the traditional peanut oil used in Chinese cooking. And if your diet indicates that less fat be used in cooking, you can reduce the amount of oil suggested in the recipes. Using a wok for cooking Chinese food—or any other kind of food—is ideal because its unique shape enables you to cook and stir quickly over high heat using very little oil.

Rice is an accompaniment for 90 percent of all Chinese meals. Rice provides significant amounts of protein, B vitamins, and iron and is low in fat content. Soybean curd (tofu) is used in some of Chef Chu's recipes and it is an excellent source of protein and minerals particularly calcium, iron, magnesium, and phosphorus. The combination of rice and soybean products, such as a bean curd or soybean products, such as a bean curd or bean sprouts, provides a good quality protein even without meat.

Chinese food can add interest and variety to your diet. Garlic, ginger, and soy sauce contribute a variety of flavors as do the hot Szechuan-style seasonings of chili oil and paste. And the array of fresh vegetables, such as snow peas, broccoli, bean sprouts, and bok choy plus the unusual texture and crunch of water chestnuts and bamboo shoots, offer such an assortment of flavors, you'll be amazed how tasty "diet food" can be.

Try teaching yourself how to use chopsticks! It will take longer to eat your meal and you will finish feeling well-fed. Eating fast often means that you eat too much so use chopsticks, eat slowly, and ENJOY your Chinese meal.

The following table showing calories, grams of protein, fat, and carbohydrate is calculated using the large number of portions for each recipe indicated. Remember—even though the recipes listed below are lower in calories than those requiring deep-frying or ones containing food with more calories, the size of the portion is important. You need to know the number of calories, protein, fat, and carbohydrate that you eat and this table will help you calculate it. Our suggested menu includes: a soup or cold plate item; an entrée of fish or meat, and a vegetable dish.

Molly Olive, R.D.

	Calories	Protein	Fat	Carbohydrate
		(grams per serving)		
Appetizers				
Chinese Barbecued Pork	29	1	1	3
Swordstick Beef	35	5	2	0.3
Cold Plate				
Buddhist Vegetarian Chicken	77	6	5	3
Szechuan Cold Cucumbers	61	2	3	10
Soups				
Won-ton	120	5	4	15
Egg Flower	37	3	2	2
Hot & Sour	166	10	11	7
Vegetarian version	125	8	8	7

	Calories	Protein	Fat	Carbohydrate
		(grams per serving)		

Poultry

	Calories	Protein	Fat	Carbohydrate
Pong-pong Chicken	136	13	7	5
Szechuan Steamed Beef With Anise				
Rice (using chicken)	216	16	7	19
General's Spicy Hot Chicken	110	15	4	2

Seafood

Hangchow Poached Fish	213	16	16	2
Foochow Steamed Clams	112	7	6	6
Spicy Hot Braised Fish	258	16	19	5
Cantonese Sautéed Fresh Squid	123	15	6	2

Pork

Lion's Head In Clay Pot	175	8	13	7
Soochow Pearl Meatballs	35	1	2	3
Cucumber Cups	76	4	4	6
Peking Meat Sauce	227	9	10	27
Mu Shu Pork	250	10	19	15

Beef

Mongolian Beef	244	16	17.5	5
Szechuan Beef With Anise Rice	213	14	8	19
Dry-sautéed Beef Strips	196	12	15	2
Chef Chu's Chinese Steak	166	17	6	10

Vegetables

Lettuce With Oyster Sauce	84	7	8	3
Hunan Bean Curd	109	49	8	3
Snow Peas With Water Chestnuts	73	1	5	6
Mixed Chinese Vegetables	79	3	5	7
Vegetarian Mu Shu Pork	221	8	16	15
(Mu Shu Eggs)				

Eggs, Noodles & Rice

Fresh Noodles	234	6	4	43
Chow Mein	307	7	11	46
Simple Boiled Rice	143	3	0.8	31
Fancy Fried Rice	143	4	7	17

Pastries & Desserts

Butterfly Steamed Bread	100	3	12	18
Potstickers	96	3	5	9
Mandarin Pancakes	95	2	5	12
Lichee Nut Blossoms	67	0.5	0.2	13

Chinese Ingredients

This glossary lists some 100 different Chinese ingredients—and I have only just begun to mention the great variety of spices, vegetables, and exotic items used in Chinese cooking. Nevertheless, the following is designed to help you understand the ingredients, how to select them, how to prepare them, and how they should be stored. Because the most often-asked question in my cooking classes is: "What do you recommend?", I have noted my preferences of brand names or source of ingredient when important or appropriate.

Abalone is available fresh (particularly in California), canned, and dried. Fresh abalone offers the best flavor, but is expensive. Canned abalone—I think the best comes from Mexico—is precooked and ready to use in soup, in an appetizer cold plate, and in stir-fried dishes. The liquid from canned abalone is excellent in soup, too. Dried abalone needs to be reconstituted. Be careful not to overcook abalone as it becomes tough and rubbery. To store unused portion of canned abalone, drain liquid, rinse in cold water, place in a jar filled with fresh water, and refrigerate, changing water daily, for up to 1 week.

Agar-agar is a tasteless, dried seaweed used like unflavored gelatin. It resembles bean thread noodles, is usually sold in strips or sticks, and is used in sweet dishes. Soak agar-agar in warm water for a few minutes to soften before using. Store, tightly wrapped, in a dry location and it will last almost indefinitely.

Anise (Chinese star) is a five-pointed, woody spice with a very distinctive flavor similar to licorice. There is no satisfactory substitute for this spice. Sold loose or packaged in plastic bags, it can be found in Oriental markets or in some gourmet shops. Store in a tightly-sealed jar for up to 1 year.

Bamboo Shoots come in cans, either sliced, shredded, or whole. They are actually the edible young fibrous shoots from tropical bamboo and are named after the harvest season: *Winter bamboo shoots* are dug out of the earth earlier and are more tender; *Spring shoots* are larger and easier to slice finely. Store unused bamboo shoots in a jar filled with water and refrigerate, changing the water every few days, for up to 1 week.

Bean Curd (Fresh), also called bean cake, or tofu, is made from puréed soybeans pressed into blocks about 3 inches square. I've heard it likened to cottage cheese for its texture and bland taste. It is a staple in the Chinese diet high in protein, inexpensive, very versatile as the following by-products show, and when cooked with other ingredients, fresh bean curd readily absorbs all the delicious flavors of sauces. Store unusued fresh bean cake in a jar filled with water and refrigerate, changing the water daily, for up to 1 week.

Bean Curd (Fermented red and yellow) is the same bean curd but fermented in Chinese wine. Available in jars and cans, it has a strong flavor something like a strong cheese. Although is usually served as a condiment, it may be used in cooking, too. To get the taste of it, try red fermented bean curd as a thin spread on toast for an appetizer. It's good! Store almost indefinitely in the refrigerator.

Bean Curd (Pressed) is compressed to a firm texture and has a delicately fragrant aroma. It is coffee-colored and usually comes in 2-inch squares cut about ¼-inch thick. Store, tightly wrapped, in the refrigerator for 2 or 3 days.

Bean Curd Skins are paper-thin sheets made from the dried residue that floats on soybean milk. Available in packages, they usually come trimmed to a size of 6 by 10 inches and are used in soup, in vegetable dishes, and as a pastry shell for sweet desserts. Store, tightly wrapped, in the freezer for up to 6 months.

Bean Paste (Red) is a sweet-tasting paste made from red beans; it is often used as a filling for pastries and buns. Available in cans, it can be kept in a sealed jar and refrigerated for many weeks.

Bean Sauce, also called brown bean paste, is a thick brown sauce with a pungent, rather salty taste made from fermented soybeans. It is available in both cans and jars. Store, tightly sealed in the refrigerator, amost indefinintely. (For hot bean sauce, see Chili Paste.)

Bean Sprouts come in two varieties: *yellow soy bean sprouts* are topped by a large yellow bean and are usually found only in Oriental markets while the *green mung bean sprouts* are available in most supermarkets all year round. When selecting sprouts, make sure they are quite fresh with a nice white body; no odor or brownish tinge should be present. Store in the refrigerator for 3 to 4 days. (Bean sprouts are available in cans but lack the crunchy texture, so I don't recommend them.)

Bean Thread is a transparent, dry, wiry noodle made from mung beans which must be soaked in warm water for 15 minutes before using. Available in small packages from 4 ounces to one pound, it is used in soup, in stir-fried dishes, and for deep-frying. Store, tightly wrapped, in a dry location almost indefinitely.

Black Beans (Fermented)
are soybeans preserved in
garlic, ginger, and salt; they are
black and oval in shape and primarily used as a seasoning. Sold
in packages, they must be
rinsed and drained before using. To store, moisten with oil
and place in a tightly sealed jar
for up to 1 month.

Cabbages are varied and plentiful in China but, outside of
Chinatowns in major cities, only
two or three kinds may be generally found: *Bok Choy*
(Chinese green), which means
"white vegetable," has a long,
smooth white stem and large,
dark green crinkly leaves. Its flavor is delicate and is used in
stir-frying and in soup (I also
shred the leaves and deep-fry
them to use as a garnish around
Chicken in a Phoenix Nest).
Napa or *Chinese* cabbage has
firmly packed, yellow-white
leaves fringed at the top with
pale green and a nice fresh taste
which holds up when lightly
cooked. *Mustard Greens* are
jade in color, with curly fluted
leaves, and a slightly bitter
taste—excellent in stir-fried
dishes or when water-blanched
for a simple, decorative vegetable ensemble as noted in my
recipes.

Cardomom is a small, aromatic, pod-shaped fruit with
seeds inside. Sold packaged
either as whole pods, seeds, or
ground, it is used as a seasoning
or condiment. Store in a tightly
sealed jar for up to a year.

Cassia Blossom or *kuei-hua* is
a tiny, fragrant yellow blossom,
available dried or preserved in
a sweet syrup, that is used to
sweeten speciality dishes such
as Hunan Honey-glazed Ham.
Store dried cassia blossom,
tightly wrapped, in a dry location almost indefinitely.

Caul Fat is the fatty tissue, resembling lace or netting, that
comes from the inner organs of
pigs. It is used to wrap food
during cooking to retain shape

and flavor. It is available from
good butchers, but they often
need advance notice. Store unused portion, tightly wrapped,
in the freezer for up to 4
months.

Chili Oil is a combination of
oil and red hot chili peppers. It
is easy to make your own (see
page 212) though it is readily
available in Oriental markets
and some supermarkets. Store,
tightly sealed, for up to 1 year.

Chili Paste, also called Hot
Bean Sauce, is used as a condiment or seasoning in Szechuan
dishes. Its main ingredients are
soybeans, chilies, and sesame
oil. Store, tightly sealed, in the
refrigerator for 3 to 4 months.

Chili Pods are just that—dried,
red chili pods, available whole
or crushed. If crushed, the seed
produces a hotter flavor. Store,
tighly wrapped, in a dry location almost indefinitely.

Chinese Barbecue Sauce,
sup-tsou, has a paste-like consistency and is made from krill
fish, oil, garlic, shallots, and
chiles. Available in jars, it is
used for dipping or in stir-fried
dishes. Store, tightly sealed, in
the refrigerator for 3 to 4
months.

Chinese Parsley, also called
cilantro or coriander, is a flat
leafy vegetable which resembles parsley but isn't. It has a
distinctive, fragrant taste and is
excellent as a garnish. Store in
the refrigerator for 3 to 4 days.

Chinese Cinnamon is the
strong, aromatic tree bark used
as a spice in such recipes as
Master Sauce. Slightly thicker
and darker than conventional
cinnamon sticks, it is available
in pieces or ground.

Corn (Baby) is a miniature ear
of corn, 1½- to 2-inches long.
Available in jars or cans, it is
used as a condiment, or in stir-
fried dishes. Store in a jar filled
with water and refrigerate,
changing water daily, for up to 2
weeks.

Cornstarch Paste is a thin
paste made from equal parts of
cold water and cornstarch. It is
essential as a thickening agent
in many Chinese dishes (but be
careful not to over-thicken). Stir
just before using. Store, covered, in the refrigerator for 1 or
2 days.

Curing Salt, also known as salt
peter, is an optional spice used
to firm up texture of meat and
to prolong storage life. Store in
a tightly-sealed jar for up to 1
year.

Dates (Chinese Red), also
called jujube nuts, are dried
dates with shiny red skin, similar in size to a prune. Soaking in
warm water for about 15 minutes is necessary before using.
Store in a tightly-sealed jar for 3
to 4 months.

Dragon Eyes, or longans, are
white, shiny tropical fruit resembling a lichee nut but not as
scented. Available in cans or
dried, they are used in flavoring
soup or in desserts. Store,
tightly-sealed, in the refrigerator for up to 1 week.

Eggs are served by Chinese
cooks in the most fascinating
ways: *Marble Eggs,* also called
tea eggs, are hard-cooked,
cracked but not peeled, and
then simmered in strong tea for
a most unusual effect when
peeled. Served as an appetizer,
either whole or cut in wedges,
they can be stored in the refrigerator for up to 1 week; *Quail
Eggs,* available in cans, or occasionally fresh in specialty shops,
are used as an appetizer or as a
garnish. Store, tightly sealed in
a jar, in the refrigerator for up to
1 week. *Salty Eggs* begin as uncooked duck eggs that are
soaked in salt water for a
month. When cooked, the white
becomes very firm and the yolk
turns a golden orange color and
appears oily. Store in a cool
place for 1 to 2 months. *Thousand-year-old Eggs* also start out
as uncooked duck eggs. They
are coated with a mixture of

clay, ashes, lime, and rice husks and then buried in an earthenware pot for about 3 months. The egg white becomes firm and amber colored and the yolk turns dark green. Store in a cool place for 1 to 2 months.

Egg Roll Wrappers are 7-inch-square sheets of paper-thin pastry made from flour, water, and eggs. Available frozen or fresh from most Oriental markets and some supermarkets. Store, tightly wrapped, in the freezer for up to 3 months.

Fennel Seeds come from the celery-like herb fennel. They have a taste and fragrance similar to anice or licorice. Available in plastic bags or in jars, fennel is used to season. Store in a tightly-sealed jar for up to 1 year.

Five Spice Powder, also called Chinese five-spice, is a strongly flavored combination of ground anise, cinnamon, fennel, cloves, and Szechuan peppercorns. Available in plastic bags or jars, it is a common spice in Chinese cooking. Store in a tightly-sealed jar for 1 to 2 years.

Five Spice Salt is a simple combination of Five Spice Powder and salt. (The directions for making it appear on page 212.) Store in a tightly-sealed jar for 1 to 2 years.

Ginger is an aromatic, pungently-spiced gnarled root. The skin, resembling a potato's, is fairly thin and ginger should be peeled before using; the root is knobby. Ginger is usually crushed or minced, or occasionally sliced such as when seasoning a wok. Dry ginger and ground ginger powder are not satisfactory substitutes. Store fresh ginger in the refrigerator for 1 to 2 weeks.

Ginger (Preserved) may be found in jars and comes in long strips, tinted red, and packaged in syrup. It is used as a garnish or in sauces. Store, tightly sealed, in the refrigerator for 3 to 4 months.

Gingko Nuts are small, white-colored nuts with hard beige-colored shells; they are the fruit of the gingko tree. A little bitter tasting, they come dried or in cans, and are used in soup or braised dishes. Store, uncracked, in the refrigerator for 3 to 4 months.

Gluten Puff, or *kou-fu,* is made from high gluten flour and water and when deep-fried, puffs up to create a chewy texture. It is used in various dishes where it delicately absorbs the flavor of the sauce and adds its own unique texture. Available frozen or in cans. Store frozen unused portion for up to 3 months.

Green Onion, scallion or spring onion, is a widely used vegetable in Chinese cuisine. It will enrich the flavor and add to the aroma of any dish. Wash, dry, and store wrapped in plastic in the refrigerator for up to 1 week.

Hair Seaweed, is black seaweed in fine strands resembling hair. It is used mainly in Buddhist vegetarian dishes and must be soaked in warm water for one hour, then rinsed in cold water.

Ham (Smithfield) is the "Virginia" smoked ham that comes closest to the Yunnan ham so treasured in China. It is lean, has a distinctive flavor and texture, and is rather salty. Consult your butcher as to availability and source. Store, tightly wrapped, in the refrigerator for several weeks.

Hoisin Sauce is a very popular reddish-brown sauce made from flour, vinegar, soybeans, and spices; it is used as a dipping sauce for some Chinese dishes including Mu Shu Pork. The brand I prefer is *Koon-Chun.* Store, tightly sealed, in the refrigerator for 3 to 4 months.

Kuei-hua, see Cassia Blossom.

Kumquats are orange-colored, oval citrus fruit about the size of large olives. Very sweet in taste with a spicy aroma, they are available fresh in the spring, or are packed in syrup in cans or jars. Used mostly in desserts, they are a colorful addition to holiday spreads. Store fresh ones in the refrigerator for 1 to 2 weeks. Store opened kumquats, tightly sealed, in the refrigerator for 1 to 2 months.

Leeks, widely used as a vegetable in China, are tougher and larger than green onions and stronger in flavor. Wash thoroughly and store in a plastic bag in refrigerator for up to 1 week.

Lichee Nut, also called lychee, is a crimson-red, crusted tropical fruit native to Southern China. The meat is firm, sweet, and almost a translucent white. Available (occasionally) fresh in specialty stores or canned in light syrup, it is also available dried, resembling raisins. Popularly used as the sweet counterpoint in dishes, such as Sweet & Sour Pork, or served chilled as a refreshing dessert. Store, tightly sealed in a jar with syrup, in the refrigerator for 2 or 3 days.

Lily Buds (Tiger), also called gold needles, are available mostly in dried form. Light gold in color, about 2- to 3-inches long, they add a delicately sweet flavor and aroma to soup, poultry, fish, or meat. They must be washed and soaked in warm water for 1 hour before using. Store dry lily buds, tightly wrapped, in a dry location almost indefinitely.

Loquats, similar in appearance to apricots, are orange-yellow fruit with thin skins and a sweet taste. Packed in light syrup in cans or jars, they may be added to stir-fried dishes or desserts. Store opened loquats, tightly sealed in a jar with syrup, in the refrigerator for up to 1 week.

Lotus Leaves, available dried, are used most often as a wrapper for food and to impart flavor during baking or steaming. Store, tightly wrapped, in a dry location for up to 1 year.

Lotus Seeds, available dried or canned, are seeds from a water lily; they must be soaked in warm water before using, most often in soup and sweet dishes. Store, tightly wrapped, in a dry location almost indefinitely.

Maltose, also called malt sugar, is a natural, heavy, syrupy sugar similar to light molasses; used for preparing Peking Duck. Store, tightly sealed in a jar, at room temperature for up to 1 year.

Master Sauce (see page 42), a concentrated spicy sauce used for simmering partially-cooked food such as meat, is used over and over again and may be kept for years. Before storing, replenish it by adding more spices and water (to bring back the original flavor and volume). Remove and discard spice bag, strain sauce into a jar, seal tightly, and store in the refrigerator almost indefinitely.

MSG, or monosodium glutamate, is a crystalline extract from soybeans used as a flavor enhancer in Chinese cooking. *We don't use MSG,* either in my restaurant or in the recipes in this book. It's considered hazardous to the health by some scientists, some people are allergic to it, and I think it can destroy subtle flavors in a dish, especially when overused.

Mushrooms are plentiful in China and they all have a different flavor and use: *Abalone-shaped mushrooms,* resembling little fans, are thick, tender, and the canned ones are quite tasty; *Button mushrooms* are similar to champignons in size and flavor (in cans); *Dried Black mushrooms* are quite aromatic with a woodsy taste and must be soaked in warm water for an hour and then rinsed before using; *Flower mushrooms* are another member of the dried black mushroom family except

lighter in color with a pattern which appears on the domed cap; *Straw mushrooms,* also called grass mushrooms, have a subtle flavor and a crunchy texture (in cans); *Tree mushrooms,* also called edible black fungus, cloud ears, or wooden ears, must be soaked in warm water for 30 minutes, washed, and rinsed several times before using. Cloud ears are smaller and more delicate in flavor; wooden ears are larger, firmer, and crunchier. All are available, dried, in small packages. Store dried mushrooms, tightly wrapped, in a dry location almost indefinitely. Unused canned mushrooms should be stored in a covered jar in the refrigerator for up to 2 weeks.

Mustard Green (Preserved Szechuan), called *jah choy,* has its own distinctive spicy hot, salty taste and texture. Available in cans or sealed plastic bags, it is used in soups and stir-fried dishes. Store, tightly sealed in plastic bags, in refrigerator for up to 1 month.

Noodles are popular throughout China, but particularly in the North where wheat is harvested. Egg noodles (see recipe on page 162) are available fresh or dried, and when boiled, are served with meat, poultry, or vegetables or used in soup. Store dried noodles, tightly wrapped, in a dry location for up to 6 months.

Oil is used in Chinese cooking for blanching, deep-frying, and stir-frying. Many Chinese cooks use peanut oil but you can use any good vegetable oil, such as corn oil, safflower oil, or cottonseed oil, as long as it does not impart a taste to the food. Store unused oil, tightly sealed, in a dry location for up to 6 months. Discard if it darkens and/or has an odor as oil can become rancid.

Oyster Sauce is made from oyster extract, salt, water, and seasonings. A pungent, aromatic

brown sauce, it is used to add a subtle, flavorful taste to meats, poultry, and vegetables. Used in most Chinese kitchens for dipping, seasoning, and marinating, it is available in bottles or cans and may be stored almost indefinitely without any refrigeration.

Plum Sauce is a sweet, spicy sauce made from yellow plums, vinegar, and spices. Available in jars or cans, it is used as a condiment for dipping, especially with roasted duck. Store, tightly sealed in a jar, in the refrigerator for 3 to 4 months.

Preserved Vegetables, packed in a lightly sweetened syrup in cans and jars, are pieces of vegetables such as carrots and cucumber plus papaya that are used as a relish or when making sweet and sour dishes. Store unused vegetables, tightly sealed in a jar, in the refrigerator for up to 1 month.

Rice is most basic to the Chinese diet. There are three common types: *Glutenous* (or sweet) is short-grained, milky white, and becomes sticky when cooked. It is used for stuffings, pastries, and dessert and must be soaked for an hour before using. *Long-grain rice* is most commonly used in Chinese cooking and served with meals. It is fluffier than *short-grain* rice which tends to be softer and slightly more starchy; more frequently served with Japanese meals, but also used by Chinese when preparing congee.

Rice (Spicy Mixture) is long-grain rice and star anise seed combined, then ground together. Available ready-mixed in small packages at some specialty stores. Used most often mixed with beef, pork, or poultry. Store in a tightly-sealed jar at room temperature for up to a year.

Rice Sticks, also called rice noodles, are thin, long, brittle sticks made from rice flour and sold in 4- to 6-ounce packages. When deep-fried, they puff up and become lightly crunchy. Or, soaked in water to become soft and noodle-like, they are used in soup or Chow Mein. Store dry rice sticks, tightly wrapped, in a dry location almost indefinitely.

Rice Wine Paste, see Wine Sauce.

Sauces for dipping follow the glossary of ingredients and appear on pages 212–213.

Scallops (Dried) are just that—small, round scallops that have been dried and packaged for use in soup or to add a delicate flavor to vegetable dishes. You must soak in hot water before using. Store, tightly wrapped, in a dry location almost indefinitely.

Sea Cucumber, or *beche-de-mer,* is available in dried form measuring some 3- to 8-inches long. When soaked, it expands and becomes rather gelatinous. Used in soup and special banquet dishes.

Seaweed (Dried) is available in tissue-thin sheets and must be soaked in cold water before using. It is very nutritious and most often used in soup.

Sesame Oil is aromatic, flavorful, and extracted from roasted white sesame seeds. Use lightly to season foods; a wonderful flavor enhancer. Store, tightly sealed, in refrigerator for up to 2 weeks.

Sesame Seeds are flat with a nutty flavor and available in black and white varieties. Toasting improves the flavor. They are used most often in pastries or as a garnish, or as a last-minute addition to dishes such as Shredded Chicken Salad. Store in a tightly sealed jar for up to 1 year.

Sesame Seed Paste is a thick, dark paste made from ground sesame seeds and is used as a dipping sauce or in cold-mix salads when diluted with broth, soy sauce, and spices. Use sparingly as it is strong in flavor. Store, tightly sealed in a jar, in refrigerator for up to 6 months.

Shark's Fin is the cartilage or gristle from the shark's fin. Packaged in 8-ounce boxes, the fins look like thread-like balls. Once reconstituted (by soaking overnight), they look like translucent needles. Used in soup generally served at banquets, this item is expensive but if you intend to cook shark's fin soup, I recommend buying the best available. Store, tightly wrapped, at room temperature almost indefinintely.

Shrimp (Dried) are available in small plastic bags and are used to add a delicate flavor to soup or to steamed vegetables. Must be softened in hot water for at least ½ hour before using. Store in dried form, in a tightly sealed jar almost indefinintely.

Shrimp Paste (Salty) is available in jars at Oriental markets. It is made from fermented shrimp and has a strong fish smell and a salty taste. Use sparingly for dipping. Store, tightly sealed in a jar, in refrigerator for up to 6 months.

Snow Peas, also called Chinese pea pods, are flat, waxy, bright green peas with edible pods. Be sure to select the young ones because they will be sweet, crispy, and more delectable (the older ones are larger, tend to yellow, and have a tougher skin). Store, wrapped in a plastic bag, in refrigerator for up to 1 week.

Soy Sauce is the fundamental seasoning in Chinese cooking. Made from fermented soy beans, flour, salt, and water, it comes in various ways: *Extra Dark* is used for stewing or red-cooking; *Black* or *Dark,* which is slightly sweeter, is used for general stir-frying, marinating, and dipping; *Light* or *Thin* does not have caramel coloring and so is used for dipping and mari-nating light-colored foods such as seafood and vegetables. *In our recipes,* whenever we call for soy sauce, we mean Black or Dark except where otherwise noted. For those on low-sodium diets, there is a Light/Lite Soy made by Kikkoman which is good. Store at room temperature for up to 6 months.

Spring Roll Wrapper is similar to but not the same as Egg Roll Wrapper. These are translucent, paper-thin crepes made from a flour batter and are used for wrapping vegetables, cooked meat, or seafood that is to be deep-fried; I especially recommend it for Mu Shu Pork wrappers. They are available frozen in most Oriental markets. Steam, wrapped in a cloth, to serve. Store unused wrappers, tightly wrapped in a freezer bag, in freezer for up to 2 weeks.

Szechuan Peppercorns are also called wild peppercorns and have a subtle delicate smell and mildly hot taste. They are spicier than black peppercorns. Store in a tightly-sealed jar for up to 1 year.

Tangerine Peel (Preserved) is coffee-colored, dried peel with a sweet citrus smell. Pieces are used in soup, stew, as an ingredient in master sauces, or in specialty dishes such as Tangerine Peel Beef. Store in a tightly sealed jar almost indefinitely.

Tea is consumed all day long in China. Although there are well in excess of 200 varieties, we think of them in three groups: *Unfermented tea,* which is green tea, the most famous of which is Dragon Well from the Chekiang province; *Semi-fermented tea* which we know as oolong; and *Fermented tea* to which the black tea belongs such as Keemun. Tea is not usually served with banquet meals because it has a neutralizing effect and will alter one's sensitivity to tastes somewhat. Instead it is served at the end of a meal so that its acidic and neutralizing quality break down the oils used in cooking. However, Chinese restaurants in the United States often bring a pot of tea to the table at the onset of a meal.

Vinegar (Chinese) comes in three types: *Black Rice vinegar* is used with braised dishes and as a dipping sauce; *Red Rice vinegar* is used with sweet and pungent dishes and for dipping steamed crab; and *White Rice vinegar* is used for sweet and pungent dishes.

Water Chestnuts are available in cans, peeled, and packed in water. They are available fresh in early spring and are particularly delicious. Crunchy in texture and mild in taste, they are used in vegetable combinations or cooked with poultry or meat. Store in a jar filled with water and refrigerate, changing water daily, for up to 1 week.

Water Chestnut Powder is a grayish powder made from water chestnuts and used for making a batter for deep-frying. (It is better in quality than cornstarch or flour-based batters.) Combine equal parts of powder to water to make this simple batter. Store powder, tightly wrapped, in a dry location for up to 1 year.

Wine is often used in Chinese cooking. If Chinese rice wine is available, I recommend it because it has such a unique aroma. I use "Shaosing" rice wine. If that isn't available, try using dry sherry or Japanese *sake*.

Wine Sauce, also called sweet wine rice, is glutinous rice that has been fermented with a wine starter. After a few days, the rice turns soft and the sauce becomes sweet. Its wonderful flavor is used in seafood dishes and sweet desserts. Available in jars. Store, tightly covered in a jar, in refrigerator for 3 to 4 months.

Winter Melon is green on the outside with a tough, waxy skin and yet soft white flesh inside. Sold by weight, either whole or in sections, its mild delicate flavor is used most often in soup. Wrap unused melon in plastic and store in a dry location for 1 to 2 weeks.

Won-ton Wrappers are similar to Egg Roll Wrappers but smaller, about 3½-inches square. Made from flour, water, and eggs, they are available fresh (usually located in the vegetable section of most markets) or frozen. Store unused wrappers, wrapped in plastic, in the refrigerator for 3 to 4 days or freeze wrappers for up to 6 months.

Utensils & Equipment   *Pictured on pages 210 and 211*

Owning a large assortment of cooking utensils is not essential for cooking Chinese food. In fact, when my students ask me about the various types of equipment and which ones I consider necessary, I tell them that their best investment when starting to cook Chinese food is probably a wok set.

A good-quality wok set contains a wok made of carbon steel, a tight-fitting lid with handle, a spatula, a slotted spoon or a wire strainer, and perhaps a rack for steaming.

Other less essential pieces of equipment such as cleavers, bamboo steamers, chopping blocks, and clay pots are often used by Chinese cooks and add that extra touch of authenticity you may want to recreate in your own kitchen.

Here is a brief description of some of the items found in a Chinese kitchen:

Wok

Nothing compares with a wok. Such a simple shape—just a wide bowl with high, sloping sides—has withstood the test of time and remained virtually unchanged throughout centuries of Chinese cooking. What other utensil allows you to cook so many different ways, from stir-frying and braising to deep-frying and poaching? And when fitted with a domed lid, a wok is ideal for steaming, too.

Woks come in various sizes, from 12 inches in diameter on up. For home cooking, I recommend a 14-inch one; it's the most practical because it conducts the maximum amount of heat from a stovetop's heating element.

Traditionally, woks have rounded bottoms and they rest in a metal ring, positioned over the heat source. This method works well over a gas burner but if you are cooking on an electric stove, I recommend using a flat-bottomed wok.

Woks are manufactured in stainless steel (usually with a copper bottom) and aluminum, too, but carbon steel is my preference because it conducts heat evenly and is moderately priced. Just remember to dry it thoroughly after washing because it will rust. When brand new, woks should be seasoned with a little oil after each use. Wipe 1 tablespoon oil inside the wok and then place it over high heat for just a few minutes. Swirl the pan to coat the sides with oil and let cool; then wipe out any excess with a paper towel.

Electric woks are only good for deep frying, poaching, steaming, oil-blanching, and stewing, but *not* good for stir-frying because Chinese food is cooked to perfection and you cannot stop the heat the exact time you want to with an electric wok where you can remove a regular wok from the source of heat.

Spatula, Spoon & Strainer

Spatulas found in wok sets or those sold with Oriental kitchenware are designed to fit the curvature of a wok and are useful for tossing and mixing food. They have long handles and are helpful when stir-frying and braising.

Slotted spoons and wire strainers are often used for the same purpose: to raise and lower food into a liquid. If you're choosing just one, an 8-inch-wide wire strainer fitted with a bamboo handle is your best choice. You can use it for deep-frying, oil or water-blanching, and to remove any particles left behind in the liquid.

Steamer

If your wok set included a steaming rack, you probably won't want to get a separate steamer unit. However, for steaming large quantities of food or for cooking food that requires a long steaming time, you may want to consider getting a steamer.

A metal steamer, made of stainless steel or aluminum, consists of two or three tiered racks that stack and rest on top of a pot containing boiling water. A tight-fitting lid seals in the steam and allows the food to slowly cook inside. It is used as a unit, in place of a wok fitted with a bamboo rack inside.

A bamboo steamer is recommended for steaming pastries and is appropriate for steaming other types of food as well. The steamer consists of stackable trays of woven bamboo and a lid. Since the steam escapes through the holes in between the woven bamboo strips, water can't condense and drop onto the food during steaming. (This is very important when making pastries or some breads.)

Although bamboo steamers will wear out after prolonged use, they are reasonably priced. Available in many different sizes, from 4 inches wide (for dim sum) on up, I find that a 10-inch one fits nicely inside a regular wok and works quite well. Bamboo also adds a pleasant aroma to the food and lends that extra Oriental touch most cooks prefer. After steaming, rinse a bamboo steamer well and let dry in the air completely before storing.

Cleaver

Like a wok, a Chinese cleaver is very versatile. It serves the function of many knives and can do almost anything: slice, chop, mince, crush, and scrape food up off a chopping block.

Cleavers come in different sizes (or weights). A medium-size one (called #2) is a good, all-purpose utensil used for cutting vegetables. A #1 cleaver has a heavier blade and is used for chopping meat and bones.

Both sizes come in stainless steel and carbon steel. I prefer the carbon steel because it holds a sharp edge better; but remember, just like with a wok, a carbon steel cleaver will rust if not dried after each use.

Chopping Block
A round chopping block, actually a "slice" or cross-section cut from a tree trunk, is a traditional piece of equipment for Chinese cooks. I've found that the most useful size is one measuring 14 inches across. Because American chopping boards are made from hard woods, knife blades tend to slip away from you during cutting, especially if you're using a cleaver. So if you do lots of heavy chopping and feel comfortable using it, why not consider an Oriental chopping block?

Clay Pot & Porcelain Steaming Pot
An earthenware or clay pot is frequently used in Chinese cooking. Made of heat-resistant clay, it can be placed directly on the heat as well as in the oven. Clay pots are used primarily for slow-cooking, such as in stews, and are brought to the table directly for serving.

Porcelain cookware is decorative so its main purpose is for serving. It's used to hold food that is steamed inside a wok or steamer. Depending on what you're cooking, procelain pots or dishes can be bowl-shaped with sloping sides (if gravy or other cooking liquids are used) or flat with a footed pedestal. In either case, since steamed food goes directly to the table for serving, fancier porcelain cookware is often used. However, you may substitute any oven-ware or heat-resistant cookware if you prefer.

Electric Deep-fryer & Thermometer
Using an electric deep-fat fryer instead of a traditional wok enables you to cook some Chinese food faster and more efficiently. It is handy for oil blanching, deep-frying, and for storing left-over oil. When choosing a deep-fryer, the most important feature to look for is a thermostat or dial labeled with the exact temperature, such as 350°, rather than a dial that merely says "High" or "Medium-low."

A deep-fat frying thermometer for measuring the exact temperature of oil when frying is another utensil most cooks find handy. Because our recipes call

for a specific oil temperature ("Heat 4 cups of oil to 300°"), I recommend using a thermometer to be sure.

Firepot
A Mongolian firepot (pictured on page 113) is a nice way to serve warm food over a long period of time because you do the cooking right at the table. Similar to a fondue pot, a fire-pot consists of a lower "stove" section or bowl that stores the burning charcoal and a wide, shallow pot on top filled with hot broth. Thin slices of raw vegetables and uncooked meat are lowered into the boiling broth and cooked to desired doneness. Later the broth is consumed like soup.

Chopsticks
Long chopsticks made of bamboo are helpful for transferring ingredients, testing for doneness, stirring, or simply picking up food for tasting.

Shorter chopsticks, used for eating, are made of many materials from bamboo and other woods to plastic and ivory. They are relatively easy to master and add that final touch of authenticity to a Chinese meal. Simple directions for how-to use chopsticks appear on page 216.

Common Chinese cooking equipment includes (clockwise, from top): brass Mongolian firepot; pair of small earthenware pots; bamboo tongs resting on covered wok set; wire strainers; cooking (long) chopsticks; three-tiered bamboo steamer; ladle and spatula; small covered bamboo steamer; and large earthenware cooking pot. In center are wooden grater and medium and large carbon steel cleavers.

Dipping Sauces & Condiments

You might notice a little saucer set before your place setting when you sit down to a meal at a Chinese home or restaurant. That saucer is for dipping sauces or condiments, such as hot mustard or soy sauce. Other sauces are designed to accompany certain dishes, to further enhance the flavor—such as Hoisin sauce or Chinese five-spice salt—and these, too, are meant to occupy the little saucer. Recipes throughout the book refer to the sauces below.

Chef Chu's Dipping Sauce

- 3 tablespoons catsup
- 1 tablespoon soy sauce
- 1 teaspoon sugar
- ½ teaspoon minced fresh ginger
- ½ small clove garlic, minced

Combine all ingredients well in a small bowl.

Ground Szechuan Peppercorns

- 1 tablespoon Szechuan peppercorns

Place peppercorns in a small skillet. Place over moderate heat, shaking pan to agitate, for about 4 to 5 minutes or until peppercorns turn brown. Cool and then grind in a pepper mill.

Hoisin Sauce

Flour, vinegar, soybeans, and spices combine to make hoisin sauce. Available ready-made in jars or cans, I prefer to use a brand called Koon-Chun.

Chili Paste

Red chili peppers, soybeans, garlic and sesame oil combine to make chili paste. Available in jars and cans; I often add a dash of sesame oil just before using.

Oyster Sauce

Many good, prepared oyster sauces are available, in cans or jars, from Oriental markets and some supermarkets.

Chili Oil

- 1 cup vegetable oil
- 3 or 4 dried chili pods, crushed

Heat oil in a wok to 375°. Remove from heat and drop in chili pieces. Allow oil to cool completely.

Notes

1. You might want to enhance the flavor by adding a few slices of fresh ginger or onion.
2. If the oil is too hot, you will burn the chili pods before the color comes out.
3. If the oil isn't hot enough, the flavor won't be strong enough.

Chinese Hot Mustard Sauce

- 3 to 6 tablespoons Colman's Hot Mustard Powder (or other spicy mustard powder)
- Water
- Dash vegetable oil

In a small bowl, place mustard. Stir in enough cold water until consistency becomes paste-like. Add a dash of vegetable oil to add sheen and prolong the shelf life.

Chinese Five-spice Salt

- 2 tablespoons salt
- ¼ teaspoon Chinese five-spice

Combine salt and five-spice powder in a small skillet. Place over moderate heat, shaking pan to agitate ingredients, for about 1 minute. Transfer to a condiment dish.

Ginger Sauce

¼ cup red rice vinegar
1 teaspoon minced fresh ginger

Combine both ingredients well in a small bowl.

Pong-pong Sauce

2 tablespoons soy sauce
1 tablespoon creamy peanut butter (or sesame seed paste)
1 teaspoon red rice vinegar
1 teaspoon hot chili oil
½ teaspoon sugar
½ teaspoon sesame oil
½ teaspoon minced fresh ginger
1 green onion (white part), minced
½ clove garlic, minced

Combine all ingredients well in a small bowl.

Szechuan Peppercorn Salt

2 tablespoons salt
¼ teaspoon ground Szechuan peppercorns

Combine salt and ground peppercorns. Place over moderate heat, shaking pan to agitate ingredients, for 4 to 5 minutes. Transfer to a condiment bowl.

Plum Sauce (Duck Sauce)

Plums, chili peppers, vinegar, sugar, and other ingredients are combined to make plum sauce. Available in jars or cans from Oriental markets and some supermarkets.

Peking Duck Sauce

2 tablespoons hoisin sauce
¼ teaspoon sesame oil
¼ teaspoon sugar

Combine all ingredients well in a small bowl.

Sweet & Sour Sauce

1 orange
1 lemon
1 thumb-size chunk fresh ginger, crushed
1 cup catsup
1 cup sugar
¾ cup distilled white vinegar
2 cups water
Pinch salt
¼ teaspoon red food coloring (optional)
¼ teaspoon yellow food coloring (optional)
Cornstarch paste

Squeeze juice from orange and lemon into a saucepan. Drop in rinds and ginger. Stir in catsup, sugar, vinegar, water, salt, and food colorings (if used).

Bring to a boil, reduce heat, and simmer for 5 minutes. Cool and then remove rinds and pieces of ginger.

Note

This recipe makes 1 quart. When ready to use, pour as much sauce as needed into a saucepan. Heat to simmering and add enough cornstarch paste to make the consistency of pancake syrup (it thickens further as it cools).

Hot Spicy Sauce

3 tablespoons soy sauce
1 teaspoon hot chili oil
1 teaspoon red rice vinegar
½ teaspoon sugar
1 small clove garlic, minced
1 green onion (white part), minced
Pinch ground roasted Szechuan peppercorns
Dash sesame oil

Combine all ingredients well in a small bowl.

Chinese Menus

A good Chinese meal should please, if not elevate, your senses! That it does depends on the proper combination of dishes. Variety is the key to an interesting meal—variety in tastes, textures, and ingredients. If you have a spicy dish, it should be complimented by a mild one, a crunchy textured dish with one which has tender ingredients. The number of dishes selected depends largely on the number of people dining. A good rule of thumb is to have the same number of dishes as people served, plus rice and perhaps a soup. Try not to duplicate the ingredients; for example, instead of two beef dishes make one of them chicken or pork. Seafood generally appears as a standard dish in a combination of dishes. The menus below adhere to these guidelines and might, in themselves, be more instructive than further suggestions:

Dinner For Two Menu

Asparagus with Oyster Sauce
Chicken in Phoenix Nest
Boiled Rice

Firepot Menu

Pieces of:
fish, lamb, beef, pork,
prawns, spinach, Chinese
cabbage, bean curd, bean
threads
Sauces For Dipping
Fancy Fried Rice

Diet Menu

Szechuan Cold Cucumbers
Egg Flower Soup
Tomato Beef
Ma Po Bean Curd
Fresh Fruit

Dinner For Two Menu

Minced Chicken in Lettuce Cups
Chef Chu's Hot & Sour Beef
Boiled Rice

Family-style Chinese Dinner

Lion's Head in Clay Pot
Canton Salt-baked Prawns
Minced Chicken in Lettuce Cups
Beef & Assorted Vegetables
Boiled Rice

Four-star Dinner

Sizzling Rice Soup
Mu Shu Pork
Snow White Chicken
Szechuan Dry-braised Prawns
Mongolian Beef
Stir-fried Bean Sprouts
Boiled Rice

Vegetarian Menu

Sweet & Sour Cold Radishes
Buddhist Vegetarian Chicken
Hot & Sour Soup (without meat)
Mu Shu Eggs
Four Seasons Vegetables
Boiled Rice
Almond Cream Squares

Congee Breakfast Menu

Marble Eggs
1000-year-old Eggs
Salty Eggs
Fermented Bean Curd
Congee

Picnic Menu
Sweet & Sour Cold Radishes
Marble Eggs
Phoenix Wings
Five-spice Beef Sandwiches
Chef Chu's Pork Chops
Butterfly Steamed Bread
Fresh Fruit

Seafood Menu
Seaweed Soup
Foochow Steamed Clams
Hangchow Poached Fish
Hunan Lichee Squid
Asparagus with Oyster Sauce
Fancy Fried Rice

Shanghai (East)
Shanghai Smoked Fish
Sweet & Sour Cold Radishes
Velvet Prawns
Sauteed Ginger Duck
Hangchow Poached Fish
Boiled Rice

Peking (North)
Potstickers
Hot & Sour Soup
Mu Shu Pork
Chicken in Phoenix Nest
Four Seasons Vegetables
Butterfly Steamed Bread
Glazed Apples

Four-star Dinner for Six
*Mandarin Tidbits: fried
prawns, barbecued pork,
crab & cheese puff*
Won-ton Soup
Canton Salt-baked Prawns
Lemon Chicken
Canton Oyster Beef Strips
Mixed Chinese Vegetables
Boiled Rice

New Year's Menu
Barbecued Suckling Pig (purchased)
Roast Peking Duck (purchased)
Steamed Kirin Fish
Fragrant Duck
Hunan Honey-glazed Ham
Mixed Chinese Vegetables
Eight Treasure Rice Pudding
*Condiments: candy, nuts,
sweet meats (purchased)*

Canton (South)
Crispy Shrimp Balls
Winter Melon Blossom Soup
Lemon Chicken
Chef Chu's Chinese Steak
Snow Peas with Water Chestnuts
Lichee Nut Blossoms

Szechuan/Hunan (West)
Sizzling Rice Soup
Pong-pong Chicken
Tea-smoked Duck
Dry-braised Prawns
Hot & Sour Beef
Boiled Rice
Almond Cream Squares

How to...

Use chopsticks

These simplist of utensils, chopsticks are easy to master—really, and in just two minutes if you are relaxed and attentive to

1) Hold one chopstick like you would a pencil. 2) Slide second stick through cradle formed by thumb and index finger; let stick rest on fourth finger. 3) Move top stick, up and down, in writing motion, bring tip in contact with stationary stick.

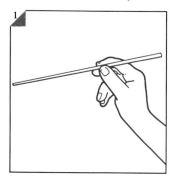

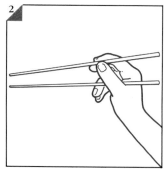

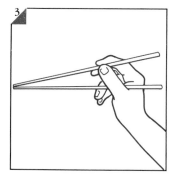

these instructions! First, place the pair of chopsticks the way you would find them at your place setting with the sticks parallel, touching, and the smaller points facing away from you. Take one stick and hold it in your hand as you would hold a pencil, small point down and your fingers holding it a third of the way up to the top blunt end. Now move the stick as though you are writing with it. Relax and hold the stick comfortably (if your grasp is tense, tight and cramped, your dexterity will be impaired).

Now, while holding the first stick take the second stick and slide it through the cradle formed by your thumb and index finger of the same hand. Let the stick rest in the cradle and against the tip of your fourth finger. A relaxed, natural pressure will keep this second stick in place. Make sure the small points of both sticks are even and meet. Move the first stick in an up and down writing motion, bringing its tip in contact with the stationary stick. Now you are set to pick up something. Ready?

Chopsticks serve as "signals" at a meal. The host will raise his chopsticks over the rice bowl or plate and invite guests to begin. Chopsticks are placed even and parallel over the rice bowl at the end of the meal to indicate that one is finished.

Order in a restaurant

A good Chinese meal should please, if not elevate, your senses! That it does depends on the proper combination of dishes. Variety is the key to an interesting meal—variety in tastes, textures, and ingredients. If you have a spicy dish, it should be complimented by a mild one, a crunchy textured dish with one which has tender ingredients. The number of dishes selected depends largely on the number of people dining. A good rule of thumb is to have the same number of dishes as people served,

plus rice and perhaps a soup. Try not to duplicate the ingredients, for example, instead of two beef dishes make one of them chicken or pork. Seafood generally appears as a standard dish in a combination of dishes. Menus (pages 214–215) adhere to these guidelines and might, in themselves, be more instructive than further suggestions.

Give a Chinese New Year's party

The Chinese Calendar follows the lunar year and Chinese New Year's Day falls on the first day of the first moon which occurs at the outset of the second new moon following the winter solstice (or mid-February).

This first day of the first moon is an auspicious date as it marks the end of winter and the beginning of spring, of new life, hopes, good fortune, and prosperity. It is celebrated with great enthusiasm in China, and by Chinese living abroad. During this time the God of the Kitchen is sent to Heaven to report the year that has passed. He returns on New Year's Eve, a day commemorated by a great feast.

In the week surrounding New Year's Day, homes are brightened by pots of flowers, such as azaleas and the sweet-smelling hyacinths to turn thoughts to spring, and by baskets of oranges and plates of candied fruits and roasted melon seeds. It is a time for friends to visit, and, of course, to eat—snacking all day long and feasting at heavily-laden tables.

The photograph on pages 6-7 shows an elegant New Year's buffet spread (the menu follows). You may wish to go all-out in this manner, or plan something simpler. Just remember that a New Year's celebration must include long life noodles (page 166), fish for prosperity, fruits to suggest the coming of spring with a new beginning of new opportunities, and enough food to convey to all the wish for a life of plenty.

Chinese adults will give children gifts of money tucked into bright red envelopes. You might decorate your table with these envelopes (available at Oriental stores), tuck in a shiny penny, or a pair of chopsticks which may be used during the meal then taken home, or a fortune you could write. The table setting should have the look of joy and prosperity.

If you live in or near a cosmopolitan city with a Chinatown, take advantage of all the special snacks which appear at this time of year and add them to your feast: Moon cakes (pastries filled with lotus seed or melon or sweet bean), the candied fruits, tangerines, freshly roasted pork and duck.

Cut fancy-shaped vegetables

Pictured below are three ways to cut fancy-shaped vegetables —an onion brush, bamboo shoot trees, and notched carrot slices.

Set a Chinese table

The Chinese table setting is rather simple. The basic everyday service consists of a salad-size plate, a rice bowl, and a pair of chopsticks. To these may be added a small saucer for dipping ingredients and a small cup for tea.

Banquets require only a few more items: a large serving spoon and spoon rest (usually in silver) and a second bowl, smaller than but similar to the rice bowl, to be used for soup or soupy dishes, and a deepset soup spoon to scoop soup or hold a juicy morsel. These items are simple when compared to the table setting of a multi-course European meal; however, in the most elaborate Chinese banquet meals, the main plate is changed after every course in anticipation of a new entreé with a distinctively new taste—and there may be 12 to 14 such main dishes. (Rice is generally not served at banquets, but if it is, it appears only before the last few courses. Tea is also not served until the end of the meal.)

In a family setting, all dishes may appear at once, including rice and the soup, which is consumed along with the meal much like a beverage.

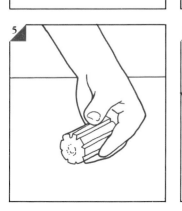

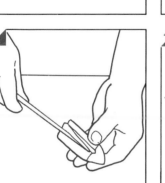

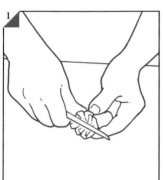

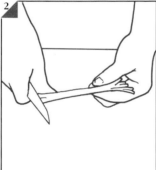

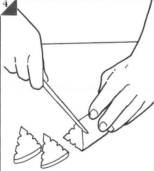

To make onion brush, trim off root and top, leaving 2½-inches of stem. 1) Make 3 or 4 lengthwise cuts, 1-inch deep at one end. 2) Repeat at other end and place in cold water. To make bamboo shoot trees, trim bamboo shoot into triangular pieces. 3) Notch 4 or 5 V-shaped grooves, lengthwise, on 2 sides. 4) Slice thinly. To make fancy carrots, 5) notch V-shaped grooves lengthwise, equally spaced, around carrot. 6) Thinly slice.

Plan a Chinese dinner party

If you are planning to give a Chinese dinner party, select dishes which do not require much of your last-minute attention. Check the notes of the recipes you think you'd like to try; they'll tell you what may or may not be done ahead of time.

I've often told my cooking class students that they should order eight dishes from me and prepare the last two at home! While this is suggested in a joking manner, it's not a bad idea and some of my students have done this a number of times. You might consider involving your favorite nearby Chinese restaurant in this scheme. The two dishes you could prepare at home are Hot & Sour soup (it gives off a great aroma) and Steamed Kirin Fish (or any seafood dish as they do not transport well).

Or, have a Chinese potluck dinner. Each guest can bring one item that travels well, such as Pong-pong Chicken, Barbecued Pork, Mandarin Beef Stew, or Tea-smoked Duck, and the host family can provide soup, a vegetable, and a seafood dish.

Or, have your guests do the cooking right at the table with the dramatic Mongolian Hot Pot.

Boxes, boxes... or what to do with leftovers you take home

No other ethnic restaurant is as prepared as the Chinese restaurant in America to package up for you the leftovers of your meal. (Can you imagine telling your waiter at an elegant Continental restaurant that you wish to take home tidbits of all the courses you ordered?) Even the fanciest of Chinese restaurants is prepared for this request; chefs and waiters of Chinese restaurants are complimented by your request and appreciate your desire not to be wasteful—the fundamental philosophy of Chinese cuisine is against waste and for the best use of all parts of all ingredients at hand.

So what do you do with these ingredients when you get home? Or, for that matter, what do you do with leftovers from your own cooking?

Chinese people love leftovers because they can be served cold, as condiments to *congee* (served as a light regular meal or late snack); stir-fried dishes can be used as toppings or fried noodles; and other dishes can be combined with new ingredients to create totally new dishes. Here are a few suggestions for the following leftovers:

Steamed rice may be resteamed or used to make fried rice, or reboiled into a delicious congee (see index for recipes). To add flavor to congee, add to the basic recipe your leftover duck.

Leftover rice may also be the base for a more Western meal of a pilaf when tossed together with a beef or pork stir-fry dish you may have brought home. Mix them together and steam until heated through. Serve with cold cucumbers or chutney on the side. (Kung Pao Chicken, Minced Chicken, Szechaun Beef, Curry Beef, and other similar dishes combined with rice make a terrific pilaf.)

Boiled Noodles may be turned into delicious pan-fried noodles. Drain the boiled noodles and follow the recipe you wish.

Soups are the easiest to reheat and to bring back to their original flavor. In fact, clear based soups are better tasting if cooked longer, such as beef stew in broth. To make a rich congee, combine a clear soup with your leftover boiled rice and follow the boiling procedure.

However there are a couple of cautions. Soups thickened with cornstarch are not recommended for reheating. For example, Hot & Sour soup is difficult to reheat because the vinegar starts to separate from the cornstarch, will lose its thickness, color, and flavor.

In Won-ton soup, boiled won-tons easily break when reheating, so take out the wontons from the broth, mix them in oil and refrigerate. Store the broth until ready to use. When reheating the soup, return the won-tons at the last minute after the broth has reached the boiling point.

Stir-fry dishes are more difficult to reheat because they usually contain fresh vegetables and lose their flavor and texture when reheated. If you have a microwave oven, reheat the dish for not more than 3 minutes so that the juices will be retained.

Serve left over stir-fried dishes cold—as toppings to soup noodles (it will enhance the quick-cooking "ramen" varieties) or as a condiment to congee.

Braised foods, such as stew, red-cooked and associated dishes, are best to reheat. There are plenty of juices, large pieces of meat and fewer fresh vegetables involved. You can also add new ingredients to replenish the dish as the remaining juices will penetrate these ingredients as well.

Braised fish, however, will not do well reheated but it does taste delicious when you combine it with bean cake. Lightly sauté soft bean cake, add the fish, a little water if necessary, adjust seasonings to taste, and reheat but do not overcook.

Steamed foods can be resteamed easily without much sacrifice of flavor; deep-fried foods are difficult to reheat and are best handled if reheated in the oven at 300°.

The trick to leftover food is to make it reappear in a new form, and your imagination and good cooking sense are your best guides.

Index